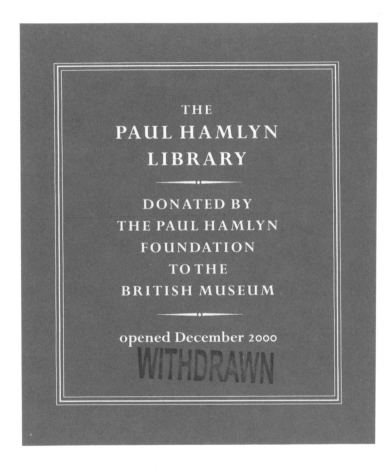

MEDIEVAL PALACES

AN ARCHAEOLOGY

GRAHAM D. KEEVILL

MEDIEVAL PALACES

AN ARCHAEOLOGY

GRAHAM D. KEEVILL

TEMPUS

First published 2000

PUBLISHED IN THE UNITED KINGDOM BY:

Tempus Publishing Ltd
The Mill, Brimscombe Port
Stroud, Gloucestershire GL5 2QG

PUBLISHED IN THE UNITED STATES OF AMERICA BY:

Arcadia Publishing Inc.
A division of Tempus Publishing Inc.
2 Cumberland Street
Charleston, SC 29401
1-888-313-2665

Tempus books are available in France, Germany and Belgium
from the following addresses:

Tempus Publishing Group	Tempus Publishing Group	Tempus Publishing Group
21 Avenue de la République	Gustav-Adolf-Straße 3	Place de L'Alma 4/5
37300 Joué-lès-Tours	99084 Erfurt	1200 Brussels
FRANCE	GERMANY	BELGIUM

British Library Cataloguing in Publication Data.
A catalogue record for this book is available from the British Library.

ISBN 0 7524 1454 2

Typesetting and origination by Tempus Publishing.
PRINTED AND BOUND IN GREAT BRITAIN

Contents

Preface

Most archaeologists are used to writing reports of one sort or another, and many of us have had the onerous task of preparing lengthy articles for publication or even whole books dedicated to a single subject. This is all part and parcel of the job — part of the territory, one might say — in a profession that thrives on and is hungry for information. Indeed academically speaking there could be little or no progress without such publications, as they provide the raw material for wider research. Nevertheless I am very far from being the first field archaeologist who has wondered what might lie beyond the horizon of such report-writing and longed wistfully for the opportunity to stand back, just for a while, from project-based work. As much as anything I wanted to see whether I had a book in me — whether I would be able to dedicate the time, thought and effort necessary to do the research, seek out the illustrations and above all write the text. The subject matter was easily chosen: I had spent most of the mid-late 1990s in charge of excavations and other archaeological work at the Tower of London and Hampton Court Palace. Quite naturally I had already looked at many other medieval palaces for comparative purposes, and most family holidays during this period tended to include a visit to one or more of them. I therefore wrote a synopsis of what such a book might contain, and fortunately found an interested publisher. That was the easy bit. Work continued to 'get in the way' of research and writing, but gradually the text began to take shape and some solid work in the first half of this year saw the bulk of the book completed. Inevitably it will be for others to decide whether the effort has produced a worthwhile contribution to the subject, but at least I have achieved my basic objective.

The research for this book (and indeed before it) involved discussions with many colleagues, and it is a pleasure to be able to thank them all for sharing ideas and information with me. Needless to say any mistakes in the text should be laid at my door, not theirs. Many of them have also been instrumental in providing or helping with illustrations. It is invidious to place my thanks in any particular order, but it seems reasonable to start with the team at Tempus Publishing who have made the book possible: Peter Kemmis Betty showed his commitment to my work from the start, while Della Cantillion, Anne Phipps and Tim Clarke have seen me through the production process. Among my archaeological and other colleagues it is a huge pleasure to acknowledge the debt I owe to Leigh and Tim Allen, Prof Martin Biddle, Robert Bowles, the late Martin Caroe, John Charlton, Dr Glyn Coppack, Brian Durham, Daphne Ford, Jonathan Foyle, Antony Gibb, Vince Griffin, Dr Roland Harris, Dave Howell, Prof Tom Beaumont James (especially for allowing the use of his illustrations and for access to the Clarendon archive), David Jennings, Neil Johnstone, Mick Jones, Brian Kerr, Neil and Paul Linford, Dr Ellen McAdam, David Miles, Nick Mitchell, Clare Murphy, Andy Payne, John

Pidgeon, Prof Philip Rahtz, Andy Smith, John Steane, Dr David Stocker, Dr Simon Thurley, Dr Ian Tyers, David Wilkinson, Duncan Wood and Dr Bernard Worssam. I hope I have not forgotten anyone, but if I have may they forgive me.

My greatest thanks among professional colleagues, however, must be reserved for a trio whose help and friendship has been incomparably important to me in recent years: Dr Steven Brindle of English Heritage, and Dr Edward Impey and Jeremy Ashbee of Historic Royal Palaces. Last, but as far from least as it is possible to be, I will be eternally grateful to my wife and children for all their help and support: Cathy undertook a great deal of research for me, found many of the references and helped with various aspects of the text, while Melissa, Alexander and Penelope had to put up with an even grumpier father than usual. Hopefully they won't have taken much harm from visiting so many 'broken' palaces, castles etc. in their formative years.

I have not provided extensive cross-referencing to the bibliography in the text, unless it seemed particularly important to direct the reader to a specific page or illustration in a publication. It seemed to me that to do otherwise (eg. through footnotes or Harvard-style referencing) would be unnecessarily distracting. Hopefully it will be reasonably easy to find references to specific sites in the bibliography. The gazetteer itself is not intended to provide an exhaustive guide to medieval palaces — that would be a book in its own right — but rather to suggest sites which both can be visited and will repay the effort involved in making such a visit. The short entries attempt to provide a flavour of what visitors can expect to see, but again space precludes extensive descriptions. Excellent guidebooks are available at many sites, especially those run by CADW, English Heritage and Historic Scotland. Anyone requiring information about sites not included in my list should refer to the *History of the King's Works* (Colvin ed) for royal residences and Thompson 1998 for a comprehensive list of bishops' palaces.

Graham D. Keevill
June 2000

The illustrations

Text figures

70   Messing about on the river: public access was allowed to the Thames foreshore at the Tower of London during a weekend in July 1998

71   Tower Hamlets schoolchildren exploring the Salt Tower at the Tower of London with Chris Gidlow of Historic Royal Palaces, November 1999

Colour plates

Front Cover

    Bishop William Waynflete's magnificent entrance tower of 1470-5 at the west end of the medieval hall range at Farnham Castle

1   The brick entrance tower at Farnham Castle, built in 1470-5
2   Geophysical surveying on a possible palace site. © Crown copyright: English Heritage
3   Results of dendrochronology work on timbers from the Great Kitchen roof damaged by the fire at Windsor Castle on 20 November 1992. © Crown copyright: English Heritage
4   St Mary's Guildhall, Lincoln, seen from the south-west. Photograph by J. Ashbee
5   The Tower of London as it might have looked during Henry III's extension of the defences in the 1230s and 1240s. © Crown copyright: Historic Royal Palaces
6   A view across the Tower of London today from the west, with the White Tower prominent
7   Hampton Court Palace (Surrey)
8   The Henry III masonry and oak timbers in the west moat at the Tower of London being excavated in 1996. Photograph by Oxford Archaeological Unit/Historic Royal Palaces
9   Edward I's Postern Gate at the Tower of London
10   L'Echequier, Caen, Normandy (France). Photograph by Dr E. Impey
11   View of the massive solar tower at the Witney manor house or palace of the bishops of Winchester during excavations in 1984. Photograph by Oxford Archaeological Unit
12   Henry de Blois's East Hall at Wolvesey Palace, Winchester (Hants), viewed from the southern (chamber block) end
13   The Jewel Tower, Palace of Westminster, with the Abbey in the background
14   Elevation of the west end of St George's Hall, Windsor Castle with medieval and later features revealed during post-fire restoration in the 1990s. © Crown Copyright: English Heritage
15   Clarendon Palace today
16   The medieval *llys* at Aber under excavation, looking north along the palace building with the motte in the background. Photograph by N. Johnstone
17   The Great Hall at Hampton Court Palace. © Crown copyright: Historic Royal Palaces
18   The Tudor Chapel at Hampton Court Palace. © Crown copyright: Historic Royal Palaces
19   Edward I's Gloriette at Leeds Castle (Kent). Photograph by J. Ashbee
20   Oven range in the fourteenth-century kitchen at Bishop's Waltham Palace
21   The moat at Hampton Court Palace in front of the great west front
22   The 'keep' and palace at Sherborne (Dorset)
23   Fete day at Bishop's Waltham Palace, July 1997

1 Medieval palaces

Introduction: the purpose of this book

The exercise of power in medieval Britain and Europe was often a precarious business, depending on a mixture of diplomacy, familial relationships, personal magnetism and not a little luck. There were, to be sure, secure dynasties and long reigns, but there were also periods of considerable instability. These could veer towards outright anarchy, exemplified in England during the reign of Stephen, and even long-lived potentates such as Henry III could have problems of loyalty and trust at many levels of society. It is not surprising, then, to find that medieval kings, bishops and great lords spent much of their lives on the move rather than in static locations.

This very mobility caused an extraordinary vitality in the construction of accommodation for these powerful but often insecure people. Palaces, castles and smaller residences such as hunting lodges were built in great numbers in Britain throughout the medieval period (always remembering, of course, that Scotland was an independent kingdom throughout this time while Wales aspired to be so whenever it came under English dominance). These houses, whether built for kings, bishops or other magnates, form an important part of our building stock where they survive substantially above ground as at the Tower of London. They are often very well documented as well, and therefore provide excellent source material for medieval historians. This is nowhere better exemplified than in the *History of the King's Works*, an undertaking in the research and publication of England's royal building campaigns unrivalled in its scope and depth of coverage. This historical resource is often under-exploited, however, and much remains to be done in writing equivalent histories for the medieval episcopate in most bishoprics, or in researching the works of the great temporal magnates.

Such matters are to some extent incidental to the purpose of this book, for the focus here is on the archaeological evidence for medieval palaces and other important residences. Surviving buildings themselves contain an invaluable archaeological 'gene pool' of information in their fabric, decoration and contents, whether for their period of construction or subsequent use. Ruinous buildings such as the royal and episcopal palaces of (respectively) Clarendon or Wolvesey retain some of this information in their fabric, but the greater part of their value lies in and beneath the soil, where the discipline of archaeology comes into its own in researching sites. Many of these, of course, have little or no sign above ground of their former use: perhaps a few earthworks, even a motte, but otherwise their secrets lie firmly below the ground. It is still possible for such sites to occur within the historical record, for there are relatively few royal, episcopal or magnate residences with no source material at all. It is inherently likely, though, that archaeologists will discover more about such a site through fieldwork than history alone will allow. Having said that, the greatest understanding of any site (regardless of its current condition) inevitably comes through an integrated approach to research, where archaeologists, historians and others come together and share their knowledge rather than keeping it to themselves.

This book shows how archaeologists undertake research on palaces and equivalent residences, irrespective of their builders. It has been written to fill a gap on the bookshelves, there being no general text specifically on the archaeology of medieval palaces in print. Anyone with an interest in the medieval period should find the book useful, whether professional or amateur, and it should be particularly valuable for those who like to cast a critical eye over a site when they visit it. The gazetteer has been designed to provide a brief summary of the most important and accessible palatial sites so that readers can plan visits and itineraries for themselves, with or without the book in their hands.

The text is largely biased towards British sites and projects, largely because of practical considerations in undertaking the background research which necessarily precedes writing. The wider European context is not ignored, however, and work in other countries is mentioned where appropriate. It would be absurd to maintain an insular perspective when British events, whether secular or religious, occurred within a European framework of cross-fertilisation and competition between royal houses and dynasties. Where necessary, archaeological evidence is placed within its proper context by reference to parallel work in other specialisms such as art history and documentary research. All kinds of sites are looked at, from surviving palaces which are still in use through ruins to greenfield sites where there is no hint of anything special above the ground. Evidence from various types of archaeological investigation will be used, ranging from non-destructive techniques such as geophysical, building and earthwork surveys through to excavations of all shapes and sizes. Many of the projects described here have yet to be published in full, often because they only took place recently or are still in progress, while others are better known through excavation reports and guide books.

Defining palaces and other residences

Hundreds of palaces were built or occupied during the medieval period by monarchs and bishops alike. Locations were chosen for a variety of reasons, including convenience, situation along regularly-used travel routes, position relative to other estate properties such as farms, and in some cases sheer delight in some special aspect like hunting. The concept of a palace may seem familiar to us today, used as we are to images of sumptuous decoration and royal ceremony in Britain and elsewhere. A palace to us is virtually synonymous with the great country houses of the seventeenth to the twentieth centuries, and we recognise Buckingham Palace as such at least partly because we are familiar with the architectural language and scale of these great houses. Even a cursory glance into the past makes it abundantly clear that palaces have changed beyond recognition in style, form, and to some extent purpose since the days of William I, Edward I or even Henry

1 Wolvesey Palace as a direct link with the past. Bishop William Giffard's West Hall is viewed here from the north-west, across the garderobe block added by Henry de Blois. Buildings still in use as part of the Bishop of Winchester's palace can be seen in the top right of the picture

VIII. Indeed, any one of those kings may well have found the houses of the others alien to his own needs and desires for accommodation. Even so there are a few crucial aspects of palaces' use which continue to link them across the centuries: in particular, their private residential functions, and their role in very public ceremonial occasions. In the latter respect the banquets, visits by foreign heads-of-state and other grand occasions hosted at Buckingham Palace are redolent of times when the monarch held far more direct power than is the case under modern parliamentary democracy. Within the ecclesiastical sphere one could argue that the episcopate has a more direct linkage with the past than royalty, especially in those cases such as Durham, Lambeth (Canterbury's palace in London) and Wolvesey (Winchester) where modern bishops' palaces offer a direct physical link with past ones (**1**).

What, then, defined a medieval palace? This is by no means an easy question to answer, though many residences (royal and episcopal) were acknowledged and described as such by contemporary authorities. Giraldus Cambrensis (Gerald the Welshman), for instance, stated that Henry de Blois built sumptuous palaces (*palatia sumptuosissima*) and the Winchester Annals for 1238 describe Henry's new East Hall at Wolvesey as a house like a palace (*domum quasi palatium*; Biddle 1986, 8-10). Similarly the Tower of London was famously described as the fortified palace (*Arx Palatina*) by William Fitzstephen in the late twelfth century, though a more full reading might involve greater emphasis on the defences with *Palatina* being more of an adjectival qualification. There are also several late eleventh- and early twelfth-century French references which make the degree of social differentiation in such buildings absolutely clear (information from Jeremy Ashbee).

At one level any royal or episcopal residence (ie. a place lodged in overnight) could be defined as palatial, but this appears too simplistic and would lead to a veritable host of sites being accepted. Even so, ownership seems to be a sensible place to start, although this is not as straightforward as it sounds: the stock of royal property was rarely static for very long, with sites being acquired and disposed of according to the needs and preferences of particular monarchs. The bishops were perhaps less affected by this fluidity of estate, especially as the largely unchanging geographical extent of the bishoprics from the beginning of the twelfth century up to the Dissolution gave them a clearly defined 'core territory'. Even here, though, the bishops often gained new sites through new grants of land, or exchanged one property for another, but the number of their residences stayed fairly constant at around 150 throughout the medieval period.

In the early thirteenth century King John built up the largest personal stock of palatial residences of any medieval English monarch (around 29 properties, 23 of which he had inherited on his ascendancy) until Henry VIII enlarged the estate (**2**). Later in the thirteenth century Henry III and his son Edward I were conspicuous royal builders, but many of their sites are more traditionally regarded as castles and the number of recognised royal palaces actually fell during their reigns to around 20. By 1485 only Baynard's Castle, Eltham, Greenwich, Sheen and Westminster remained in the vicinity of London, with Clarendon (Wilts), King's Langley (Herts) and Woodstock (Oxon) a little further afield. The early Tudors re-enlarged the royal portfolio through purchase or other means — there were remarkable numbers of propitiatory 'gifts' to Henry VIII — so that there were almost twice as many palaces in the middle of the sixteenth century as there had been in the early thirteenth. In common with the concentration of late fifteenth-century properties, this expansion was heavily biased towards London and the Thames valley, with outlying sites to the north and west. Palaces were conspicuously absent in Wales, East Anglia, and the far south-west, north and north-west. Henry VIII, meanwhile, was quite happy to begin construction on his new palaces at Bridewell (London) and Nonsuch (Surrey) before the relevant properties had legally become his.

Different though related circumstances prevailed in Wales which survived as an independent principality until the reign of Edward I. The kings of Gwynedd in north-west Wales and Anglesey established a sophisticated system of land tenure and duties based around townships (*trefi*) grouped into the commote (*cwmwd*) or the larger *cantref* (100 townships). Two townships in each commote were held directly by the king, and these were the *maerdref* (eg. township of the king's reeve) and the *fridd* (in effect, waste or summer pasture). There are historical and archaeological reasons for believing that the origins of the tenurial system with its central places lie quite early in the post-Roman era, certainly well before 1000, while both the system and its centres seem to have remained stable (and in the latter case static) until the late thirteenth century. There is also a notable relationship between early Norman mottes (which were, of course, thoroughly intrusive and militarily offensive elements here as much as in England) in the area and existing

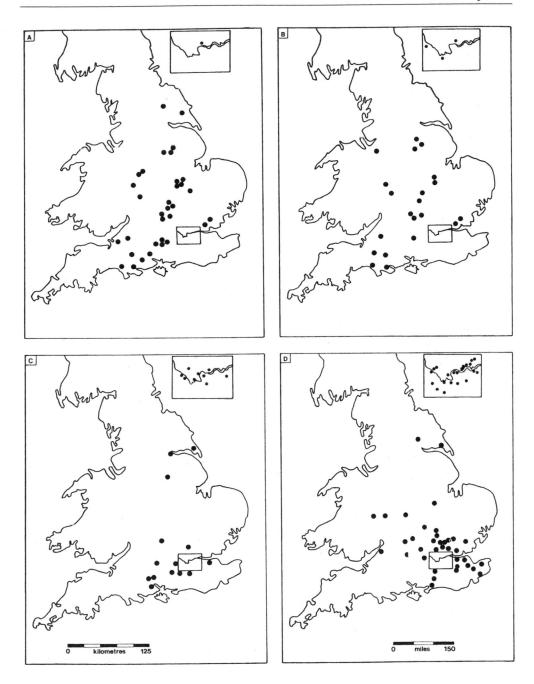

2   The distribution of medieval royal residences:
    A, 1154-1216; B, 1216-72; C, 1327-77; D, c.1550.
    From James 1990; drawn by Alex Turner

maerdrefi such as Rhuddlan and Degannwy (both of which were early) (**3**). The Norman conquest was unsuccessful in this period (which is why a capital C is inappropriate until Edward I's time), but several of the English mottes were turned to good use by the Welsh princes (who also subsequently built a few of their own; Longley 1997).

The critical locus in the *maerdref* was the *llys*, a complex of royal buildings equating to a palace. As Longley very aptly puts it (1997, 42), 'the king would periodically visit his *llysoedd*, meeting the people he needed to meet, doing business, dispensing justice and, with his retinue, eating his way through his taxes', which provides a rather neat description of the use of medieval palaces everywhere. The system all but collapsed with the Edwardian conquest in 1283, for the Welsh royal lands passed to the English crown and the *maerdrefi* etc. ceased to function or be looked after (though elements of the tenurial pattern which went with them proved to be much more stubborn and survived into modern times). It is difficult to reconstruct the full pattern of the royal Gwynedd estates for this reason, and the specific location of most *llysoed* has proved difficult to determine. There have been important advances in this respect in recent years, including the discovery of several *llys* complexes through archaeological fieldwork (**3**; see Longley 1997, Johnstone 1997 and 1999).

The stock of Scottish palaces seems to have been as fluid as those south of the border during the medieval period, and when James I returned to the throne from his English captivity in 1424 he found the royal properties severely depleted. The major residences in the Forth valley remained (Edinburgh and Stirling Castles, and Linlithgow Palace), but otherwise the Stewart estate was just about all that he could still lay claim to. Over the coming decades, however, the king and his successors annexed numerous earldoms through the forfeiture of disgraced nobles (eg. Fife, Mentieth, Mar and Methven), bringing places like Falkland, Doune and Kindrochit into royal hands. The lands of the Black Douglases came by the same route in 1455, with the important castle at Threave among others in the Forest of Etterick. The Scottish crown lands reached their greatest extent when James V took the earldom of Angus and the lordship of Glamis. Even then the number of major royal residences was not great, and around 36 properties were used with a degree of regularity (Dunbar 1999, 1-3).

On occasion the figures for English palaces must be treated with a degree of caution, as the Tower of London is a notable absentee in the 1485 list along with others such as Windsor because of their 'castle' status. It seems unlikely that contemporaries drew such fine distinctions, and Windsor was certainly a favourite residence of successive kings and the focus of at times enormous expenditure. The distribution of the sites is more telling, for the pronounced south-eastern bias and the focus on London were ever-present from the early post-Conquest period onwards. Admittedly there were more sites owned and used in the north and west through to the early fourteenth century, and there were 'outliers' even in later reigns, but the overall pattern is clear enough.

The next qualifying standard should be residence, in the sense that a site should be intended for reasonably regular visits of one or several nights over a prolonged period. We certainly should not expect a king or bishop to spend a whole year in one place only — indeed such an occurrence would have been unthinkable — although as we shall see in chapter 4 there could be favoured residences which would be lived in for weeks or even

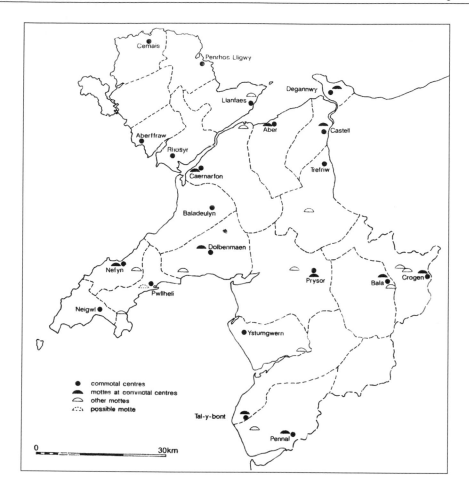

Cemais

Penrhos Lligwy

Degannwy

Llanfaes

Aber

Castell

Aberffraw

Rhosyr

Trefriw

Caernarfon

Baladeulyn

Dolbenmaen

Nefyn

Prysor

Bala

Crogen

Pwllheli

Neigwl

Ystumgwern

● commotal centres
▲ mottes at commotal centres
⌒ other mottes
⟨⟩ possible motte

Tal-y-bont

Pennal

0   30km

3   Commotes and llysoedd *of medieval Gwynedd. After Johnstone 1997*

months at a time if circumstances allowed. Residence implies certain standards of comfort and quality in accommodation which can be recognised in the scale and type of materials used in the ranges and chambers lived in by the monarchy and bishops (and indeed by others of similarly high status in the secular and religious worlds such as abbots). While monarchs in particular might find it difficult to find time away from the public eye (just as they do today) such rooms always had an element of privacy about them, and this became more important, and recognisable, as the medieval period progressed. Some of the smaller palaces can be seen as avowedly private: many hunting lodges certainly fall into this category, and some bishops' houses, including many of the London 'inns' which provided episcopal residence when attending Court and government in the capital, can be seen in a similar light. Many of these smaller sites, including most of the London inns, fell out of fashion in time, and generally they have not survived well into the modern era. Despite this there are some remarkable survivals, such as the Court House at East Meon (Hants) where the late fourteenth-century great hall, solar and garderobe built by

Winchester's Bishop William of Wykeham survive largely intact (Roberts 1993).

Were there other strong defining functions in medieval palaces besides residence? The exercise of governance was certainly one, both in ceremonial terms and through the provision of space for major offices such as the Exchequer and Wardrobe until they began to settle into more permanent buildings towards the end of our period. It is difficult to over-estimate the imperative for kings and queens to travel and be seen around their country, especially in the often-volatile politics of the period and given the questionable legitimacy of some monarchs' claims to the throne. Equally, though, security must have been at a premium during such turbulent times and a degree of strength or defence is to be expected in this context. To a large degree Court and Government moved with the monarch. Bishops had an equivalent need to circulate and be seen within their diocese, whether by the clergy, wealthy patrons or the public who formed their flock. Palaces could provide the stage for public displays of regal or mitred style and justice. It is scarcely surprising, therefore, that the importance of ceremony is patent in the care and expense lavished on great halls by monarchs and bishops alike. The very act of building a palace could be a statement in this regard. We need to allow some overlap here between palaces and castles: some, such as Windsor, were clearly intended as much for palace accommodation as defence, while the capacity for a fortress and its buildings to impart powerful messages of control and dominance should never be overlooked (the Tower of London is probably the best example of this phenomenon in England). Others were primarily military, and long-term residence or use was usually less important than strategic location and impact. Most of the thirteenth-century Welsh castles (on both sides) could be seen in this context, though the royal suites at such strongholds as Conwy (Gwynedd) show that care would still be taken for comfort even in campaigning areas.

As the medieval period wore on, the idea of palaces as pleasure-grounds — places where those in power could escape briefly from the intense pressures which came with their positions — gained in strength. Interiors could be sumptuously decorated, while outside gardens became an increasingly important element in their own right as well as providing links into the wider landscape. The latter might well be exploited for hunting, while the development of tournaments and other sporting spectacles led to space and buildings being dedicated to them. Here the private interests of the potentate might link in very well with court and public life. Thus we are obliged to look at the settings of palaces as well as the buildings themselves.

A brief summary of chronological developments

This section looks briefly at the ways palaces changed through the centuries, from the pre-Norman timber structures of locally-based Anglo-Saxon petty kingdoms through William the Conqueror's White Tower to Henry VIII's great palaces in and around London. The study of structural development is one which archaeology is particularly well suited to, as so much of the evidence rests firmly in physical remains, both in surviving buildings and buried in the ground.

Anglo-Saxon palaces

Palaces, or something very like them, are quite common from the sixth/seventh century onwards in the Anglo-Saxon period, especially when England was divided up into a series of separate regionally-based kingdoms such as Wessex, Mercia and Northumbria. These might even have smaller, localised 'petty' kingdoms within or associated with them, such as that of the Hwicce on the Worcestershire edge of Mercia. Thereafter the more unified English and Danelaw estates continued to maintain royal enclaves, culminating in the royal seat at Westminster and the single-nation capital in London in the early eleventh century. For virtually all of the period, palaces (in as much as we can define them) consisted of timber buildings, often of considerable complexity in their ground plan, and thus by implication in their superstructures as well. The division of long rectangular buildings into two or more rooms by constructing timber partitions is particularly notable. Paired doors in the centre of the two long sides are also quite common: examples at Cowdery's Down (Hants), Doon Hill (Scotland) and Yeavering (Northumbria) are associated with a partition to one side reminiscent of medieval screen passages. The buildings were usually grouped in ranges, often contained within fenced and/or ditched enclosures, and some of the sites display complex phasing which demonstrates that individual buildings or whole areas had been rebuilt on several occasions; in other words, they were long-lived sites where high status was maintained, though it is not always possible to establish a 'royal' presence. A distinctive insular Anglo-Saxon timber building tradition can be discerned, owing something to continental Germanic and native Romano-British influences but not definitively or solely rooted in either of them (James *et al* 1984).

Examples can be found on many sites throughout the country, from Cheddar (Somerset; Rahtz 1979) and Chalton (Cunliffe 1973) or Cowdery's Down (Hants; Marshall and James 1984) to Yeavering (Hope-Taylor 1977). The first and last are generally accepted as palaces, not least because of the overall complex of buildings, some of which are unusual or at Yeavering even unique in any context of this date, but the other two are not, although the high status of Cowdery's Down is scarcely in doubt. Similar sites have been located through archaeological fieldwork, and the tendency has been to accept that they are also of high status. Drayton (Oxon; Hassall 1986, 109-16 and especially plate 8c), and Cowage Farm, Foxley (Wilts; Hinchcliffe 1986) are examples of this, and both have been tentatively identified as palace sites. This has relied as much on Saxon documentary references to the centres of minor kingdoms in the vicinity, with all the problems they entail, as on the archaeological evidence. The sites are largely known from non-intrusive work (air photographs and geophysical survey), and ascriptions to palatial status will remain difficult to support unless and until extensive archaeological excavations have taken place (**4**).

Yeavering and Cheddar are still the best-known and most readily acknowledged Saxon palaces in England outside London, both with direct, documented links with the royal houses of the day (and, in Cheddar's case, later as well). The former was the earlier of the two, having belonged to king Edwin of Northumbria during the early seventh century. There was a large and complicated hall as well as smaller timber buildings, but perhaps most remarkable was the wedge-shaped structure which probably served as an assembly

ANGLO SAXON HIGH STATUS SITES

Archaeological evidence

DOON HILL
SPROUSTON
MILFIELD
YEAVERING

NUNBURNHOLME

ATCHAM
TAMWORTH
HATTON ROCK · LONG ITCHINGTON
NORTHAMPTON
SUTTON HOO
GLOUCESTER
· SUTTON COURTENAY
FOXLEY/BREMILHAM
OLD WINDSOR · LONDON
EASTRY
WESTENHANGER
CHEDDAR

4 *The distribution of middle to late Saxon high-status or palace sites. After Rahtz 1979*

point cum platform for addresses. The great late ninth-century king Alfred may have been associated with Cheddar, although Asser's claim that he built many palaces has yet to be substantiated archaeologically, not that it would necessarily be easy to do so given the problems of dating evidence from sources such as pottery in this period. There is certainly evidence from coin finds that the site was in use in Alfred's time, and it was undoubtedly a royal site subsequently (eg. under king Edgar). The principal building in the ninth and early tenth century was a timber hall, 78ft (23m) long and 20ft (6.5m) wide, with opposed central entrances in the long, slightly bowed sides. At least one other timber building was contemporary with it, and there was a large drainage ditch running along the north side of the site. The hall falls within the general pattern of carpentry construction techniques of the period, though if anything Cheddar's late Saxon buildings are less complex and impressive than the earlier ones of Yeavering or Cowdery's Down; it would have been substantial for its day, though not by comparison with medieval halls or even with Edward the Confessor's great hall at Westminster, although the latter was exceptional. It was subsequently replaced (after 930) by a rectangular hall to the west, shorter but wider and

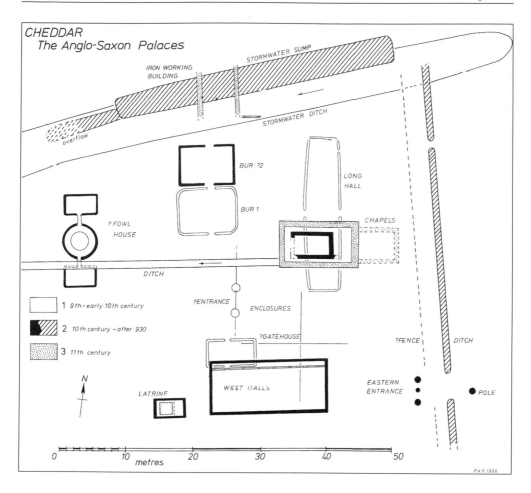

5   Plan of the middle to late Saxon palace site at Cheddar (Somerset). After Rahtz 1979

associated with the first of a series of chapels and an unusual building which has been variously interpreted as a fowl-house or a corn mill. At about the same time the built area seems to have been defined by a fence and ditch (**5**).

We have already seen that many of the *maerdrefi* of Gwynedd appear to have pre-Norman or post-Roman origins. Longley (1997, 45-52) points out that some sites which definitely enjoyed this status in the eleventh century and later 'can, either on direct evidence or by association, be considered as significant power bases during the early centuries of the kingdom of Gwynedd'. Sites like Aberffraw, Caernarfon, Degannwy (possibly the *arx Decantorum* besieged and burned in the ninth century), Dinorben and Rhuddlan provide such evidence in varying degrees, while there are several strongly-defended upland/hilltop sites containing small citadel-like enclosures which may also qualify as early royal centres. The 'citadels' tend to be distinctively located in the middle of a long side (eg. Carn Fadrun, Garn Bodrun) or at the end of a promontory (Castell Caer Lleion, Pen y Castell) and the plan form is similar in some respects to the motte and bailey of later centuries. The upland locations meant that building stone was readily available at these sites, and several of them (notably Carn Fadrun, Castell Caer Lleion and Garn Bodrun) retain impressive stone walls around their 'citadels'.

Anglo-Saxon bishoprics developed slowly, perhaps even hesitantly, not least because Christianity took time to gain widespread acceptance in the early-middle Saxon period, and occasionally there were serious setbacks as in early seventh-century Northumbria when the converted king Edwin lost out in conflict with the pagan Penda of Mercia and was slain. Even though Penda tolerated the 'new' religion, Northumbrian conversion took a step backwards in the confusion following his death. Despite this a system of 15 diocese had been established by the end of the seventh century, although subsequent Scandinavian incursions continued to cause problems for the church. We know a great deal of the ecclesiastical buildings of this era — cathedrals, monasteries and minsters, churches and chapels — from their timber origins through to the magnificent edifices which were being erected by the period's end, but we know far less of the episcopal palaces which we may presume existed from the eighth century onwards.

Signs of pre-Norman activity have been found at a number of episcopal palaces belonging to the Bishops of Winchester. At their home palace of Wolvesey in the south-eastern corner of the old Roman city defences, for instance, excavations in the 1960s revealed traces of a possible chapel with apses at both the eastern and western ends, along with a range of timber buildings to its west, all of late Saxon date. A wide but shallow ditch ran around the south and west sides of the structures, which lay partially underneath the north range of the medieval palace (eg. Woodman's Gate and the rooms/areas to its east), and no further late Saxon buildings were found anywhere to the south. This shows that the Saxon palace, if these buildings do represent it, lay mostly to the north of the post-Conquest site; it is possible that the earlier ranges were retained while Bishop William Giffard was building his hall in the early twelfth century. A similar situation has been found at Bishop's Waltham Palace, where the bishops of Winchester had one of their most important residences. Here a timber building, perhaps a hall, went through at least two phases of construction during the late Saxon period, and as at Wolvesey it may well have continued in use after the Conquest. Unfortunately it is difficult to be certain of this, not least because it can be difficult to date archaeological events around the Conquest, especially as the pottery of the period does not change to any significant degree with the coming of the Normans. The Bishop's Waltham hall was not especially large (36ft x 14ft 8in, or 11m x 4.5m, though it did have additional structures/rooms attached to it), but it was associated with external yards and pits. The late Saxon building was found to the north of the medieval palace, though on this occasion it was outside of the moated Inner Court, where no evidence has yet been found for pre-Conquest buildings.

The post-Conquest period and the twelfth century

The years immediately after 1066 had to be dedicated to the establishment and consolidation of Norman rule. During this period it is easy to imagine that many late Saxon palaces, including such important royal centres as Old Windsor, Westminster and Kingsholm in Gloucester, would have continued in use. There would not have been time, quite apart from the necessary human and financial resources, to embark on extensive building campaigns in stone while the fundamentals of controlling a numerically dominant population were still being dealt with. Much of the initial work was in earth and timber, because extensive and heavily-defended sites could be established quickly using such materials. There was a degree of native precedent to such sites, not so much at palaces like Cheddar and Yeavering as at lower-status but still lordly (or 'thegnly') places like Goltho (Lincs; Beresford 1987) and Sulgrave (Northants; Davison 1977), where substantial ranges of timber buildings have been excavated within areas enclosed by substantial banks and ditches. The latter may not have been truly defensible, and the post-Conquest earthworks which replaced these late Saxon sites were noticeably larger, but they must have been obvious and impressive central places even so. Indeed it has recently been suggested that the insular Anglo-Saxon tradition of timber buildings represented a major influence on the masonry 'hall and chamber-block' model developed on seigneurial sites in Normandy in the post-Conquest period and then brought back into England in stone (Impey 1999). There is no strong precedent for this model in Normandy itself, but the Saxon timber structures both individually and in their disposition may well have influenced the conquering hierarchy sufficiently for them to have adapted the wooden template in stone.

Setting aside timber sites for the moment, a number of existing palaces were put to use or new ones established soon after the Conquest. Westminster is undoubtedly the best-known of the former; Cheddar is another good example, and we have already seen evidence for continuing use (if with a slight shift of location) at Wolvesey and Bishop's Waltham. As for new sites, ditching work may have been under way to create the equivalent of a motte around London's White Tower a decade before the latter's generally accepted commencement in 1077/8. The stone keep at Colchester, meanwhile, was not only the direct contemporary of the White Tower but also virtually identical in size and plan. At about the same time the likes of Clarendon (Wilts) began to attract attention, in this case as early as 1072 when it was little more than a hunting lodge close to the royal castle being established at Old Sarum. The lodge would eventually grow to become one of the most important, consistently popular and long-lived of all medieval palaces.

The location of pre-Conquest 'palace' buildings mostly beyond and to the north of the later moated areas at both Wolvesey and Bishop's Waltham may be little more than coincidence — two swallows do not make a summer. In many sees, of course, there can be no expectation of an earlier palace phase under a medieval episcopal site because several of the post-Conquest diocesan centres were newly-created as the Normans brought formerly rural cathedrals into cities (eg. North Elmham to Norwich via Thetford, or Selsey to Chichester). When the Salisbury diocese was moved from Sherborne in 1075, for instance, its new cathedral and palace at Old Sarum was placed within the old Iron Age hillfort. This had seen use during Roman and Saxon times as well, and there was a mint there at the beginning of the eleventh century which continued to strike coins until the early days of Henry II's reign (1154-89). The site was probably in the hands of the diocese already (the manor of Salisbury was a temporality of the Bishop of Sherborne) but the establishment of a royal castle very soon after the Conquest was probably a greater spur for the re-siting of the cathedral here; the site was much closer to the centre of the diocese as well. Despite this there has been no hint to date of an episcopal residence pre-dating 1075 at Old Sarum (**6**).

6   *The Inner Bailey at Old Sarum (Wilts) viewed from the east. The massive ramparts of an Iron Age hillfort offered a good choice of site for a new royal castle, cathedral and bishop's palace, the latter occupying the Inner Bailey*

A similar situation exists at Lincoln, which became the seat of a vast and ancient central English diocese in or soon after 1073 (the move was agreed in May 1072, receiving papal and royal approval in April of the following year). The cathedral had previously been based at Dorchester on Thames, a former Roman town that could scarcely have been described as a thriving and vibrant place in the late eleventh century. It was also in the extreme south-western corner of the diocese; if Lincoln was only slightly more central in the north-east, it did offer the advantages of a major urban site which still had important land ripe for development on high and very visible ground. As with Old Sarum William I established a royal castle in the old Roman city soon after the Conquest, and the castle and cathedral together covered the greater part of the northern half of the walled area. Curiously the bishops themselves did not have a residence in Lincoln until the second decade of the twelfth century, though the whereabouts of this first house is unknown, and the medieval bishop's palace whose ruins can still be visited immediately to the south of the cathedral was not established until the 1150s. There would appear to have been some activity on this site beforehand, as pottery sherds of the late Saxon period have been found during excavations. The nature of the activity is unknown, although there is little or no likelihood that it had anything to do with the episcopate.

The early twelfth century saw a significant expansion in the number of palaces being built, especially by the episcopate. The likes of Roger of Caen, Bishop of Salisbury (1103-39), and William Giffard or his successor Henry de Blois as bishops of Winchester in 1107-29 and 1129-71 respectively enjoyed long, though by no means uneventful, periods in office within wealthy diocese over whose resources they had control. Moreover many bishops brought significant wealth and position of their own to the job, and individually they could rival the monarch in their ability to invest heavily in ostentatious new building programmes. The new *domus* built by Giffard at Wolvesey, for instance, represented 'the largest non-monastic domestic structure of its date in England, exceeded only by Westminster Hall' (Biddle 1986, 6) (*see* **1**), though unlike the latter, Giffard's building seems to have contained a full residential suite rather than just a hall. Collectively their property and resources would outstrip even the Crown's, though for the most part the balance of power was firmly with the king and even the likes of Henry de Blois could find themselves reduced to exile for part of their term. Interestingly, though, de Blois was not removed from office when Stephen died in 1154 and was replaced by Henry II (though the order went out for his castles to be destroyed); instead he had to retire to Cluny until Henry allowed him to return from exile to Winchester in 1158. The masonry halls, chambers, service ranges and other accommodation built by kings and bishops across the land at this time represent an astonishing explosion of secular construction, particularly when seen against the background of monastic expansion and other ecclesiastical building work at the same time, not least at the bishops' own cathedrals.

It is well to remember that palaces did not exist in isolation. Those who built them were equally interested in the lands around about, partly because there was great economic value to be had from their exploitation. To that extent the farm centres associated with the Winchester palaces at Wolvesey, Bishop's Waltham and Witney (Oxon) may be typical, though sadly they are also typical in having received far less archaeological attention than the palaces themselves. It is astonishing, for instance, that the sports field and open ground which now occupy the medieval farm area between the palace buildings at Wolvesey and the city defences to the south and east have not even been the subject of geophysical survey, let alone anything more intrusive (see chapter 2). Not all of the interest in palace estates was economic: monarchs and bishops alike were great enthusiasts for the hunt, and the relationship between palaces and deer parks or other hunting grounds, such as the great swathes of forest, was established early in the Norman period (**7**). As we have seen, Clarendon started out as a hunting lodge, and sites of this type have been excavated (notably the Writtle, Essex; Rahtz 1969) while others survive, usually showing evidence for later building works as well (eg. Tollard Royal, Wilts).

Thirteenth-century palaces

The reigns of Henry III and his son Edward I covered all but the first 15 years of the thirteenth century (Edward lived on until 1307), an astonishingly long period in the context of medieval reigns anywhere in contemporary Europe. This is not to say that England was a haven of peace at the time: Henry had ascended to the throne as a minor, while campaigns occupied both monarchs. Internally the situation in Wales had to be dealt with, and Henry in particular spent the greater part of several years in France. Despite this, or perhaps in part as a result of it, both kings spent lavishly on building campaigns. Their work at Westminster, for instance on the Painted Chamber, is justly famed despite its destruction in the first half of the nineteenth century (fortunately excellent record drawings were made before this occurred), while most of what they achieved at the Tower

**THE KING'S HOUSES
1154 - 1216**

▨ ROYAL FORESTS

▲ ROYAL HOUSES

🏰 CASTLES ASSOCIATED
WITH ROYAL FORESTS

Pickering

Easingwold

York   Driffield

Peak

Kingshaugh
Clipstone   Laxton

Nottingham

Radmore
Cannock

Rockingham   Kingscliffe
Brigstock
Kinver   Geddington

Feckenham   Northampton   Brampton

Silverstone
Finmere   Wakefield
Woodstock
St Briavels   Brill   Writtle
Oxford
Havering
Westminster
Windsor

Bath   Freemantle   Wolverton
Cheddar   Hurstbourne   Tidgrove
Gillingham   Clarendon
Cranbourne   Stansted
Poorstock   Beaulieu
Bere   Portsmouth

100   100

MILES   KMS

7   *The relationship of royal residences and forests in the late twelfth and early thirteenth centuries.*
    Drawing by J. Steane

of London can still be seen or reconstructed (see chapters 3 and 4). Henry was especially fond of Clarendon, being responsible for extensive building and internal decorative works there, and again both were active at Winchester Castle (eg. the Great Hall). The royal works in Wales were also a defining factor in their reigns, especially so for Edward. It was also at this time that the gradual move began towards increased privacy for the monarch and his family, usually with separate accommodation for king and queen with their attendants. Privacy was to become a common theme in virtually all areas of society, secular and religious.

The bishops were not idle during this period either, although there was much less work done during the thirteenth century than either before or later in the Winchester diocese at the likes of Bishop's Waltham, Farnham or Wolvesey. The Salisbury residence at Sherborne, meanwhile, had been confiscated by the Crown in 1135 and stayed as royal property for more than 200 years. Work here during the thirteenth century was restricted to maintenance, though the defences underwent substantial remodelling early in the century (White 1986). At this stage the diocese would doubtless have been fully occupied with the planning and execution of the removal of their cathedral from Old Sarum to its new site on the east bank of the Avon little more than 2 miles (3.2km) to the south. This involved not only the construction of one of the finest ecclesiastical buildings of that or any other era in Europe, but also the development of a new residence for the bishop within the cathedral close.

Others were active later in the century, notably Robert Burnell, Bishop of Bath and Wells from 1275-92. This extremely wealthy prelate was denied the highest church office of Canterbury by his somewhat less than godly fathering of illegitimate offspring which led to acerbic comments at the time. Nevertheless, the riches he accrued in office and personally would have impressed in any age: he controlled 82 manors either in his own right or through the see (this compares with Winchester's 50 — they were the wealthiest bishopric — or Canterbury's 34). Burnell was not slow to expend the fruits of these manors on his personal comfort, not only in his 'home' palace at Wells but also, perhaps especially, at the site which still bears his name, Acton Burnell in Shropshire. The impression of strength given here by the corner towers and crenellated walls is just that: this was very much a residence built for style and comfort with fine accommodation for the bishop himself and his senior officers such as the constable, along with smaller attic rooms for lesser officials such as clerks and secretaries. It is highly unlikely that defence was ever a serious consideration in its design and construction even if it was close to the Welsh border (**8**).

The later medieval period

The redevelopment of Westminster and Windsor is a defining element of royal works in the later medieval period. As noted above, Henry III and Edward I undertook extensive work at Westminster, at which time it was still very much in palatial use. Gradually, however, arms of government such as the Chancery and King's Bench began to take up accommodation in the great hall there. Richard II's rebuilding of the hall has been seen as an attempt to restate the absolute quality of the monarchy's power, and the commissioning of 13 statues of the kings from Edward the Confessor down to Richard

8   Bishop Robert Burnell's late thirteenth-century palace at Acton Burnell, Shropshire

himself was powerfully symbolic in this context. More impressive still, however, was the rebuilding of the hall itself from 1393 onwards. Recent work has shown that the earlier Norman hall, of virtually the same plan, had been of a single span (there is no physical evidence to suggest that it had been aisled), so Richard's structure was not quite as revolutionary as had been thought, and contemporary references make it clear that the old hall had been in need of serious remedial work (**9**). No doubt the massive single span of the roof had put severe pressure on the outer walls, and the east side had been buttressed in 1385-7. Even so the hammer beam and arch-braced structure put up by the master carpenter Hugh Herland during 1393-9 remains as one of the great achievements of the medieval world, and there can be little doubt that it was equally or more impressive in its own time as it is today.

Windsor, meanwhile, had been much favoured by Henry III who stayed there regularly from 1224 onwards, rarely missing the chance to visit. In the early years he might be there for only a few days per year, but from the 1230s he was regularly in residence for 20 days or more (in 1247 he managed 73 days). It was not uncommon for these days to be spread about across the year, and then as subsequently Windsor was clearly a very convenient stop on journeys west from London (or on the return). Henry's enthusiasm does not seem to have been shared by all monarchs, and when the great chamber he had built burnt down in 1295/6 it was not restored straight away. During the middle of the fourteenth century, however, Edward III spent over £50,000 on the old castle, a vast sum by any standards of the day and 'the most expensive secular building project of the entire

9 *Ground plan of*
the Great Hall
at Westminster
Palace.
Drawing by
R. Harris

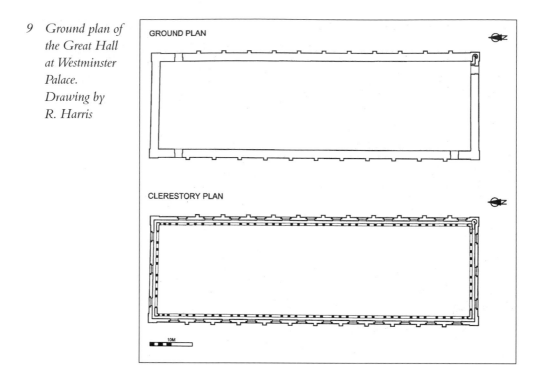

Middle Ages in England' (Brindle and Kerr 1997, 39). He had been born there and clearly felt great affinity for the place. Much of his expenditure went on rebuilding the palatial apartments in the Upper Ward, lining the existing defences with lodgings to create what amounted to a courtyard plan. Though to a degree dictated by the pre-existence of the curtain wall, this regularity stands in marked contrast to the way in which so many earlier palace plans developed (eg. Clarendon) and points forward to the formality and regularity of layout which were to become the norm in the late fifteenth century and into the sixteenth. Edward also remodelled Henry III's chapel in the lower bailey, while also deciding to establish the centre of his Order of the Round Table at the castle as well. William of Wykeham was the Surveyor of the king's works at Windsor from 1356-61, but his name is as familiar for the great building campaigns he embarked on while Bishop of Winchester either in the name of the diocese or his own (as at New College, Oxford, or Winchester College).

Episcopal palaces could also witness extensive new building works or refurbishments, though few brand new sites were developed. As one might expect, the wealthiest diocese took the lead, and substantial construction went on in the Winchester diocese at (for instance) Bishop's Waltham and Farnham. At the former, William of Wykeham, bishop from 1367-1404, transformed the prelate's residential and hall ranges along the south and west sides respectively of the moated Inner Court at the end of the fourteenth century. His successor, Thomas Beaufort (1405-47) built a new gatehouse at the court's north-west corner and, more importantly, the great range of lodgings which provided modern accommodation for courtiers and guests along the entire northern side of the moat platform. Beaufort and Wykeham were jointly responsible for the impressively large bakehouse/brewhouse which ran south from the east end of the guest range. Wykeham also put new life into Wolvesey, which does not seem to have been a favoured palace of the bishopric in the century following the death of Henry III. Various parts of the palace saw substantial renovation during his episcopate, but new work concentrated on the refurbishment of the bishop's quarters. Beaufort's successor was William Waynflete, one of the great builders of his age.

The Tudors and their palaces

Eltham and Oatlands Palaces and the Manor of More at Rickmansworth on the south-east, south-west, and north-west sides of London respectively, epitomise much of transition from the late medieval into the Tudor period. Eltham and the Manor of More had already been transformed under episcopal authority, in the former case during the late thirteenth and early fourteenth century by Bishop Anthony Bek of Durham and in the latter by an unusual joint venture between the bishops of Winchester and Durham in the 1460s. Oatlands (House) was a secular venture initiated in the early fifteenth century, but no less impressive for that. All three sites were already moated, Eltham massively so, and had already been built on with impressive accommodation ranged around courtyards before they were taken over by the Crown. Edward IV had made significant additions to Eltham in 1475-83 — his great hall survives there but his chapel does not — and a new entrance courtyard (the Green Court) was established immediately to the north-east of the moat in the sixteenth century. Both of the other sites were taken over by Henry VIII and further developed along courtyard lines, though the king seems to have done less at Rickmansworth than he did at many of his other acquisitions. As we shall see in chapter 4, Eltham (especially its new hall) also seems to have exerted a powerful influence over palace building in Scotland in the late fifteenth and early sixteenth centuries. The longevity of the basic hall and chamber model seems clear in this context, though both elements had undergone significant changes by this time.

This tendency to acquire residences in a ring around central London became steadily more marked, especially under Henry VIII. At the time episcopal estates in particular were coming under increasing pressure as the public displeasure at ecclesiastical excesses grew and the Reformation loomed. Several bishops sought to jump before they were pushed by offloading properties to the Crown in an attempt to buy safety, or at least time. They were not the only ones to feel under threat, however, as the secular example of Oatlands demonstrates. This process reached its zenith at Nonsuch, which in many ways also marked the peak of the Henrician pursuit of comfort and sporting pleasure. Like Hampton Court the site was attractive for its fine countryside and especially for its hunting potential, though given Henry's corpulence in later years the game tended increasingly to be brought to the king rather than the other way round. New diversions were also embraced, such as tennis and bowling, and buildings dedicated to these sports became features of Henrician palaces such as Hampton Court. Interest in gardens and landscape design expanded alongside the continued drive to tame and kill nature's wild beasts, and produced exquisite gardens (again at Hampton Court, but perhaps best of all at Nonsuch). Sadly very little of this aspect of Tudor palace design has survived directly into the present, though contemporary and later descriptions and depictions often make up for this and archaeological investigations can and do make very significant contributions as well.

The Tudor age straddled the end of the medieval and the early post-medieval periods. It can be misleading to place too much emphasis (in archaeological terms at least) on the break between the periods, but the pivotal position of the era between the ancient and modern worlds is scarcely deniable. If the Tudor period harked back into earlier medieval centuries in some respects, in many others it looked forwards into the modern world.

2 Studying medieval palaces

Introduction

Medieval palaces and their surroundings have attracted the attention of people with an interest in the past for hundreds of years. Great antiquarians such as John Aubrey, who was active in the later seventeenth century, have left us with vital records of sites which no longer exist above ground (eg. Woodstock and Everswell within what is now the Blenheim estate, Oxon). Many other sites have remained available for study, of course, both above and below ground. Research has become increasingly methodical, especially during the twentieth century, and the main archaeological techniques will be described and assessed in this chapter. It will become apparent that most of the techniques are generic and can be applied to archaeological sites of most periods, but their use specifically on medieval palaces is undoubtedly of considerable interest in its own right.

First principles: using history

Any archaeologist who approaches a medieval or later site of any type without first considering the value of historical sources is rash indeed, and is likely to commit basic errors of commission or omission. Many (but by no means all) medieval sites are referred to in contemporary documents while later sources can also provide invaluable information. This is nowhere more true than with palaces, whether built by kings or bishops, and huge amounts of data can be available for the best-known sites. The various houses of the bishops of Winchester, for instance, can be studied in the bishops' pipe rolls, annual financial and works accounts which have survived (albeit patchily) for this diocese from 1208/9 onwards (Riall 1994). The various royal building campaigns of the medieval period, meanwhile, tend to be extremely well documented because of the contemporary need to maintain financial control over the works (though inevitably there are gaps, often in particularly frustrating places). All students of the period are in debt to Sir Howard Colvin and his team of researchers who produced the monumental *History of the King's Works* in several volumes from 1963-84, and this must be the first port of call for anyone looking at a royal palace, castle, hunting lodge or other house.

Such documents can be a rather hit-and-miss affair in that some sites might not be described at all while the names used in referring to parts of others are often different to those in currency today — the various mural towers at the Tower in London are a good case in point. Equally the historical record may not be reflected within the archaeology of a site. Clarendon Palace offers a good example of this: there are numerous mid- and later thirteenth-century references to buttresses against the king's great hall, which had been built on steeply-sloping ground, but 'none of the excavations round the walls of the great hall revealed archaeological evidence of buttressing' (James and Robinson 1988, 10). It seems inconceivable that the great hall has been misidentified given the scale of the structure concerned, especially in comparison to the remaining buildings and their layout. Either the 1930s excavations missed the buttresses, which seems equally unlikely given the scale of the work involved and the likely size of the buttresses, or the medieval references are wrong or have been misinterpreted.

Pictorial sources can help to fill in some of these gaps, but again there are problems with any medieval depictions of sites. The accuracy is often questionable — drawings and plans of the time were often highly schematic — and the original purpose of the illustration may have affected its execution: property surveys, whether cartographic or written, may well be deliberately misleading in an attempt to justify one party's ownership of a given area. Fortunately the numbers of reasonably trustworthy pictorial documents available increases for the late medieval period, and especially afterwards. The art and science of surveying (early maps demonstrate that it can be both) improved rapidly in the late sixteenth and seventeenth centuries, and by the early decades of the eighteenth century many excellent plans of royal/governmental sites were being drawn up by the likes of the Board of Ordnance and the Office of Works. While these are obviously not medieval sources they do commonly show buildings and features of that period, which might have subsequently disappeared. Accordingly they can be of great value in reconstructing the medieval appearance of a palace. There appear to be fewer accurate surveys of this sort extant for bishops' houses, but it may be that they survive undiscovered in diocesan archives.

Using such sources is no mere academic exercise: it is important for a proper understanding of a place, and essential if work on site today is not to cause unnecessary and irreparable damage to historic fabric or archaeological remains. This is as true for urban tenements or rural villages as it is for medieval palaces, but the exceptional importance of many of the latter undoubtedly increases the need for an appreciation of the historical development of a site. One example among many will suffice.

Using historical sources at the Tower of London

In most ways the Tower of London is the best-known of all our medieval palaces, and it is certainly the most visited. Around 2.5 million people pay to enter the Tower every year, and as many more come to look at the castle from the outside but do not go in. The site is an icon of British (or perhaps more correctly English) national history, and has borne witness to countless important events. This legacy of historic resonance is etched into the fabric of the place, above and below ground, and there is scarcely a part of it which is of anything less than high archaeological potential. Having said that it is all too easy for visitors to assume that the castle we see today is much as it has always been. Nothing could be further from the truth: it is one of our most complex historic monuments, with secrets still to be told. Several parts of the site retain evidence for several generations of buildings, and the features such as gardens and yards which go with them. If the Tower of London we see today is at least partly a product of Victorian artifice (Parnell 1993, 98-108), the evidence for its true past is still available to us in a variety of forms.

The White Tower is a particularly good example of this. William the Conqueror's massive stone keep stands today in splendid isolation at the literal and conceptual heart of the castle, but it was not always thus. Indeed it had buildings against one or more sides from the middle of the twelfth century onwards, when Henry II added a forebuilding at the west end of the keep's south side to provide protection for its entrance. Such structures survive and are well known at several other twelfth and thirteenth-century castles (eg. Dover and Scarborough, both with strong royal connections, and Rochester), but the example at the Tower of London was demolished in 1674. Fortunately it is shown clearly on Haiward and Gascoyne's survey of 1597 (**10**), the best of the early depictions of the Tower and a reasonable representation of how it must have looked at the end of the medieval period. The plan also shows that a Jewel House had been added to the south side of the White Tower, running east to the Queen's Lodgings, while another low range had been built along the east face, but separated from it by a narrow courtyard. This range seems to have been put up during the reign of Edward III (1327-77), while the Jewel House was probably built during 1396-9. Like the forebuilding these fourteenth-century structures were removed in the 1670s (the east range was left in place), and plans of the following decade show that they had been replaced with stockade fences and timber sheds (Parnell, 1993). Those on the south side of the White Tower were replaced with the Carriage Storehouse in 1717; this in turn made way for the Horse Armoury in 1825. The latter and the east range were demolished in the late 1870s and early 1880s (Parnell, 1993), with the loss of much medieval masonry in the process, leaving us with the White Tower largely as we see it now.

Much the same process of repeated reconstruction on the same place can be seen elsewhere around the Tower on the same surveys. Haiward and Gascoyne, for instance, show a range of stores lying perpendicular to and abutting Henry III's inner curtain wall to the north of the White Tower. Elements of the royal accommodation such as the Wardrobe, running east from the Wardrobe Tower to the Broad Arrow Tower, and open space, probably gardens, lay to the east of the keep. During 1663-4 the New Armouries was erected on the open space (the Wardrobe was probably removed at the same time), and in 1688-91/2 the Grand Storehouse replaced the old stores ranges. The two new buildings were among the finest post-medieval constructions at the Tower, and the New Armouries still survives. Sadly the Grand Storehouse was gutted in a major fire on 31 October 1841, and was replaced four years later by the Waterloo Barracks, intended (as the name implies) for the permanent garrison but now principally famed as the house of the Crown Jewels.

The popularity of the Tower naturally places great strains upon it: the pressure of numbers alone would cause wear and tear to any historic site, and paying visitors quite properly expect to receive top-quality facilities (eg. catering and retail) as well as value for their admission fee. Furthermore the site itself and its resident community needs to be serviced, while security and fire prevention have risen to the top of the agenda in the light of disasters in the late 1980s and 1990s at Hampton Court Palace, Uppark House and Windsor Castle. Such factors can create a need for substantial building programmes, and these must be added to the ongoing round of routine maintenance which happens at any set of buildings. How can the requirements for such works be squared with the

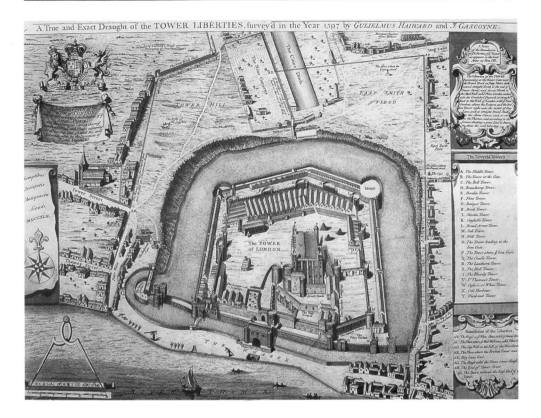

10 *Haiward and Gascoyne's 1597 survey of the Tower of London, showing the castle very much as it would have appeared at the end of the medieval period. © Crown copyright: Historic Royal Palaces*

overwhelming need to preserve and sustain the history and archaeology of the site into the future?

Foreknowledge and careful planning are the inevitable answer. During the early 1990s, for instance, it had become obvious that the existing electricity cables at the Tower were getting close to the end of their active lives. At the same time plans were well advanced to move and re-display the Crown Jewels, and this would require a massive increase in demand for electricity. These imperatives could only be satisfied by complete replacement of the existing supply with a new set of cables, and these were to run around the site in a continuous ring. The Tower bears many scars from the insertions of services such as cables and drains in days gone by when historical and archaeological sensitivities were either not appreciated or sat too far down the list of priorities to provide protection for the fabric of the site. The electricity main being planned in the early 1990s was different, however, because the Tower's authorities did take full account of the needs of the castle's past as well as its present and future. To this end various options for the cable routes were studied against the excellent historic mapping of the site. The results of earlier archaeological works were also looked at, while the location and course of existing service runs were also checked. It was therefore possible to predict which areas crossed by the ring main would be the most sensitive, and also to establish where the new cables could be lain in the footprint of old services. The latter prevented any new damage, and the focus on sensitive areas allowed archaeological resources to be concentrated there to prevent unnecessary or accidental damage.

Surviving buildings

The next and equally obvious source to look at is the buildings themselves. Many medieval palaces have survived into the current land- or townscape, although what is left can vary from low earthworks to near-complete complexes. Two reasonably distinct groups can be recognised: sites which are no longer in use (except perhaps as visitor attractions), and those where part or all of the palace is still operational (though not necessarily as a palace). In general the former group usually comprises earthworks or ruinous sites, whereas the latter will include some intact buildings. There is some overlap: at Farnham Castle (Surrey), for instance, the late twelfth-century shell keep is maintained by English Heritage as one of its Properties in Care, while the hall and other medieval buildings which continued to function as the bishop's palace into the twentieth century are now used for conference facilities. The latter buildings also display plentiful evidence of their continued use, and the high medieval fabric sits alongside several other building phases which are clearly visible today (cover and **colour plate 1**).

Ruinous buildings can display an equal complexity of phases, though usually without more modern 'overlays' to confuse the picture, and this can be evident in both ground plans and elevations. Plan evidence often takes the form of one wall or building butting against or cutting through other masonry which is therefore demonstrably earlier in date. Looking again at Farnham Castle, the fourteenth-century lodgings added to the back of the shell keep's West Turret is a good example of this. In some cases, however, the effects of stone-robbing (especially the removal of ashlar facing stones, leaving only the rubble core behind) can make these relationships difficult to understand; much of Old Sarum falls into this category. The problem has often been exacerbated by modern consolidation using thick layers of cement and in some cases rebuilding the core work.

Building elevations tend to provide plentiful evidence for structural development, assuming that the building itself is not in essence of a single phase, such as Acton Burnell. This might be evident in the straight joint between original masonry and a new build, and any modern extension to a house will display as much. Alternatively one might see evidence for the wholesale replacement of windows in one or more storeys, as in the West Tower and great hall at Bishop's Waltham Palace where Bishop William of Wykeham inserted new windows in the late fourteenth century, removing most traces of the original twelfth-century arrangements as he did so. The grand new Perpendicular windows can best be appreciated from the west (ie. outside the palace), from where one

11 Bishop's Waltham Palace (Hants) seen from the west, with the twelfth-century window visible to the right of the lamp-post

also gets a good view of the single surviving late twelfth-century window at the palace, in the outer wall of a passage range between the hall and the West Tower (**11**). The hall at Bishop's Waltham also contains other evidence of the radical overhaul effected upon it by William of Wykeham in 1378-81. Blind arcading in the south wall is the only feature left of the twelfth-century arrangements, though the lower walls are largely of this date as well, while the later work is evident in the masonry itself, the windows, and the signs of a new roof (corbelling, and slots in the wall face where vertical timber posts once rose from the corbels to support the roof).

Bishop's Waltham also provides excellent evidence for the service buildings and lodgings that would have formed such an important element of any palace complex. The massive bakehouse and brewhouse erected by William of Wykeham in the diagonally-opposite corner of the moated Inner Court is the most immediately impressive of these at Waltham, not least because it is one of the first sights to confront the modern visitor on the somewhat inappropriate approach to the ruins from the car park. It is still an imposing structure when seen from the more correct entrance point at the gatehouse over the north-west corner of the moat, however, at which point the bishop's lodgings are hidden from view by other service buildings — the substantial kitchen and other rooms to the north of the hall. Today's visitor buys a ticket in a ground-floor room which gives little hint of the splendour of the guest lodgings on the first floor above, built by Cardinal Henry Beaufort in 1438-42. The masonry of the service ranges and the

12 The bakehouse/brewhouse at Bishop's Waltham palace with putlog holes rising through four stages to the right of the window

timberwork of the lodgings also contain plenty of archaeological evidence, whether in the form of putlog holes which show how the walls of the bakehouse/brewhouse were raised, or the complex of ovens in the kitchen (**12**, *see* **colour plate 20**).

Archaeological evidence

Archaeological study of palaces can of course apply to surviving buildings, whether ruinous or not, but it is a subject which becomes uniquely important when looking at or below the ground. Earthwork or cropmark sites can be examined by measured survey, aerial photography and geophysical methods to provide a level of information about a site which might, at first glance, seem to have little or no potential for study. Then, if necessary and desirable, the site can be excavated, in stages ranging from small test pits through trial trenches up to large areas (even, in extremis, whole sites). Many of the techniques involved in such research are not only used as a matter of routine by modern archaeologists, but are also familiar to a wider public because of media coverage. This book is not the place for detailed description of archaeological techniques, though it is worth looking at their applicability to palaces: in other words, how and where archaeological evidence for such sites can be found today.

Existing evidence and where to look for it

It is easy to understand the suggestion that 'the activities and preoccupations of kings, their families and courtiers [have] been given inadequate treatment by medieval archaeologists' (Steane 1993, 10-11), as many textbooks do indeed skate over the subject (and that of episcopal estates). Nevertheless a great deal of archaeological work has been done on palatial sites over the last 50 years or so. The evidence can be found in museums, record offices and archives around Britain, and these sources must be the first port of call for anyone wanting to study a palace. They can be divided into two main groups, national and local. This applies both to catalogues of data (lists of sites and excavations), archives (eg. the documentation of archaeological projects themselves) and publications (excavation reports etc.). The main national catalogues in Britain are the National Monuments Records (NMRs) which are maintained by English Heritage, CADW, Historic Scotland and DoENI. These contain major collections of air photographs, copies of thousands of excavation archives, and original documentation. Depositing copies of archaeological archives in the NMRs is not only good for anyone pursuing research interests, but also invaluable for the security of the information itself. Data security is a major social issue in the digital age, but information which is largely held on paper (as most archaeological records have been to date) is highly vulnerable to disaster or loss. Many excavators would offer a silent 'there but for the grace of God' when reading of the loss of the excavation records for work in 1982 at the episcopal palace at Kirkwall on Orkney (Cox *et al* 1998, 569). The sheer volume of information can be daunting, but searches on key elements such as the date and type of site in which one is interested (eg. *medieval palaces* as opposed to *Roman villas*) make the resources more manageable. These archives include computerised data catalogues, and they are contactable via the Internet; subject searches can be initiated there as well.

The local equivalent to the NMRs is the Sites and Monuments Record (SMR). All England's administrative counties, most Scottish Regions and the administrative areas of Wales maintain such catalogues, and they can be immensely valuable sources of information. They can be more up-to-date than the national archives because they are usually integral to the local planning process and thus have to be as comprehensive as possible; the results of virtually all modern archaeological work will be copied into the SMR, usually rapidly by means of a detailed report. It is usually possible to search the records using key words, as with the national archives, although by no means all SMRs are computerised and so the process can take longer. The local archives score heavily over the national ones, however, in their coverage of earlier work: late nineteenth and earlier twentieth-century discoveries may not appear in the national catalogues, especially if no formal records of the work survive, but they usually will have been included in the local archives through references to published descriptions (often obscure in their own right).

These catalogues do not usually incorporate the original data from archaeological projects such as site notebooks, photographs, drawings or the finds, though copies may be included, especially on microfiche. These records, commonly referred to as project archives, may be stored nationally either by the same organisations that look after the NMRs or by one of the national museums such as the British Museum. More often than not, however, such material will be held locally, in the stores of the county museum or the nearest local equivalent (even in England not all counties maintain such a service). Those responsible for such stores are naturally enough very security-conscious given the irreplaceable nature of their collections and the often high intrinsic value of individual pieces, but the archives are usually readily accessible to bona fide researchers. Public accessibility is usually an important point of principle to those responsible for looking after the collections as well. Some important archives are held outside these national and local collections: Historic Royal Palaces, for instance, look after virtually all archaeological material from the Tower of London and Hampton Court Palace, maintaining special stores at both site.

Publications on palaces come in many shapes and forms from guide books produced by English Heritage and its equivalent national bodies through to highly detailed technical reports on excavations. National publications including the journals of major learned groups such as the Societies of Antiquaries of London and Scotland, the Royal Archaeological Institute and the Society for Medieval Archaeology often have articles about palaces, and individual books or series may be produced by English Heritage et al, various University Presses, and commercial publishers. Local works include articles in journals from county or other archaeological and historical societies, the Victoria County Histories, county/regional inventories, and a wealth of locally published work. The gathering pace of information technology, meanwhile, has already seen information on palaces posted on a variety of individual and organisational web sites.

Fieldwork techniques in practice

It should be possible, then, to find out whether any fieldwork has taken place on any given site in the past, and use this as the starting point for further work where this is envisaged or necessary. Such fieldwork might arise through dedicated research, although it must be admitted that this is relatively rare nowadays. Most work now occurs within the framework of local planning and development control, and royal, episcopal or other high-status sites are not exempt from such considerations. Many of the most important archaeological projects on such sites in recent times have arisen precisely because of development pressure. To be fair, some of these projects have been as much to do with the long-term preservation of sites, such as the archaeological excavations in advance of underpinning the Round Tower at Windsor Castle, or have been necessitated by catastrophes and their aftermath (we need look no further than Windsor Castle for an example of this). How, then, are archaeological techniques applied to palaces?

In many ways the answer is 'no differently than for any other type of site', though that would be too simplistic a position. For one thing a relatively high proportion of royal and episcopal sites in Britain are designated in law as Scheduled Ancient Monuments, and they are thus given more protection than most; even quite simple activities such as laying new drains will tend to need some archaeological input. This is not to say that the sites are sacrosanct, to be preserved untouched and unalterable for all time; far from it, but any activity which might damage the monument must be rigorously justified, and executed under appropriate archaeological scrutiny.

It is common now for archaeological studies of a site (the type and period is virtually irrelevant) to begin with non-destructive techniques such as analysis of air photograph evidence, measured survey, fieldwalking and geophysical prospection. The first two or three seem less relevant to palaces than to other types of site if one looks no further than ruined or surviving palaces, but there are plenty which survive mostly or only as earthworks and cropmarks; others do not even provide that much visible evidence but instead survive solely below the surface. Such sites are still highly susceptible to damage, especially from ploughing. Aerial photographs of earthworks can be both impressive and highly informative, such as the well-known pictures of Henry V's Pleasance and Mere at Kenilworth Castle which have also been the subject of a measured survey (Taylor 1997 fig 5 and 1998 fig 2). Some sites such as Merdon Castle (Hursley, Wilts; a property of the Bishops of Winchester) can be appreciated as well from air photographs as from the ground (Riall 1994, fig 11), but such images take on crucial importance in a few cases where ploughing or similar damage has removed earthworks and left behind only cropmarks. This is probably less common with palaces than for most categories of archaeological site. Even so the potential value is demonstrated at Somersham (Cambs) where impressive features (including terraced walks and what appears to be a moated gazebo) of medieval gardens belonging to the Bishops of Ely have been reduced to cropmarks but can still be seen on aerial photographs (Taylor 1989, and 1997 fig 6).

Sometimes earthworks are difficult to photograph, for instance because of tree cover, but it should still be possible to carry out a measured topographical survey. This can range from a simple plan of major features to the sort of highly-detailed coverage of even the most subtle surface variations which has become a familiar trait of Britain's Royal Commissions on Historical Monuments. At Hamstead Marshall (Berks), for instance, two motte and bailey earthworks with strong royal connections (both Henry III and Edward I stayed here) became features of a post-medieval planned landscape and, at least partly because of this, were covered in trees. Thus air photographs from the 1940s onwards often provided good coverage of the late seventeenth-century formal gardens, but the medieval earthworks were largely invisible. The site is clearly a complex one, however, and a survey by the RCHME in the mid-1980s not only covered the main earthworks, where there are possible traces of buildings, but also located fishponds and features from an associated medieval village; the latter was transplanted as part of the post-medieval landscaping (see Bonney and Dunn 1989, Keevill and Linford 1998) (**13**). Fishponds and building platforms have also been surveyed at Llanddew, Powys, on a site belonging to the bishops of St David's (Nenk *et al* 1992, 305). Fieldwalking is one of the simplest of all archaeological methods, involving the controlled collection and recording of artefacts which have been brought to the field surface by ploughing. It is not often relevant on palace sites, though it was used on the potential sites of several royal *llysoedd* in Gwynedd during the early to mid-1990s. Then, as in most cases, fieldwalking proved most valuable when used in conjunction with other techniques of archaeological and historical investigation (Johnstone 1997, 55).

One of the other techniques used in Gwynedd was geophysical surveying. This has developed into one of the most potent and successful means of examining archaeological sites without recourse to excavation, with the two main techniques (magnetometry and resistivity) being largely complementary and frequently used together. A third method,

13 Hamstead Marshall (Berks) with a motte to the right and the Kennet valley in the background. The reedy growth across the centre ground marks the position of a silted up fishpond

ground-penetrating radar, has yet to find widespread acceptance in the same way, but it is valuable so long as some limitations are recognised. Radar also offers the potential to look inside and through the fabric of buildings, though little use has been made of this yet (**14**). Perhaps surprisingly, palaces have not received a great deal of attention from geophysical surveyors, though this may reflect the protected status of many palaces, as the majority of geophysical surveys occur as development-led work. English Heritage's database, however, lists only 22 geophysical surveys covering nine palace sites (one of which is the Roman Governor's 'palace' in London), and most of these seem to have had distinctly limited success. One exception was at Freens Court, Hereford and Worcester, where buildings seen on aerial photographs in 1990 were examined by resistivity in the following year with exceptionally clear results. The site may be a Mercian royal palace of the eighth century (such a site is located here in historical sources), but this has yet to be demonstrated conclusively. Alternatively the structures could be agricultural and later twelfth or thirteenth century, though they would still probably belong to a royal estate centre (**colour plate 2**).

Admittedly the database is not comprehensive (work at the Tower of London and Hampton Court Palace is not included), and some sites probably do not appear because the palatial part of a site was secondary or even peripheral to the reasons for carrying out a survey. At Hamstead Marshall, for instance, work was carried out with only limited success on one of the two motte and bailey earthworks with strong royal connections in

14 *Using radar survey to detect ancient features behind Victorian refacing of the thirteenth-century inner curtain wall at the Tower of London*

the thirteenth century, but the project's main focus was on the formal gardens of the post-medieval period (Keevill and Linford 1998). Equally the remarkable survey of the Privy Garden at Hampton Court presumably does not appear on the list because its main focus was the garden itself; it would be absurd, however, to view this in isolation from the palace (Thurley 1995, fig 106). Even if we take account of these cautions, the general picture of relatively little geophysical work being done on palaces seems to be true. Nevertheless we can look at an example from the Tower of London for an indication of the potential, and pitfalls, of geophysics.

At first site the Tower may not appear to be a good choice for surveys of any kind. Much of the castle's interior is covered with buildings, and most of the remaining space

15 *Excavating a late thirteenth-century building in the east moat at the Tower of London. The building showed up very clearly on resistivity and radar surveys, partly because the masonry lay just below the grass surface*

is paved or cobbled over (magnetometry and resistivity are virtually inoperable on such surfaces, though radar can be used). There are some lawned areas, of which the moat is the most obvious, and this has been examined comprehensively in recent years. The whole circuit was surveyed using resistivity and radar in 1996, following on from more limited work using all three geophysical techniques in 1995. The work identified a number of medieval and later masonry structures built out into the moat, and these were subsequently trial-trenched (**15**). This might seem like a major success, but these features were already known through historic plans, and even photographs in the case of one

Victorian building which stood until it took a direct bomb hit in 1940, and they survive only just below the grass. What of more deeply buried archaeology, and unexpected discoveries? Magnetometry and resistivity were at a serious disadvantage here, because the techniques cannot 'see' much (if at all) below 3ft 3in (1m) in normal circumstances. Radar, however, can provide much deeper penetration and seemed to be the ideal way of assessing the lower limits of the moat, which was already known to be around 10ft (3m) deep. Unfortunately the saturation of the moat fills caused by a very high water table severely affected the radar signals, and even structures which had already been identified by trial trenching at depths of between 6ft (1.82m) and 8ft (2.44m) could not be located with any confidence in the survey results. Obviously we cannot conclude, therefore, that blank areas on the survey do not contain archaeological remains.

The example of Freens Court illustrates the drawback of all non-intrusive archaeological survey techniques: by their very nature they cannot provide dating evidence for a site, except perhaps by comparison to similar sites, and such an approach can be fraught with dangers of misidentification and interpretation. At some point, therefore, we have to go below the surface physically if we are to achieve an adequate understanding of a site. This need not mean full-scale excavation, of course: a great deal can be found out by trial trenching or even through boreholes. The latter are too small to give more than an extremely general picture of a site, but they have been used successfully on many archaeological sites including the Tower of London.

Trial trenching sounds simple enough, but it can vary from one or a few small excavations 6ft 6in (2m) square, or even less in some circumstances, up to multiple arrays of trenches which can be 100ft (30m) long or more. Sometimes, as in the moat at the Tower of London, the approach can be to mix small and larger excavations as appropriate to the particular needs of each, but in many palace sites the combined restrictions of space and protection leads to a presumption for smaller-scale work. Once again, ignoring the Tower for the moment, a few examples will suffice.

Hampton Court Palace also had a moat, though this was a Tudor feature (for our purposes we must ignore the potential for such a feature associated with the medieval manorial complex of the Knights Hospitallers). While the palace's Tudor moat was certainly an important feature around three sides of the building complex (with the Thames on the other), it is by no means clear that it was intended to be wet throughout its length. Contemporary references to a pheasant yard in the moat, for instance, suggest otherwise, and by this time defence would scarcely have been a major reason for such a feature anyway. Even so a wide and deep ditch could have numerous functions, not least drainage. Gradually, however, the moat was completely backfilled: the process was already under way in the seventeenth century and had been completed early in the Victorian era. The process was partly reversed in 1908-10 when the stretch of moat in front of the Great Gatehouse on the west side of the palace was re-excavated, thus exposing the fine bridge across it once again. The rest remains as a backfilled feature, scarcely recognisable among the gardens today. A 10m-long trial trench was dug into the northern arm of the moat in 1994, providing a section across roughly half of the ditch (**16**). This was found to be 13ft 9in (4.2m) deep from the current ground level (the original depth would probably have been 11ft 6in/3.5m or thereabouts), and important evidence for the past environment both

16 *Trial trenching the Tudor moat at Hampton Court Palace*

of the ditch and its environs were recovered (see page 156).

Several trial trenches were excavated at Spynie Palace in 1986 (Youngs *et al* 1987, 186-7) in advance of large-scale excavation in subsequent years. This was the main residence of the bishops of Moray during the medieval period. Walls, floors, drains and other features were found. Structures such as latrines and a possible stable block were located in the trenches, along with precinct walls and cobbled roads. Clearly these trenches were very successful in achieving their aims, but less positive results are not uncommon in trial trenches. Their limited extent renders them vulnerable to localised changes in site characteristics, and sometimes the site itself will prove disappointing. At Bishop's Waltham, for instance, trial trenches were dug close to the palace in 1978 in the hope that further traces of Saxon-Norman or later buildings related to it would be found. Unfortunately parts of the site had been destroyed by the construction of houses and stores in the late eighteenth century, while other areas contained evidence only for gardens and orchards unrelated to the palace. The only features of any interest were two fifteenth-century rubbish pits which had been succeeded by a post-medieval timber-framed building (Lewis 1985, 118-20).

Trial excavations can be extremely valuable, and even small trenches can provide remarkably rich detail in the right circumstances. In general, however, it remains true that the larger the excavation, the greater the information gained from it, and of a higher quality. We need not expect to see total excavation, though the example of Martin Biddle's work within Wolvesey Palace shows that this is possible, but there have been many very large-scale excavations on royal and episcopal palaces over the last 50 years. Some of these have been major research projects (eg. Nonsuch Palace, again excavated by Martin Biddle) while others have had an origin, at least, in rescue work (eg. the Bishop of Winchester's site at Mount House, Witney). The gradual piecing together of evidence out of many disparate excavations, often spread across many years, is perhaps more

17 *Excavations in 1996-7 showed that beech piles had been used to provide a firm foundation for Edward I's south-western entrance causeway at the Tower of London*

47

common than either of these circumstances, and seems likely to continue to be so. We will reserve any more extensive description of the results of large-scale excavations for subsequent chapters.

Dendrochronology (or tree-ring dating) has developed into one of the archaeologist's most powerful tools, not least on medieval sites and buildings where evidence for successive phases of timberwork may survive. The technique relies on the measurable properties of the annual growth cycle of trees by which new layers of wood are added each year. Two seasons are identifiable: the spring/summer when growth is vigorous, and the autumn/winter when it slows down to virtually nothing. The growth has to be reasonably uniform all around the trunk for the species to be usable, largely because tree-fellers and carpenters tend to reduce the whole trunk down to a series of smaller sections. These are unlikely to keep the full pattern of growth rings, and so any gross irregularities from one side of the tree to another will render it useless for ring dating. This affects a number of trees sometimes used by medieval and later builders such as the elm, but fortunately the most commonly used materials, oak and beech, are also just about the best for dendrochronology (English Heritage 1998) (**17**). There have been a number of spectacular successes with tree-ring dating at medieval sites in recent years, including two of the very greatest: the Tower of London and Windsor Castle. Further consideration of both will be found in chapters 3 and 4, but here we will look briefly at results from the White Tower and the kitchen roof at Windsor.

The White Tower contains a great deal of historic timberwork, but much of it appears at first sight to be relatively late. The great piers which support the sequence of timber floors and their joists are a good example of this, and they can be easily understood both in their own right and in relation to the roofs. Clement Lemprière's cross-section through the building in 1729 gives a particularly good view of the structural relationship of the timbers. Although early woodwork is very hard to come by within the building, several Norman timbers were found embedded in the walls during restoration works in 1996-8, particularly oak planks lining the sockets for drawbars to seal the doors, and the lintels of cupboards set in the walls. It was very difficult to obtain samples from timbers which were so integral to the fabric of the building itself, but this was achieved and several dendrochronology dates were obtained. None of the samples could be dated precisely to a specific year, and it was usually only possible to say that the tree had been felled after a given date (described in the Latin phrase *terminus post quem*). One of the planks, however, was shown to come from a tree cut down in 1081 at the latest, and brought to site after that. This timber came from the entrance level (ie. above the basement where building work started) and so can only have been inserted several years into the construction programme. This therefore fits very well with the traditionally accepted commencement date of 1077/8 given in the contemporary Rochester Priory chronicle, the *Textus Roffensis*.

The results from Windsor's great kitchen in the Upper Ward are if anything more remarkable, though it is sad that such a terrible event as the fire of 1992 had to provide the context in which the archaeological research could be carried out. Hitherto it had been assumed that the medieval roof had already been lost during seventeenth-century rebuilding and Sir Jeffry Wyatville's extensive work in 1828. The fire caused extensive damage to the roof, and especially to the lantern which ran along the ridge and lit the interior of the kitchen, but when some of the badly charred timbers were examined after they had been taken down an extraordinary discovery was made: the softwood decoration on the surface was just that — little more than a nineteenth-century veneer nailed onto oak timbers which were clearly of an earlier date.

How much earlier could not be appreciated until samples had been dated by dendrochronology, but this soon showed that there was evidence not merely for one phase of roof construction but for several. The first period was in the later fourteenth century: at least one timber was felled after 1337, but it was not possible to be more precise and the actual date could have been decades later than this. It is likely that this period relates to Edward III's documented works on the kitchen in 1362-3. The next period was represented by timbers dated to the fifteenth/early sixteenth century, and in one specific case, where the sapwood was complete, to 1489 (**colour plate 3**). This probably reflects necessary repairs accounted for between July of that year and the following April which involved not only a carpenter but also a mason and a plumber who undertook leadwork. The third group of timbers belonged to the late sixteenth/early seventeenth century and again included one sample with all its sapwood, in this case dated to 1577 and matching further repairs for which documentary correlation was available: on this occasion the kitchen roof was singled out as an urgent priority. Finally various timbers were dated to the eighteenth century, reflecting the known period of rebuilding. It could now be appreciated that the latter had been but one in a series of great repairs necessitated by what was evidently seen in each instance as the imminent structural failure of the roof. This had, after all, been a major and highly ambitious piece of work for its age, especially in the utilitarian confines of a kitchen, albeit one of the greatest to be built in medieval England. Far from failing, and far from having been totally replaced as thought, the latest research has shown that the roof survived through its several alterations through to 1992. Fortunately the story did not end in the drama of the fire on 20 November of that year: though badly damaged it was possible to save the greater part of the roof and reconstruct what could not be salvaged. Windsor's great kitchen and its roof have survived for the future, and one more phase of construction can be added, with a date in the mid-1990s (Brindle and Kerr 1997, 14-17).

Putting it all in perspective: research frameworks

National and regional research frameworks and overviews are critically important for anyone researching medieval palaces, whether individually or in groups. The localised view is important, of course, and at any given site, no matter how grand, there will be things which can only be appreciated at the site-specific level. Nevertheless it is now commonplace to refer to nationally-generated lists of research priorities such as those produced by the Society for Medieval Archaeology (1987) and English Heritage (1991). These can be problematical in practical terms, however, either because of the restricted extent of the strategies themselves, specialist input (or lack of it) to them, or the specific needs of the commissioning bodies (eg funding considerations for grant-aided works). On the other hand such documents can become little more than wish lists. At the moment one must conclude that there is no adequate national guidance for research into medieval palaces.

Curiously this is one subject which does not immediately lend itself to more localised research strategies. If the site itself is rarely (if ever) going to be a large enough canvas, a county perspective runs the danger of irrelevance if one is considering the estates and properties once managed by bishoprics such as Canterbury, St Davids, Salisbury or Winchester (most especially the latter). Most of the bishops maintained a house in London; even those from the poorer, less powerful dioceses had one, though perhaps not all would have recognised them as palatial. The wealthiest managed vast property portfolios (it seems reasonable to use such a word even with its modern overtones), and it is surely at this level that we should view them first. So much the better if this happens to coincide with a broadly recognisable locale such as a county. When one looks at the royal palaces, of course, a national focus seems to be a prerequisite. This topic will be returned to in the final chapter of the book.

A moveable feast: the art of palace living

The medieval palaces we see today, whether as ruins, archaeological sites or intact buildings, are in many ways little more than shadows of their former selves — perhaps shells would be a better word. The way buildings were arranged, both internally and in relation to each other, very often gives us evidence for their former use (eg. hall, chamber, chapel etc.). Internal features such as hearths, ovens and floors of various kinds can be particularly helpful here. In most cases, however, it is far more difficult to gain a clear picture of what interiors actually looked like and how the royal and episcopal households operated within them. This is partly because palaces were usually used over many generations and centuries, and each one tended to alter the arrangements of its predecessors to suit then-contemporary requirements of fashion and comfort; there are relatively few palaces which have remained as essentially single-phase buildings. Naturally enough few medieval interiors survived untouched even into the post-medieval age, let alone into the modern era. It would be well not to attach too much importance to this problem, however, because there may have been relatively few palaces which housed permanently-fixed internal decoration in anything more than a small minority of rooms (if indeed in any at all).

It is axiomatic that the royal and episcopal courts carried much of their fixtures and fittings with them. Occasionally medieval documents provide specific reminders of this, as on the occasion early in 1290 when a cart in the entourage of the Bishop of Hereford overturned near Wantage (Oxon); much broken crockery had to be replaced as a result if this incident. The Wardrobe was an important office of these establishments, often with permanent central buildings or stores as at the Tower of London. Such central stores would contain fixtures and fittings such as beds and bedding, tables, wall hangings, and pots and pans, which could be sent on from palace to palace ahead of the royal or episcopal party when it was touring its domain. It is quite clear that kings and bishops could spend large parts of any given year undertaking such progresses, and a considerable infrastructure must have been required to keep track of the various wagon trains which might be carrying the households' needs around the country at any one time. By definition, of course, the various items of the Wardrobe would not be fixed at any one place, though equally many sites would have had a permanent establishment of basic needs for the use of the caretaker staff who could be resident throughout the year. The more impressive pieces would be in the Wardrobe, and are thus less likely to have found their way into the archaeological record as 'finds'. This problem is exacerbated by the perishable nature of pieces such as tables, chairs and tapestries which would largely consist of organic materials. These do not normally survive on archaeological sites in western Europe; only oxygen-free waterlogged environments provide the right conditions for the preservation of such pieces.

Ruined sites, or those which survive mostly below ground, might seem to be poor candidates for interior reconstructions. It is quite common, however, to find relevant evidence in both types of site. Thrones (or at least chairs on raised daises) are often referred to explicitly in medieval documents, for instance at Clarendon in the thirteenth century. Their positions can also be inferred from the layout and internal arrangements of ruined buildings, as in the halls at Bishop's Waltham Palace and Wolvesey where blind arcading high in the gables is usually taken to indicate the site of the bishop's chair. Moreover the remains of decorative schemes are often found during palace excavations. This might amount to little more than fragments of wall plaster, though traces of pigment might show which colours were used, and elements of the original design scheme may be reconstructable. Wall and ceiling attachments can be important as well, such as the eight-pointed stars and crescents found at Clarendon (James and Robinson 1988, 224-6). These were made of lead but they had also been gilded, and seem to coincide with Henry III's documented order (in 1251) for a room to be decorated with a scheme including *scintillae* (stars).

Combining the methods

There are occasions when truly startling new discoveries are made at a site that might seem, at first glance, to be very well known and documented. Several recent projects at the Tower of London have made this point rather well. These will be described in more detail in subsequent chapters, but the advantages of an inter-disciplinary approach to the analysis of a site can be pointed out here. The rediscovery during 1995-7 of a crucial part of Henry III's entrance to the Tower could scarcely have occurred without archaeological fieldwork (see pages 73-6). Analysis of finds such as pottery, and stylistic comparisons of (for instance) stone tooling were useful in suggesting the likely date-range of the masonry which was found. Precise dating of the remains, however, relied on the science of dendrochronology. The accuracy, down to the season of a year, was remarkable, but the significance of this lay in its ability to link the archaeology with documented events in the middle of the thirteenth century. The structural remains were to a degree comprehensible in their own right, but they could only be interpreted adequately by reference to historical sources of two quite different kinds. The combination of archaeological, architectural and historical analysis here laid bare extraordinary, if not to say catastrophic, events which took place 760 years ago.

In this case it is equally clear that the archaeological evidence has led to a re-assessment of the historical record of the events of 1240/1 at the Tower of London. Matthew Paris's description of the Henry III's gatehouse falling down has been well-known for many years. Early scholars took it as a reference to the entrance in the southern defences (eg. the Bloody Tower gate), but Colvin rejected this in favour of the western defences and the Beauchamp Tower in the 1960s. The recent work does not overturn this ascription, but it does add a significant new layer to it, and requires a major rethink of how the Tower's entire western defences developed in the thirteenth century.

A few other examples will also demonstrate the value of using more than one type of information to gain the best understanding of a palace. We have already looked at the visible evidence in the buildings at Bishop's Waltham Palace for major campaigns of improvement and reconstruction by William of Wykeham and his successor Henry Beaufort in the late fourteenth century and the first half of the fifteenth century. Until recently, however, many of these radical changes had been ascribed to Bishop Langton (1493-1501), a full half-century after even Beaufort's time, let alone Wykeham's. To some extent this reappraisal rests on the building fabric, and architectural features within it, but the problem of stone-robbing is as evident here as at many other sites; the masonry, therefore, is not always inherently dateable as it stands. The main factor in the reinterpretation of the palace's buildings and their dates is the great wealth of documentary records available for the Bishops of Winchester and their many properties. This archive is often extremely detailed, despite frustrating gaps, and the major palaces such as Wolvesey, Farnham and Bishop's Waltham are usually very well represented. Detailed analysis of these records in relation to the surviving ruins has shown that thousands of pounds were expended on new works (as opposed to relatively routine maintenance) at Bishop's Waltham during the episcopates of Wykeham and Beaufort, far more so than at the other two palaces just mentioned. In some cases the records are quite specific about expenditure on (for instance) the hall or the bishops' accommodation in and to the east of West Tower. Langton was by no means inactive at the site, but his spending was at a much lower level and may well have been more concentrated on the outer court to the north of the moated platform which contained the main episcopal and other apartments of the Inner Court. Earlier descriptions placing a very late fifteenth-century date on many of the changes at Bishop's Waltham palace have therefore had to be radically revised.

St Mary's Guildhall, Lincoln, is another good example of the combined approach (**colour plate 4**). The building itself still contains hugely impressive evidence for its original form and function. The façade fronting onto High Street is magnificent in its own right and the building as a whole is surely one of the best-preserved medieval structures not only in the city but in Britain. This is despite a long sequence of structural development and functional alterations which began during the medieval period, when an essentially domestic building became a guildhall, and continued into the modern era. Archaeological research in the 1980s included a thorough survey of the surviving elevations (**18**). Meanwhile excavation within the ground-floor rooms and elsewhere in the complex provided many significant details of the original building, not least of which were the many pieces of building stone that had clearly come from the original structure. These included many fragments of architectural features such as decorated string courses,

18 *The interior elevation of the north gable at St Mary's Guildhall, Lincoln, at first floor level with the remains of blind arcading revealed during the 1980s. The arches had been cut down in the past, showing that the roof had been lowered. Photograph copyright City of Lincoln Archaeology Unit*

doors and windows, and careful analysis of these meant that several complete features could be reconstructed. This process was taken one logical step further when these were combined with the evidence of the surviving building itself to arrive at an impressively complete and detailed picture of what a top-quality mid-thirteenth-century structure looked like (Stocker 1991) (**19**).

The largely external reconstruction of the Lincoln house is monochrome, but we know from a variety of sources that medieval interiors were often vividly colourful: many parish churches and a few other medieval buildings retain fragments or larger schemes of wall paintings. Some may still be seen at palaces, most notably the magnificent late fourteenth-century mural featuring St Michael in an upper chamber of the Byward Tower at H M Tower of London (Parnell 1993, colour plate 7). The royal apartments of Henry III at the Tower had evidently been highly decorated; the accounts for his reign record floral designs in the queen's chambers in 1238-40, while in 1251 an order was placed for a painting of the Antioch story (one of Henry's favourite themes) in the chamber used by the king's chaplain. Sadly all these have long since been lost along with the bulk of the palace buildings, but an extraordinary echo of the floral work was rediscovered at Windsor Castle during post-fire restoration in 1992. Here the removal of eighteenth-century wood panelling from a second-floor chamber in the Rose (or King John's) Tower revealed a near-intact scheme of repeating emerald green cartouches containing delicately-painted roses set against a deep crimson background covered in stars. All the painting had been

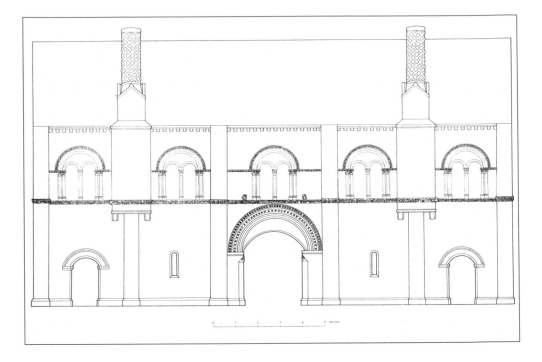

19 St Mary's Guildhall, Lincoln: a reconstruction of how it might have looked when completed c.1170 based on archaeological, historical and architectural research. Drawing copyright City of Lincoln Archaeology Unit

done freehand during the fourteenth century, perhaps in 1365-6 when various pigments and varnishes were bought for the painter William Burdon. He had been well paid, and had also employed a dozen assistants whose three levels of remuneration presumably reflect their skills and experience (Brindle and Kerr 1997, 44-5).

Elsewhere painted false ashlar jointing can be found, for example in the western antechamber to the Antioch chamber at Clarendon, though the delicate plaster can be all too susceptible to damage once uncovered (*see* **46a** and **b**). The remains of tiled pavements at Clarendon are also justly renowned, though they are not as important as Henry III's Cosmati Pavement which still survives at Westminster Abbey. Perhaps the greatest medieval interior of them all — the Painted Chamber at the Palace of Westminster — was destroyed in the fire of 1834, but at least we do have some excellent early nineteenth-century records both of the room as a whole and of specific panel details within it (Binski 1986). They give us a priceless example of both the value of accurate recording, and what we can strive to achieve through that recording: a better appreciation of the palaces themselves and how people lived within them. The following chapters will take up this theme in a detailed exploration of royal and episcopal palaces. Archaeological evidence will most often be our starting point, but it will rarely be where we finish.

3 Building medieval palaces: the archaeological evidence

Having looked at the way archaeologists study palaces, it is now time to turn to the buildings themselves in detail. In this chapter we examine the evidence for how palaces were constructed, looking at the ways in which medieval engineers and builders addressed the problems which the choice of site might present them with. It is perhaps surprising that ground conditions were often far from ideal for the kind of heavyweight, ostentatious buildings their patrons expected. Contemporary documents describing specific construction works and their cost form an invaluable background to the archaeological evidence here, as well as providing what amount to eyewitness accounts of occasions when the builders got things badly wrong.

Building palaces

Medieval palaces can tell us a great deal about the techniques employed by the people who designed and built them, both from surviving fabric and especially from archaeological evidence where sites have been excavated. It is possible to see how the buildings were put up, and to look at the solutions used when problems were encountered, such as poor ground conditions on the development site. Many of the basic techniques — anything from piles to putlogs — might well be used on many buildings other than palaces, but the sheer scale so often required by kings and bishops sets the enterprises of their builders apart from most other work of the medieval period.

Before we turn to the physical evidence, it is worth noting that we do know some names of the builders who worked on palaces, and the top craftsmen who operated alongside them; this is despite the fact that the vast majority of the considerable labour force which would have been operational at individual palaces or in the country at large will remain anonymous. The likes of Henry Yevele, William Wynford and Hugh Herland (the first two architects, the third one of the greatest carpenters of his age) were very active for the monarchy over many years during the mid-late fourteenth century, often together, but they also worked for the episcopate and other magnates. Yevele was especially active in London and the south-east of England on such important projects as the rebuilding of Canterbury Cathedral's nave, but he also worked for Winchester's Bishop William of Wykeham at the see's London palace in Southwark and at Bishop's Waltham. Wynford seems to have been Wykeham's favoured architect, however, working extensively for him on major projects in the heartland of the bishopric such as Winchester College, the new nave at the Cathedral, and New College, Oxford. Herland's best-known work is undoubtedly the spectacular 660-ton roof built over the great hall at Westminster in the 1390s, but he too did much work for Wykeham, including at Bishop's Waltham.

Many of these men could turn their hand to both design and engineering, offering practical solutions to the requirements of their exacting patrons, travelling the country to visit the sites where their services were required. Sometimes they would supervise work themselves, or they would instruct locally based masons who would be responsible for the execution of the designs. Few today would allow any of these people the title of architect, at least not as that profession is understood today; that is no doubt valid enough, but when faced with the magnificence of so much medieval architecture, and not only among the 'greatest' buildings, we must certainly acknowledge the skills of those who were responsible for its design and construction.

Foundations

Many palaces were built on perfectly good solid ground such as chalk or gravel where the bearing weights of even substantial buildings would not require special treatment in the foundations. The digging of the latter often provided a secondary benefit because they were a good source of basic materials such as flint for core work or sand and gravel for the mortar to bind stones together. This would rarely be enough for all the needs, even at a smaller site, and the bulk of requirements would be sourced elsewhere in quarries and pits at varying distances from the building site. At Henry VIII's Nonsuch Palace, for instance, extensive chalk pits were available within quarter of a mile of the site, and freestone quarries were only five miles away (probably at Merstham; Dent 1962). Basic materials could therefore be carted in at very low cost: the 1s 4d per load for the freestone and only 4d per load for the chalk contrasts starkly with the 3s 6d cost of carting stone from a Reigate quarryman. This, of course, was as nothing to the cost of shipping in material such as the 35 loads of Liége and Caen stones (quite apart from the expense of the stone itself) which were already in stock at London when work was starting in 1538. Nonsuch cost £22,631 14s 11½d, of which labour accounted for over £16,000, materials etc. £3,739, and carriage £2,764 (£353 of which went on water transport).

Nonsuch also provides an excellent example of an important phenomenon which could occur at any time in the medieval period but which became commonplace at the very end of it: the re-use of materials from earlier buildings. In earlier cases this might simply involve using whatever could be salvaged from a structure pulled down to make way for the new work, as in the re-use of stones such as Reigate limestone and Purbeck marble from Henry III's work at the Tower of London in the foundations for various parts of his son Edward I's new defences (**20**). In others extant buildings might be ransacked, as at Aberffraw in 1317 when 198 lengths of timber were removed from the former *maerdref* of the princes of Gwynedd for use at Caernarfon where Edward I had established a prominent new castle (Longley 1997, 45). Llewelyn's Hall at Conway had suffered similar ignominy when being dismantled in 1302-6 and re-erected at Caernarfon in 1315 (Johnstone 1997, 56). There must have been a strong element of symbolic display in such requisitioning of former royal buildings for the new Conqueror's own purposes, and perhaps there was something of this at Nonsuch too, although at first sight the motivation there seems more straightforward.

*20 Edward I's south-western entrance causeway at the Tower of London: the masonry incorporated some re-used stones from Henry III's building works at the Tower eg. the lighter blocks in the lowest course to the left of the arch (see also **17**)*

The suppression of Merton Priory on 16 April 1538 provided a large source of valuable materials such as stone, roof tiles and the lead with it, window glass and portable items for use at Henry VIII's new palace. His builders were particularly interested in the stone, rapidly stripping out no less than 3,600 tons of the stuff (the carters earned 8d per ton for the four-mile journey). Thus they both precluded any possibility of a re-occupation of the old monastery while also making a clear enough statement about the king's dominion over ecclesiastical powers. Something similar happened at Camber Castle (East Sussex), where priories at Winchelsea were mined for materials to build Henry's new coastal fort. At Nonsuch the cartloads included not only freestone and ashlar but also numerous carved pieces, many of very high quality. These were all but useless for exterior work at the palace, however, and during Martin Biddle's excavations in 1959 they were typically found mixed in with the chalk of the foundations or set in the below-ground walls of the great cellars with the carved faces inwards and therefore hidden. Only two blocks, both Norman roundels, had been set with their carvings showing on the face, though this may not have meant it was actually visible: the walls were lined out with racks to hold the wine and beer.

Ground conditions were not always favourable though, and in these circumstances the design of the foundations had to reflect the load-bearing capacity (or otherwise) of the soil. Unconsolidated material such as water-lain silts or dumped layers were the most common problem, particularly where waterside sites became desirable for new residences. This was especially the case on the Thames riverfront in London. Similar circumstances would apply when building or extending an existing property over a former watercourse such as a moat. In these circumstances it was imperative for the engineer to establish some contact with firm ground below the unconsolidated levels, just as it is today. Short of wholesale excavations to remove the soft material (which would rarely be practical, especially on a river edge), piling of some form was the only realistic solution. The two main methods, which could be combined, were to drive the piles (usually wooden) into place with a gravity-operated weight, or to dig out a relatively narrow-bore hole and pack it with stone or other rubble to create a newly-consolidated base.

It often surprises people to learn that such methods, especially pile-driving, were not only available to but were also used by medieval builders. It should not do, as this was by no means new technology: the Romans had used driven piles routinely to provide a secure building platform where ground conditions required them, as witnessed in the quays built along the soft, silty ground of the Thames's north bank in London *c*. 200 and the riverside defensive wall of some 55-75 years later. They also used the technique under both domestic and monumental buildings if needed, typically capping the wooden piles with a raft of rammed stone such as chalk (Blagg 1996, 45; Brigham 1998, 32). It may be that pile-driving became a forgotten technique during the Anglo-Saxon period when few stone buildings were erected outside of ecclesiastical contexts, but it was certainly brought back into use after the Norman Conquest. At Windsor Castle, for example, timber piles had to be driven into the summit of the late eleventh-century motte to stabilise it following a partial collapse of the unconsolidated chalk rubble (Brindle and Kerr 1997, 32-3).

William I's choice of site for the Tower of London must have seemed simple enough: the Roman city and riverside defences in effect provided two ready-made sides of a castle, although documentary references suggest that parts of the riverside wall may have been derelict and requiring repair by the early Norman period. William had ditches dug across the obtuse angle formed by the walls to create what amounted to a motte, probably doing this very soon after his entry into London after the Conquest. Work on the White Tower started soon afterwards and the germ was sown of the castle which was intended not only to protect but also to control and dominate the city and its inhabitants for much of the medieval period. The great keep itself was both physically and metaphorically at the centre of the castle's defensive and dominant functions. For instance recent archaeological work has shown that the upper walls (corresponding to what is now the top floor within the building) did not originally enclose a room at all: instead they were screens, rising above and obscuring twin steeply-pitched roofs (Impey and Parnell 2000, 16-17 and fig 10). In other words, the building was made to look artificially tall compared with the space within, emphasizing its height and severity at a time when it seems certain that ecclesiastical buildings would have been the only ones outside of royal control to aspire to any great elevation. Surprisingly, the Conqueror's tightly-constrained site seems to have remained unenlarged over the next 100 years or so. There are hints of an outer enclosure, in effect a bailey, but its existence remains highly conjectural either on historical or archaeological grounds. The extension of the defences seems to have begun under

Richard I's chancellor, William Longchamp, at the end of the twelfth century but it is to the successive reigns of Henry III (1216-72) and his son Edward I (1272-1307) that we must look for the most significant enlargements of the Tower and its defences (**colour plates 5 & 6; 21**). The developments they instigated are dealt with elsewhere in this book, but in the matter of foundations we may begin our encounter with them here.

Henry III came to the throne as a minor and only gradually gained full control of his inheritance in the later 1220s. He rapidly took an active interest in his estate and became one of medieval Europe's great patrons of architecture and the arts. At the Tower he massively extended the defences and therefore the area contained within them starting in 1238, pushing well to the north beyond the former limits and, importantly, abandoning the former Roman defences along the eastern side of the castle for the first time. In so doing he pushed his new walls out over the ditch which ran on the outside of the Roman defences; this ditch may already have been partly filled in or silted up, though presumably it would have been kept fairly clean and clear for as long as it functioned as part of the Tower defences. The ditch would have required filling in and consolidating, but unfortunately the two places where the new wall crossed the ditch have never been

*21 A model of the Tower of London in the early fourteenth century after Edward I's extension of the palace and defences; compare with **colour plates 5** and **6**. © Crown copyright: Historic Royal Palaces*

examined archaeologically. The rest of Henry's new circuit, now known as the inner curtain wall, lay predominantly on the drier and higher ground to the north of the river, with the exception of the short stretch between the Lanthorn and Salt Towers which ran slightly to the north and east along the river edge. A small-scale excavation against the junction of the inner curtain's external face and the west side of the Salt Tower did not reach the base of the curtain's stone foundations, though they were massive. Several small oak piles of Roman date were found in the lower levels, driven into foreshore layers of gravel, silt and peat; these piles did not act as foundations in their own right, being too small and insufficiently close together, but they do illustrate the perceived need to lend support to any activity along the river edge (Parnell 1983).

We know far more of the lengths gone to by Edward I and his builders to ensure the stability of the outer curtain wall and associated defences (1275-81) because of a major programme of archaeological research carried out in Edward's moat during 1995-7 and earlier work in the late 1950s and the 1970s-80s. These projects examined the curtain in several places, St Thomas's Tower, and the two entrances built at the south-east and south-west corners of the new circuit. These landward entrances were an absolute necessity because the Tower was still in direct contact with the Thames at this stage: the southern length of the new outer curtain and the associated water entrance with palatial accommodation in St Thomas's Tower were built out into the river. The foundations of these water-edge structures were usually underpinned with driven piles, often representing what must have been massive operations in advance of masonry construction. At St Thomas's Tower, for instance, excavations in 1958/9 demonstrated that the south wall of the tower was fronted by an apron of mortared Kentish Rag rubble, possibly associated with some piling. The central part of the raft between the tower and the fourteenth-century wharf had been cut away for the insertion of a causeway constructed of piles, some at least being halved elms; horizontal members were also found. The same timber structure was found within the tower in 1975 associated with rammed chalk, where it was dated to 1634-5 and interpreted as a solid slipway to prevent boats getting stuck in tidal muds (Parnell 1993, 62 and fig 42).

The excavations against the south curtain were generally small and quite widely spaced so that it was difficult to assess the spacing of the oak piles which were found in most of them; usually, however, no more than two were found in any pit and singles were more common. The majority of piles were linked by transverse beams across their tops and were associated with mixed rubble foundations which, strangely, did not appear to be as massive as those under the landward parts of the curtain which had been dug into London Clay. This pattern of spaced piles and linking beams was repeated a century later when the wharf was built on very similar foundations to the south. Evidence from the 1958/9 excavations around St Thomas's Tower showed that the transverse beams included some running back under the wharf at 90° to its edge wall, in effect creating a timber lacing.

Edward I's two landward entrances were provided with massively-engineered foundations. The Iron Gate causeway at the south-eastern corner of the moat was largely demolished in 1680 to allow free flow of water — the masonry had evidently been acting as an unintended dam here by this time — but its lower courses were left in place and

22 The Iron Gate causeway at the Tower of London being excavated in 1996. This bridge into the castle from the eastern suburbs was demolished in 1680 and had lain unseen since then

survive below post-medieval and later dumps of soil. Virtually the whole of the causeway's remains were exposed during excavation in 1996 and proved to be a rebuild in stone several generations later in date than Edward I's time (**22**). Excavation down the north face of the masonry, however, showed that it rested on a raft of very closely-set beech piles (**23**). Moreover a single transverse beam was found (the masonry had been built hard against it) set into rebates in some of the piles and over others. The beam had mortices in its upper and southern faces, the latter therefore facing back across the piles. The piles all retained their bark edging and so the final growth ring of the tree in the forest was preserved: this allowed for accuracy down to the year and growing season in the dendrochronology samples, proving that they had all been felled between the summer of 1276 and early in 1277 — the beam was probably contemporary, but it did not retain its final growth rings. This coincides with a reference in 1276 to the purchase of 660 beeches to be used in the foundations of the mill towards St Katherine's (ie. on the east side of the castle) where a mill was built in 1278. At the same time 600 beech trees were ordered in from the king's forest at Langley to be used under another mill 'to the west of the Tower'. Excavations in 1996-7 on either side of Edward I's entrance causeway between the Middle and Byward Towers at the south-west corner of the moat again located a continuous raft of closely-set beech piles, with a few oaks. Two beech samples provided dendrochronological felling dates of 1275/6 while 17 dated to 1277/8, the dates represent the dormant winter season in both cases (**24**; *see* **17**).

23 The beech piling found under the Iron Gate causeway at the Tower of London

The linkage between the documentary references and the dendrochronology dates here is remarkable, but it must be admitted that 600 or 660 piles would scarcely be enough to span the corners of the late thirteenth-century moat. The excavations and scientific samples provided further insights into the medieval builders' methods by establishing that the beech trees were not used whole, though unused beech tree trunks from Henry III's building campaign were found elsewhere in the excavations. Instead they were cut into lengths of around 3ft-5ft (0.9m-1.52m) before use; in this way each tree might supply three, four or more piles and each batch of 600 or so trunks would represent at least 2000 piles. Edward's engineers and builders clearly wanted to ensure that their handiwork survived the test of time, and at the south-west corner at least it did: despite a late eighteenth-century re-build the bulk of the medieval masonry is still in use. As we shall see, Edward's workforce had the chastening experience of his father's time at the Tower to look back on, and this at a time when it would not be wise to incur the wrath of an all-powerful client. Elsewhere at the Tower, elm piles were found acting as the foundations of the fourteenth-century wharf in small excavations in the 1920s. Elm piles were also used under the Jewel Tower built during 1365-6 at the Palace of Westminster. These timbers remained in situ until 1954 when they had to be replaced by reinforced concrete (Taylor 1996, 23), but a group of four piles and their wooden cap were conserved and form an impressive part of the displays within the building.

Piling was also used at the Manor of the More, Rickmansworth (Herts), though the technique was somewhat different as, indeed, was the imperative for the piling. The

24 A bar diagram of the dendrochronology dates achieved from wood (mostly beech) samples at the Tower of London, showing remarkable consistency in dates from two phases of work under Henry III (in 1240/1) and Edward I (1275-7). Chart by Dr I. Tyers, University of Sheffield

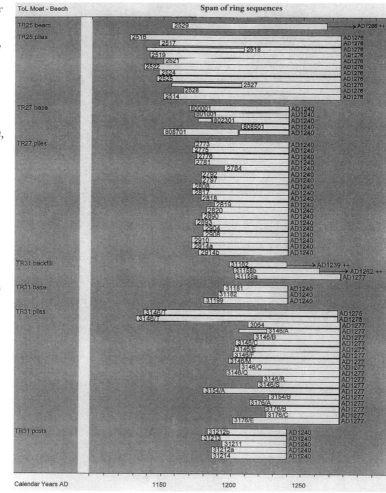

fifteenth-century building site here was not riverine but was located over a late thirteenth-century moat. In 1426 Henry Beaufort and Thomas, bishops of Winchester and Durham respectively, had been granted a joint licence (with others) by the Crown to 'enclose, crenellate, enturret and embattle with stones, lime and brik, their manor of More in Rykmersworth', and so they did. Several of their new walls ran within the thirteenth-century moat arms, and two of these at least had to be filled in before building could commence. The new backfills were obviously very poorly consolidated and utterly inadequate for founding substantial masonry. Consequently pits were dug through to the natural gravel along at least one wall and these pits were then filled in with rammed chalk to act as piles. The foundations were further strengthened by the construction of relieving arches spanning between the piles and transferring the structural load directly through them into the bearing gravel below. Cardinal Wolsey acquired the More in the early 1520s, probably through his role as Abbot of St Albans from 1522, though Henry VIII took over in 1530/1. Both of them altered or enlarged the house, though it was evidently in poor condition by 1556 and was occupied by squatters soon afterwards; it was demolished *c.* 1650 (Biddle *et al* 1959).

Similar foundation techniques were used almost 100 years after the bishops of Winchester and Durham rebuilt the Manor of More when, in 1515, Henry VIII ordered the construction of a new palace at Bridewell on land acquired from the order of the Hospital of St John of Jerusalem (Gadd and Dyson 1981). Oddly the Hospitallers retained legal title to the site until 1531 when the freehold was finally taken over by the Crown, by which time the palace had not only been finished but had also ceased to be used directly by the king. The new palace had become necessary because of the fire in 1512 at Westminster which had rendered the royal accommodation there unusable, and the new site chosen was on a fashionable riverside location just outside the south-west corner of the city wall. The Thames was met here by one of its major tributaries, the Fleet river, with what seems to have been a broad mouth extending well back inland. The Hospitallers, and their predecessors on the site, the Knights Templar, had needed to dump large quantities of soil into the confluence to turn what had been a narrow triangle of ground into a roughly rectangular block. The Templars had established a mill on the reclaimed ground, but this was ruinous by 1308 and the Hospitallers seem to have used it as little more than an orchard and garden; indeed in 1422 the site was described as vacant, waste and in need of fencing. As much as two-thirds of the ground may thus have comprised unconsolidated infill, scarcely an auspicious location for a royal house, it would seem.

Here Henry had a palace built on three courtyards at a cost of around £22,000, remarkably similar to the amount he spent at Nonsuch. At Bridewell work was concentrated on the principal courtyard (around which the main royal rooms were arranged) up to 1518, probably along with the south courtyard (**25**). The former was wholly enclosed by buildings, but the south courtyard had only a wall along its east side; the west was occupied by a long gallery and this returned east where a south range was built along the river front. Building work declined from 1519-21, after which the palace was soon completed by the construction (or perhaps completion) of an outer (service) court on the east side of the principal courtyard. This final phase involved significant changes to the original plan, and necessitated several alterations to the buildings which had already been started. Nothing survives of Bridewell above ground since its last remnants were demolished in 1863, but an engraving of 1720 and other drawings show that the principal and outer courtyards rose up to four storeys high, or about 36ft (11m). Moreover, archaeological evidence demonstrates that the great hall on the south side of the principal courtyard was built over cellars. Less is known of the long gallery and south range, but late sixteenth-century birds-eye views of the palace suggest that the former was a relatively low building, probably single-storeyed, while the riverfront range was evidently elaborate and fitted up with plinths and turreted corner and central towers. Documentary evidence further suggests that the gallery was most likely timber-framed above its foundations.

The differing scales of the various building ranges required different foundation solutions to the problems posed by the variable ground conditions. The best ground must have been in the north-western third or so which had always been dry land on the west side of the confluence. This has not been investigated archaeologically, but the south-west

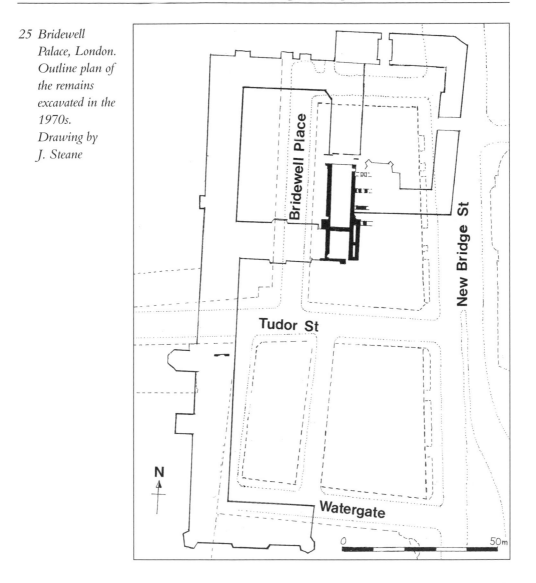

25 Bridewell Palace, London. Outline plan of the remains excavated in the 1970s. Drawing by J. Steane

corner of the principal courtyard and the central area of the long gallery were both examined in early 1978 in advance of building works which largely destroyed the relevant areas of the palace. The latter, and especially the long gallery, had already been badly affected by previous generations of development on the site, but fortunately the archaeologists were able to record important details of the palace's walls and foundations. These seem to have been simplest under the long gallery, partly because reasonable gravel could be found at shallow depth here to bear the load which would have been less than elsewhere if the range really was single-storeyed and half-timbered. Foundation pits had been dug into the gravel and planks placed on their bottoms to provide a level building surface. Piers of mortared chalk blocks, sometimes with broken bricks, had then been built over the planks to fill the pits, and low brick relieving arches spanned between the piers. The areas between the arches were infilled with mixed brick and chalk, sometimes coursed and sometimes random, and keyed in to the arches. Thin trampled layers of soil were evident in most of the foundations, showing how they had been built up in stages.

The long gallery works give an impression of shoddiness and poor quality in marked contrast to the care taken over the foundations in the principal courtyard. The intended superstructures were much more substantial here, and the ground conditions significantly worse where the buildings overlay the former confluence. Accordingly most of the foundations were trench-built and supported on large chalk-filled piles which were as much as 9ft 10in (3m) deep and perhaps 9ft 10in (3m) x 6ft 6in (2m) in plan. Some effort had been made to shore the pit sides with planks, doubtless because of the relatively loose ground they were digging into, and the chalk had been rammed in to form a compacted base from which brick relieving arches sprang. These, like the ones under the long gallery, had very little curvature but even so their shapes had been prepared in the base of the foundation trench either by leaving a lump of earth of the required profile or by inserting chalk rubble and brick form work. In at least one case the precise shape of the flattened arch had been set out in sand over such a rubble block so that the brickwork could be built to the right shape, but even where such careful preparation was in place the archwork could still be botched.

Once the piles and arches had been completed the remainder of the foundations were built up in well-coursed brickwork tight to the trench edge up to the point at which contemporary ground level was reached; construction continued above this in fair-faced brick masonry, typically with double-struck pointing (ie. the bonding mortar was smoothed out with a trowel to produce a convex 'V' section). By no means all of this fair-faced brickwork was meant to be seen, though: large quantities of earth were imported and dumped onto the site once the foundations and lower walls were in place, levelling the ground up by as much as 6ft 6in (2m) so that courtyard and other surfaces could be laid in. This also had the secondary and highly beneficial effect of allowing the cellars to be built under the south range of the principal courtyard (indeed this work was kept back until the dumping had been done) at a high enough level for the water table on this riverside site not to be a problem. There is little doubt that the cellar floor would have been at least damp and probably under water if the pit for it had been dug from the original ground level.

Wall construction and associated features

Once walls rose above foundation level a different series of practical problems arose for the builders, and the solutions to these can often be recognised in the masonry itself. It was common to build stone walls face-inwards, that is with the outer skin built first and the internal core (which was not meant to be seen, of course) put in afterwards. This worked very well for coursed masonry where each facing 'layer' was placed in a horizontally-bedded line, though it was less straightforward for uncoursed or irregularly-coursed facing (eg. random freestone). In such cases horizontal string courses or vertical quoining was commonly used at intervals to level up the masonry and add solidity. String courses can be seen at Bishop's Waltham Palace, where most of the flintwork is carefully coursed, and vertical quoins are very evident in Edward I's outer curtain wall at the Tower of London.

In either circumstance work could proceed to around shoulder height quite easily, but after this some form of timber scaffolding would be needed. There are numerous illustrations of such temporary works in medieval manuscripts and paintings, and the many surviving tall masonry structures make it clear that scaffolding could be used successfully up to considerable heights. The use of scaffolders and scaffolding is sometimes documented in works accounts as well. In physical terms the use of scaffolding can be recognised by the presence of putlog holes in either or both faces of a wall. These mark the positions where wooden poles were built into the stonework as the wall was rising; timber platforms would then be attached to the protruding poles so that the masons could continue their work at a reasonably comfortable height. Eventually the platforms and bars would be removed, and the holes where the latter had been would be filled in, sometimes with rubble (or bricks) and sometimes with carefully-selected and cut stones. In either instance the blocked-up positions are usually quite easy to pick out, as in the long walls of the late fifteenth-century brewhouse and bakehouse at Bishop's Waltham. It is usually easy to distinguish them from floor joisting: the holes or voids of the latter left behind as the timbers rotted away or were removed are usually much more closely and regularly spaced than putlogs, and can be followed across an interior at identical heights. This need not always be the case for putlogs, because construction (and therefore scaffolding) need not proceed at the same rate and height all round a building.

For the most part materials were chosen with practicality in mind; local supplies of building stone would be used where possible at least for core work and where display was unimportant (eg. service ranges, kitchens etc.), and timber continued to play a major role irrespective of the use of masonry. There were instances of lavish display in the choice of materials, of course, and the intent here could be as much the ostentatious proof of wealth and power as anything else. This was nowhere more true than in the great royal palaces and castles of the thirteenth century, especially those which were highly visible to the populace. The use of expensive materials at an essentially private site such as Clarendon would doubtless impress dignitaries and nobles (this was certainly the background to the extraordinary embellishment of Nonsuch in the middle decades of the sixteenth century) but it would have little impact on the bulk of the king's subjects who would never expect to see such a place.

How different, though, was a major castle in the corner of an important county town such as Oxford or Winchester, or most particularly in London itself, at the Tower. It is not always easy to gain a full appreciation of how this great royal castle at the south-east corner of the city looked during its long history of development. This is partly because the latter has in itself seen significant changes which often mask earlier building phases, but equally the Victorians re-faced large areas of the medieval defences to create a peculiar, bastardised version of what they believed medieval masonry 'should' look like. In some areas the new face work looks like random crazy paving, while elsewhere it has a neat, evenly-coursed appearance which is equally at odds with the thirteenth-century reality. Arrow loops also proliferated in the nineteenth century, both in re-faced and untouched masonry — indeed there are few medieval loops left intact at the castle, though fortunately the embrasures behind them have survived rather better, especially on Henry III's inner curtain wall.

Nevertheless much of the original work survives, and more of it, especially from Edward I's reign, has been examined during archaeological excavations over the last 40 years or so. This has confirmed that much of the basic wall work comprises freestone, often uncoursed, in readily and relatively cheaply available stones such as Kentish Rag. The size and regular shape of the ragstone is sometimes suggestive of material re-used from the various demolitions of the Roman city wall which were required as the castle defences expanded: the stretch of Edward I's outer curtain between the Well and Develin Towers is a good case in point (**26**). Other materials also appear, such as Bembridge limestone from the Isle of Wight, but these tend to be restricted to specific features such as quoining. The materials used, and their treatment, thus do not seem to have been a major feature in the intended impression of the curtain walls, but then they were not necessarily the focal point of the defences: the approach to and passage through the layers of defence were where materials were used to the greatest effect. We shall see shortly how Henry III's masons used a combination of relatively expensive Purbeck marble and Reigate stone to create a striking banded effect in a central feature of the new approach to the castle being built around 1240.

Edward I ordered the use of massive blocks of stone from a variety of sources (eg. the Purbeck quarries for both their limestone and marble, and the common Kentish Rag) to emphasize the monolithic visual quality of structures such as the Lion, Middle, Byward and St Thomas's Towers. Some of the stonework has been repaired or re-faced over the years, usually, as in the case of the Middle Tower, retaining the originally-intended effect, though St Thomas's Tower is surely the worst example of Victorian re-facing: the lower levels, buried throughout the post-medieval period and only re-exposed during the 1958/9 excavations, retain the original massive ashlar blocks which stand in marked contrast to the small random rubble facing put up by Antony Salvin between 1864-6. The tower was evidently in a very poor state by that time (part of the south-east turret had collapsed in June 1862), and undoubtedly remedial work was inevitable. Salvin could not have appreciated the quality of the buried basal courses which remained buried in his time, and elsewhere in this tower he was at pains to retain important historic features. Even so it is hard to look upon the Victorian facing with equanimity when it sits in such direct contrast to what rests beneath it.

The earliest uses of brick in medieval Britain involved either re-use of Roman materials (this had been a feature of Anglo-Saxon architecture as well) or the import of stocks and specialist workmen from Europe (especially Germany and the Low Countries). Until the late fifteenth century, brick remained a relatively rare, even exotic and certainly prestigious material, and its use is virtually unknown outside of wealthy, high-status sites. It is not surprising that it was incorporated into important royal works from a relatively early date. At the Tower of London, for instance, the earliest use of new brick, as opposed to the occasional re-use of Roman pieces, occurred under Edward I. He made extensive use of the material in his reconstruction of the Beauchamp Tower and adjacent stretches of the inner curtain wall. Here we can connect the surviving masonry with the purchase of almost a quarter of a million bricks from John Bardown of Ypres (in modern Belgium) recorded in the works accounts for 1276-8.

Brick was also used for Edward I's outer curtain, and several of the larger showpiece constructions such as the Postern Gate (see below), the Byward Tower, where the interior walls are brick-lined, and the Lion Tower, where recent archaeological work suggests that

26 Edward I's outer curtain wall and Develin Tower at the south-east corner of the Tower of London

brick was used quite extensively on the external face of the great half-moon bastion (some of the brick may have been from later refurbishment). In cases like the latter structures it is surely significant to see the new material being used alongside traditional but expensive and monumental stone ashlar. About 200 years later brick was virtually the only material used when Edward IV added a further layer to the defence in depth of the western approach to the castle. This was the Bulwark, built *c.*1480 as an artillery emplacement running obliquely northwards up Tower Hill from the Tower Dock to a pair of cylindrical bastions, where the bulk of the guns may have been placed, and then returning east to meet the edge of the moat. Parts of the masonry were exposed during archaeological excavation on Tower Hill in 1985 in advance of drainage works. The masonry stood to around 6ft 6in (2m) high in places and was impressive, but this had not saved it from demolition which started in 1678 in the aftermath of the Great Fire.

The face-and-core method still held good for brick so long as this was a valuable commodity reserved for facing, as at the Manor of More (Herts). Here it was used sparingly above ground in the 1426 building works: only the faces were built in brick, onto a chalk rubble core (in places the lowest courses of the face were in chalk blocks as well), and in some walls only the exterior face would be so dressed. Once brick became the material of choice for mass walling, however, it was common for the brickwork to be continuous through the masonry rather than being used solely as an outer skin. This was the case in many of the great construction programmes of the Tudor age once the monarchy had accepted its widespread use on palaces. The alternation in the way the brick headers and stretchers were bedded, either in single courses or groups of them, produced the characteristic bonding patterns on the masonry faces. Sometimes different-coloured bricks would be produced by deliberately changing the kiln firing conditions, and these could them be used to create relatively simple geometric decoration. Good examples of this can be seen in the Base Court at Hampton Court Palace.

With the Tudor monarchy's acceptance of brick as a major building material, kilns and associated features soon became a common sight on and around palace building sites. This has been well documented at palaces such as Hampton Court and Nonsuch. At the latter bricks and lime were being burnt in kilns within the park close to the site of the new palace, and 600,000 bricks had been produced by September 1538 alone. The brickmakers were paid 2s per thousand in this period, and a further £522 had spent on their supply by 1545 — this would represent a further 5,220,000 over and above the 600,000 produced in 1538. At Hampton Court Palace (**colour plate 7**), meanwhile, 'upwards of ten million bricks were burnt by brickmakers at their own kilns . . . [and] approximately sixteen million were burnt at kilns at Hampton Court by bricklayers working away from home' in 1529-38; 'home' could be as much as 40 miles away (Musty 1990, 412). Where the establishment of kilns even for short periods was less practical, as in central London, materials could be brought in from existing factories by road or, for sites such as Bridewell, by river.

Keeping it covered: vaults and roofs

Vaults are known in Anglo-Saxon architecture, but there they are restricted to the rather limited context of crypts (mostly reliquary) under churches such as Hexham and Ripon (Northumberland) and Repton (Derbyshire). After the Conquest they become more common in a secular context, typically in undercrofts (cellars) beneath halls or other chambers. The simplest form to build, the barrel vault, sprang directly off the side walls of the room and terminated on its ends, but more complex groined forms soon developed. These were supported on ribs rising at intervals from buttressing in the walls and, in vaults covering wide spans, from central piers as well.

Both types relied on the vaults being built around pre-constructed form-work — we have already seen something similar in the relieving arches of late medieval/Tudor foundations. This former, known as shuttering, would usually be timber, comprising planks supported on scaffold bars, and would replicate the final inner form (the soffit) of the structure. Once the shuttering was ready the masonry could be built over it, starting from

27 The bishop's palace at Sherborne Castle (Dorset) with the surviving groined vault in the 'keep' to the left

the outer edges and working in to the crown or rib-centre just as one would in an arch. The stone would be built onto an initial layer of mortar bedding laid onto the form-work, and it is often possible to see the positions of the latter's planks still impressed into the mortar. The technique can be seen to excellent effect in several parts of the White Tower and elsewhere at the Tower of London. Within William the Conqueror's great keep the mural passages in what is now the second floor, the vaults (barrel and groined) and arches in the successive levels of the Chapel of St John, and the embrasures behind many of the windows all display these tell-tale signs of shuttering. Southampton's twelfth-century Castle Vault also provides an excellent example of this technique (Oxley 1986, 28 and plate 3). Elsewhere there are numerous vaults to be seen at ruins such as Bishop Roger de Caen of Salisbury's early twelfth-century palaces at Old Sarum (Wilts) and Sherborne (Dorset). Evidence of both former barrel and groined vaults can be seen at the latter, along with an impressive surviving groin, probably of fifteenth-century date, supported on a re-used column (**27**).

The roofing of a building marked a critical stage in its construction: the stability of the whole structure would be enhanced, though of course the weight of the roof was an important factor which the engineer and builder had to take into account when calculating the load-bearing needs of both walls and foundations. This was largely irrespective of the roofing material, though fired clay tiles or stone slates would be heavier than thatch or shingles (small wooden tiles). In practical terms putting the roof in place also meant that the structure no longer had to be covered with temporary tarpaulins etc. if the potentially

71

destructive elements were to be kept out, and from now on attention could turn towards transforming the interior shell into habitable accommodation. Not surprisingly a great deal of care went into the design, erection and support of roofs on medieval buildings, and this is manifest both in examples which survive today, and in the structural elements such as arcade piers and corbels which might be all that remain of a lost roof. The skills of engineers were rarely up to building wide unsupported roof spans in the two centuries or so after the Norman Conquest, and consequently building ranges tended to be either narrow or wider but with the roof given additional support by stone or timber posts along its centre. This created the typical aisled plan familiar from such great buildings as Henry III's hall at Winchester Castle (*c*.1220-35; see chapter 4 for further consideration of aisled halls and associated buildings). The development of roof carpentry in the fourteenth century onwards meant that much wider spaces could be crossed by transferring the roof load outwards as well as down through the timberwork, eg. with hammer beams and bracing. This obviated the need for central structural support and thereby opened much larger internal spaces with uninterrupted sight lines. The magnificent hammer beam roof created in the 1390s at Westminster Hall and estimated to weigh 660 tons is perhaps the best-known and certainly one of the finest examples of the type in Britain and Europe.

The bases of arcade piers can still be seen in the East Hall at Wolvesey Palace, the rest of their masonry having long since been removed to a new home elsewhere. The hall and a gallery along its west side had been built *c*.1135-8, and the insertion, during the early to mid-thirteenth century, of the arcade into the solid wall which separated them converted the gallery into an aisle. This placed an additional structural burden onto the outer wall of the former gallery, so that this had to be strengthened with external buttresses marching in step with the arcades. Evidence for wall-fixed roof supports can also be seen in the vertical slots left for wall posts and the associated corbels in the hall at Bishop's Waltham; here the evidence relates to the rebuilding of the hall range and its roofs under Bishop William of Wykeham in the late fourteenth century.

While the timberwork of a roof was essentially a utilitarian matter in terms of design and construction, it did also provide a potential setting for elaborate decoration, sometimes on a vast scale. It is here that we often see the medieval master craftsman at his best, because the sheer solidity of the engineered structure could be hidden, both literally and metaphorically, by the lightness and delicacy of painted and carved artistry. Thus the cantilevered bracing of Herland's hammer beam roof at Westminster Hall becomes the vehicle for carved angels bearing shields, a common device in late-medieval roof carpentry (eg. the church of St Thomas Becket, Salisbury, Wilts, or the refectory roof at Cleeve Abbey, Somerset) but seen here to great effect. Towards the end of our period the work would be taken one stage further and the roofing timbers would be hidden entirely. There was nothing new about this — roofs over masonry vaults such as that in the White Tower's Chapel of St John would be invisible from below by definition — but the insertion of elaborately decorated plaster and/or timberwork suspended below and from the roof structure (in effect, a false ceiling) was a different matter. The complicated and impressive ensembles of pendants, bosses and ribwork on the ceilings of Hampton Court's Chapel and Great Watching Chamber are particularly good examples of this genre.

Disasters — a case study: collapsing buildings at the Tower of London

As we have seen, Royal and episcopal palaces tended to be well made, as one might expect for wealthy and powerful clients, but occasionally things could and did go spectacularly wrong even at important sites such as the Tower of London. On 23 April 1240, for instance, a grand new entrance which Henry III had just ordered to be built fell down; the king had the defences rebuilt, but exactly one year later to the day in 1241 a further collapse seems to have occurred. The events are described graphically in the contemporary *Chronica Majora* (Great Chronicle) of Matthew Paris, a Benedictine monk based at St Albans. Matthew could be a stern critic of Henry and some aspects of his account may be fanciful, but there is little reason to doubt the ultimate truth of the collapses (or at least one of them). Indeed excavation in the Tower moat during 1995-7 produced direct archaeological evidence for these very events, and it now transpires that there is a reference to what occurred (or more properly the aftermath) in the Liberate Rolls (government records) on 23 September 1241: the Constable of the Tower was ordered 'to pull out the lead and boards which lie under the Tower recently fallen, to bring together the timber and freestone and put them in a suitable place'. It is worth describing the combined historical and archaeological evidence for what occurred in further detail, but first we might well reflect on the largely accidental nature of the archaeological discovery of masonry under Edward I's moat in 1995. The first of what eventually amounted to around 60 trenches in the moat happened to strike the northern edge of what was clearly important and high-quality masonry pre-dating the 1275-81 moat (Keevill 1997, Impey 1998). The location of the trench in question was to some extent arbitrary, dictated by an overall pattern of sampling rather than any specific expectation for this precise location roughly in the centre of the moat's western arm; had the trench been as little as 6ft 6in (2m) to the north the masonry would have been missed. Only a keyhole view of the one small area was possible in 1995, but in the following year the entire building was exposed (**28**).

The structure in fact comprised two distinct but interlocked elements: a roughly square area of high-quality masonry projecting forward from a bank of clay which seemed to be partially revetted in stone as well, and a complex network of timbers continuing westwards from the stonework. The latter stood to just over 3ft 3in (1m) high on poor rubble foundations, evidently without the provision of any piling even though the rubble rested on London Clay. The core was of mortared Kentish Rag rubble, and at the north-east corner (the only place where it could be exposed) this was laid in at least four courses. The ashlar facing used two different types of stone: Purbeck marble from Dorset in the lowest three courses (the bottom one being chamfered) and Reigate from Surrey in the upper two (again the bottom of these was chamfered); further blocks of both stone types were found in the silts around the masonry. The Purbeck was a hard water-resistant stone which would retain its grey-white colour, but the Reigate was more porous and took on a green hue when damp. The effect, undoubtedly deliberate, was to provide contrasting colours in the ashlar face; a similar contrast was achieved between Reigate and white chalk at Windsor under Edward III a century later. At the north-east and south-east corners, where the masonry met the clay bank, the ashlar courses turned through 90° externally. The chamfer on the bottom Purbeck marble course stopped against the returns, but the equivalent on the Reigate above turned with them (**colour plate 8**).

28 The Tower of London: overhead view of Henry III's masonry and timber structure found unexpectedly in the west moat during 1995 and seen here fully revealed in 1996. Photograph Oxford Archaeological Unit/Historic Royal Palaces

All of the facing was of the highest quality, with fine combing (masons' dressing marks made with an iron tool) preserved in crisp condition by the muds which had buried the stone. The individual blocks were very tightly jointed and bonded with lead, clearly with the intention to resist water. There were holes in all the adjacent upper surfaces of the Reigate blocks for iron cramps (staples to hold the stones together), and these too would probably have been covered in lead (similar examples can still be seen in Edward I's south-west causeway and St Thomas's Tower) though neither the cramp nor the lead survived in any example. Cramp holes were also present on the last stones of the corner returns except on the lowest course, suggesting that the upper courses should have continued for at least one more block each; there may have been an intent to link the projecting block to some kind of curtain wall via these returns, but this could not be proved.

It was more straightforward to establish the contemporaneity of the masonry with the complex of halved and quartered oaks associated with it, because the beams along the north and south faces of the stonework were firmly and deeply bedded under the returns at the two eastern corners. It is inconceivable that this could have been achieved after the masonry was built. These side-beams were linked to a third one across the front (ie. west face) of the building with pegged mortice and tenon joints. Four more timbers were attached in the same manner to both this north-south beam and another one parallel to and 8ft 2in (2.5m) west of it; the position of a fifth linking timber was also found. Another oak was found further still to the west, and though this was not attached there was enough evidence to

*29 Oak and beech timbers exposed to the west of the masonry shown on **28**. Note the empty mortices in the two oaks*

establish that it had been once (**29**). The arrangement of these timbers was strongly reminiscent of the bases of known medieval timber bridges of trestle construction, but there was little if any evidence for the intended or actual position of uprights. Nevertheless they clearly rested within a moat running underneath and 6ft 6in (2m) deeper than Edward I's here; the south end of this earlier moat was found just over 29ft 6in (9m) north of Edward I's south-western entrance to the Tower.

Both the masonry and the timbers showed clear signs of severe structural stress. The stonework, for instance, tilted down from west to east at an angle of about 6-7°, and the timbers varied from horizontal at even more alarming angles. Indeed they had clearly been moving significantly in their own right, and there was clear evidence for strain on some of the mortice and tenon joints and even the rupturing of two of them. There can be little doubt that a substantial building of this kind using different types of material would have been hard put to withstand such strains, and modern engineering opinion confirmed that it would have fallen. Thus we have archaeological evidence, as yet without a date, for a combined masonry and timber building suffering structural failure on the one hand, and equally clear historical evidence for a fallen entrance in 1240/1 on the other. We will now start to put the evidence together.

Firstly it seems clear enough that the 'noble gateway' specified by Matthew Paris in 1240 was the Beauchamp Tower, an ascription which has been accepted for some time. The same chronicle entry also refers to the gateway's forebuildings and outworks (*antemuralibus et propugnaculis*), and there is more likelihood that these (or some part of them) are the structures found under Edward I's west moat. How, though, do we close the link between the two strands of evidence? The answer lies with beech trees and, once again, their value for dendrochronology. More than 100 beech piles had been driven down the east face of the masonry in an apparent attempt to stabilise it; unused beech trunks were found in two parts of the early west moat, recalling the instruction of 1241 to put materials in a suitable place. Virtually all of the beeches retained their bark and therefore the final growth rings as well, and the 32 dendrochronology samples (19 of which were from the piles) all returned the same date: the winter of 1240/1, a precise match with the documentary evidence. We can be reasonably certain that we found some of the *antemuralibus et propugnaculis* described by Paris. The nature of these structures will be discussed in chapter 4.

One final piece in this jigsaw of evidence deserves a mention. Chamfered Purbeck marble blocks which must have derived from the collapsed structure(s) were found during the same excavations incorporated into the foundations of Edward I's outer curtain wall immediately to the east of the masonry structure, and also in the bottom courses of the causeway built between the Middle and Byward Towers at the same time. Like the beech trees, these examples of re-use surely echo the 1241 order to the Constable to rescue and store whatever he could.

As we have already seen, Edward I's builders were careful to use timber piles when putting in foundations for masonry along the river frontage of the Tower of London. Elsewhere in the castle they provided stone foundations of enormous mass to give the same effect, as when re-building Henry III's collapsed 'noble gate' at the Beauchamp Tower and the adjacent curtain wall. Excavations of the late thirteenth-century rebuild of the inner curtain just to the south of this tower in 1958 showed that it had been given exceptionally substantial foundations. Occasionally, however, the passage of time showed that this apparent sureness of touch was deceptive. Some time after Edwards I's moat had been dug out a new twin-towered Postern Gate was added on to the city wall where the excavations had breached it, thus stopping up what would otherwise have been a severe weakness in London's defensive circuit (the first reference to the new gate comes in 1308). It sat on the outer edge of the moat ditch, and its southern tower may even have oversailed the edge somewhat: certainly arrow loops were provided on the castle side of the structure, showing that this side of the gate was as much intended to guard the moat as control access into the city.

The choice of location could scarcely be avoided but it was unfortunate, and in 1431 a landslide on the north edge of the moat tore the gateway in two: the north tower and gate passage evidently stayed where they were (and must have been consolidated afterwards), but the south tower slid down the sloping edge of the moat and came to rest about 10ft (3 m) below its original level, twisting slightly as it slipped. Some effort was made to keep the chambers of the tower in use, but obviously it could not continue to function as part of the gate; that seems to have been kept as a single-towered structure from the 1430s onwards, and the passage through or past it ultimately developed into a road onto Tower Hill. The southern tower was demolished in the post-medieval period, or perhaps in the late medieval, and was then lost under the gradual development of the northern margins of the Tower (**colour plate 9**). It was rediscovered in 1978 during a major upgrade to London's road network which created the dual carriageway which now faces visitors to the castle as they approach from the north. The Postern's existence had evidently been completely forgotten, and no provision had been made for even so much as archaeological observation, let alone an excavation, during the roadworks. Fortunately good sense prevailed, and not only was a rapid rescue excavation mounted once the importance of the structure had been realised, but it was also preserved at the southern end of a new pedestrian underpass instead of being removed. Thus today's visitors to the castle can still gaze down on one of the Tower's less successful building episodes.

The dangers of fire

Disasters could happen in other ways than through poor-quality design and engineering. In the modern age we have become used to the dangers of fire and take extensive measures to prevent, detect and control it, though this has not saved Hampton Court Palace, Uppark House and Windsor Castle from highly destructive conflagrations. These are but the latest in a long line of fires which have affected palaces over the centuries, stretching back from the destruction of so much of Westminster Palace in the early 1830s through the Great Fire of London in 1666, though many royal and episcopal palaces survived the worst effects of this, and back into the medieval period. Medieval buildings of all sorts were, and still are, highly vulnerable to fire both because of the large quantities of timber used in their construction (even for those with stone walls there would be some framing, the roof structure, and panelling) and because of the fires which were required to heat them, whether on open hearths or within fireplaces. It is interesting to note that it was the timber-framed gallery which suffered worst at Bridewell during the Great Fire, being destroyed along with the riverside range and not rebuilt. The buildings of the other courtyards were affected as well (fire-damage levels were found in the 1978 excavations), but the effects were not as serious; these ranges survived for another 200 years, though not as a palace, for Bridewell had been passed to the city authorities by Edward VI in 1552 to be used as a workhouse for the poor. Another example from 1666 demonstrated the lengths to which the authorities would go to protect an important site threatened by fire. At the Tower of London a wide swathe of ground to the west of the castle was peremptorily cleared of all buildings to act as a fire-break. This was successful — at least the fire did not reach the Tower — and the extent of the action taken is understandable given the quantities of armaments, gunpowder and other munitions stored within the castle walls (not least within the White Tower itself) at the time, to say nothing of important state and government records which had been held there since the time of Edward I.

The simplest means of heating any interior was to place a hearth somewhere close to its centre, allowing smoke to rise upwards and pass out of the room through a hole in the roof. Such simple hearths are well known archaeologically from prehistory onwards, and they are common on sites of all kinds during the medieval period. During the latter it was common for the hearth to be defined by tiles set on edge into an already-prepared shallow pit, with tile or brick edging as well. This at least defined the limits of the fire. A major drawback of the open hearth was that the space over it had to be open to the roof if smoke was to escape through a louvre (vented opening) in it. This precluded the provision of an upper floor over such a hearth unless a solid back was added to one side of the hearth so that a chimney could be raised off it and taken directly up to the roof, thus freeing the space above for more accommodation, which could also make use of the chimney. In most cases this was only realistically possible on a solid wall, either on the exterior of the building or at an internal partition. Despite the restrictiveness and risks of open hearths their very simplicity seems to have been a continuing attraction, and they were still being built well into the medieval period. At the Lincoln bishops' palace at Lyddington (Leics), for instance, a watching brief during the insertion of drains in 1980 revealed archaeological evidence for the first time of the palace's successive great halls and their hearths. The first hall was built probably in the late twelfth century with a hearth placed centrally at its south-east end, but a new and grander hall was built in the early to mid-fourteenth century: a new hearth was built directly over the original one and seems to have persisted in use for the remainder of the medieval period. Mural fireplaces were certainly being added in some other palace rooms in the late fourteenth to early fifteenth century, however, including one on an internal partition which survives within the Bede House. The latter is all that now remains of the palace, but the conservatism of the hall's heating may reflect little more than the traditional nature of its arrangement.

Fire is an ever-present hazard in any room or building where a naked flame is used, but open hearths are particularly problematic simply because there is, by definition, little or no confinement to the combustible material. Not only random sparks but also much larger pieces of burning matter could come out of the hearth, not only during the day but also at night-time if the fire was to be stoked up in readiness for the next day. There were ways in which the risk could be reduced, and the most obvious was to provide a degree of containment for the fire within a room. The main way of doing this was to remove the open fire from the centre of a hall or other chamber and instead place it against or within a wall in a clearly defined fireplace. This would have the distinct secondary advantage of controlling smoke and fumes, which passed up a chimney flue independently of the roof, while wall fireplaces also made it much easier to control and gather ash. Mural fireplaces and chimneys were available from the early Norman period onwards, and primary ones of around 1100 can still be seen in the White Tower (Tower of London). At St Mary's Guildhall in Lincoln, fireplaces were an integral element of the original twelfth-century structure probably built for Henry II between 1150-70 (**30**). They were provided in the west wall of the main building with chimneys rising through the thickness of the wall to stacks above the eaves. Only the northern features survive, the southern half of the range beyond the exquisite central gateway having been rebuilt during the post-medieval period, with fireplaces at both ground- and first-floor level. The flue is contained within a shallow buttress (1ft/0.3m deep) which carries the chimney breast for the hearth at first-floor level. The placement of the chimney/buttress equidistant between one at the north-west corner of the range and another on the north side of the central gateway shows that the original structure was symmetrically planned with considerable care.

Internally the ground-floor fireplace was blocked in the eighteenth/nineteenth century, but the centre and south half of its original lintel survived. The bottom surface had a chamfer which continued down onto the jambs, and the front comprised joggled stones; the central keystone was T-shaped with tapering stem, and the blocks to either side continued

30 St Mary's Guildhall, Lincoln: the northern fireplace flue expressed as a buttress on the outer face of the west range. Photograph by J. Ashbee

this stepped pattern, terminating it over the jambs. When the blocking was removed from the fireplace in 1982 it was found to have a firebase of tiles set on edge, and this may have been a primary feature, though most of the tiles were clearly later replacements (**31**). The first-floor fireplace had suffered more extensive alteration in the eighteenth and nineteenth centuries, but the southern jamb survived intact to the point where it was cut away when the wall height was reduced during the post-medieval period. The bases for a projecting hood also survived. Enough evidence is available in the remaining structures and dismembered fragments of them recovered during excavation to allow a paper reconstruction of how this most impressive range would have looked as-built, both inside and out.

There are many other fireplaces of a similar nature to be seen in royal and episcopal palaces. Several examples from the thirteenth-century reigns of Henry III and Edward I survive at the Tower of London, for instance, with a magnificent original hood being an important feature in Henry's Salt Tower. The reconstructed hood of similar form and the same period in the Wakefield Tower 'throne room', though controversial when put up in the early 1990s, is intended to be removable without affecting the original fabric and gives a good impression of the monarch's requirements for comfort even in ceremonial areas of a palace. Tiled fireplaces like the one at the Lincoln guildhall also survive at the Tower: there is a good example cut into the rear face of Henry III's inner curtain wall between the Salt and Broad Arrow Towers which now sits enclosed within the late seventeenth-century New

31 St Mary's Guildhall, Lincoln: the northern ground-floor fireplace as exposed during renovation in 1982. Photograph copyright City of Lincoln Archaeology Unit

Armouries building, but the base of the hearth lies well below the floor level of the latter. This hearth proves the existence of a medieval building on this spot which has long since vanished, and further evidence for buildings in this area was revealed unexpectedly during excavations late in 1999 (described in chapter 5).

Late medieval chimneys tended to be brick-built and substantial. They usually projected out from the external wall face of the building range, so that the fireplace itself was in effect a detached element of the room's interior. The use of brick was a logical extension of the tiled fireplaces we have already seen at the Lincoln guildhall and the Tower of London, which in themselves were merely versions of the end-set tiles in open hearths: brick and tile were especially good building materials to use where fire was concerned, as they had already been exposed to high heat in the kiln and could thus resist the heartiest of domestic fires. There are many excellent fifteenth- and sixteenth-century examples to be seen today, such as the two surviving chimneys and their stacks at the east end of the guest range erected by Bishop Henry Beaufort along the north side of the Inner Court at Bishop's Waltham in 1438-42. The eastern chimney was extensively rebuilt later on but the other is largely as first built, showing the diamond-shaped diaper pattern which is typical of the period picked out in black and white. The foundations of the remaining chimneys in the range can still be seen stretching westwards along the edge of the moat around the inner court. Each chimney would have had two fireplaces in it, one each for guest suites on the ground and first floors.

Similar Tudor chimneys have been excavated in the south-west range of the Middle Court at Oatlands House, perhaps pre-dating Henry VIII's acquisition of the house and its conversion into one of his palaces (Cook 1969), and Nonsuch Palace. The surviving examples at Hampton Court Palace are well-known, though many of the chimneys here have been repaired or rebuilt over the years. The Bede House at Lyddington also includes a number of Tudor fireplaces and chimneys, along with others which were also rebuilt in the post-medieval period.

In this chapter we have seen how palace-builders went about their business, and how they sometimes erred in doing so. We now go on to look at the variety of functions performed by palaces of various sizes, and some of the ancillary services or features provided within and around them.

4   The use of palaces: public and private faces

Palaces were complex, multi-functional establishments. At a basic level they provided a monarch or bishop with the comforts of home, whether close to that person's main seat of power or remote from it. They could be much more than simply a home, however, and the next two chapters explore the variety of ways in which palaces were used, and the archaeological evidence for these functions.

Residence and court

Palaces were very much the stage for the two distinct facets of private and public life, and the interplay between these sometimes became expressed within the fabric of the buildings themselves. Intermediate rooms were commonly attached to the private accommodation and public chambers, for instance, so that courtiers and visitors could wait on the presence of the monarch or prelate. This was a deliberate act of separation and control based both on the need for security and the expression of power. Such considerations can be recognised in the planning and disposition of palaces throughout the medieval period, while the private and public sides each contained distinctive elements which need to be seen in the context of the personal and social requirements of those who used the buildings. Perhaps the greatest of these was the need to be seen by one's subjects in an age when mass or rapid communication was scarcely an option. The very legitimacy of the monarch's claim to the throne was often in doubt, and if this was usually less of an issue in the episcopal sphere there were still hierarchical and other tensions in many diocese during the period. Those in power or striving for it had little option but to progress around the country if they were to establish and maintain their claim. Such imperatives found ready expression in the mobility of kings and bishops with their families and courts which lies behind the profusion of palaces and other residences they built or acquired, while the ceremonial function of the more public buildings is usually explicit in their location and internal arrangement.

The movements around the country of Norman and later medieval kings of England were partly dictated by the military campaigns necessary to control restive areas while also seeking to extend the kingdom into Wales. The far north-west also had to be re-taken from Scotland, with the royal castle founded at Carlisle around the close of the eleventh century being a potent symbol of the struggle between the two countries for control of the borders which continued for centuries afterwards. We know relatively little about the detailed movements of the early kings beyond the broad sweep of campaigning (whether in a military or political sense), but some later reigns are very well documented; as we shall see, the detailed movements of some bishops around and out of their diocese are also known. Extracting the information for these progresses can be a significant work of scholarship in its own right, but the enormous potential is nowhere better demonstrated than by the long reign of Henry III (**32**). During the early twentieth century an archivist at the Public Record Office compiled a complete itinerary of the movements of England's longest-reigning medieval monarch (he was later overtaken by George III and Victoria) from the first days of his minority in 1216 through to his death in 1272. This involved detailed searches of the Charter, Close, Fine, Liberate and Patent Rolls, and despite occasional gaps the result is what amounts to a daily diary of the king's travels within his realm.

It is interesting to compare the hard evidence from the itinerary for Henry's journeying and his residences of preference with our archaeological and other knowledge of his buildings. His time was used carefully, and can be broken down into four principal groups: time spent in the capital, in the Thames Valley/Wessex region, elsewhere in the country, and in France (details of the king's time spent there are not included in the itinerary). The length of stay varied from a day to months on end, especially at Westminster during the later years of his reign, and the shorter periods often involved either stops en route to an intended longer sojourn at a favoured house, or a distinct progress to and around one of the more distant parts of the kingdom such as Yorkshire, the north-east or south-west. While some palaces were used regularly, sites like Hamstead Marshall near Newbury (Berks) might only be used in a restricted number of years, especially earlier on when the king's position in Wessex and the West Country was being consolidated. Henry stayed at Hamstead several times in 1218, for instance, usually in transit to or from the important stronghold at Marlborough, evidently taking a conscious decision to travel along the ridge to the south of the river Kennet rather than on its north bank (Rosevear 1995, 6-7). During April, however, he seems to have made a deliberate visit to the site in between short stops at Worcester, Gloucester and Worcester again. The king also made use of monastic hospitality (for instance at Chertsey and Reading abbeys close to London) and this was a dominant feature of his time in East Anglia with stays at Bromham, Bury St Edmunds, Castle Acre, Ely, Thetford and Walsingham.

Perhaps unsurprisingly London was the dominant area of domicile, and Westminster was clearly the favoured residence as the following table shows. The Tower of London, by contrast, was scarcely used at all outside of the minority and during troubles in the 1260s (the king was there for 171 days in 1261 and 23 days in 1263) despite the enormous amounts of money expended on the castle. This is probably the best possible demonstration of the Tower's importance as a symbol to London and the kingdom of royal power and (hoped-for) dominance as much as anything else. The second area (the Thames Valley and Wessex) was also heavily used, and the royal preference for London and its surroundings even during years of uncertainty including internal and foreign campaigns is plain enough. Indeed there were many years in which the king did not venture any further than this heartland while he was in the country, and once past his minority he showed a particular liking for a few palaces such as Windsor Castle and Woodstock among the wide

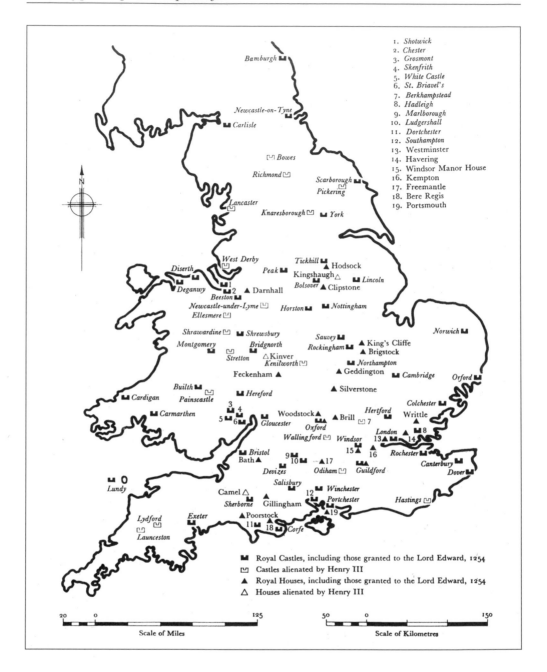

1. *Shotwick*
2. *Chester*
3. *Grosmont*
4. *Skenfrith*
5. *White Castle*
6. *St. Briavel's*
7. *Berkhampstead*
8. *Hadleigh*
9. *Marlborough*
10. *Ludgershall*
11. *Dortchester*
12. *Southampton*
13. *Westminster*
14. *Havering*
15. *Windsor Manor House*
16. *Kempton*
17. *Freemantle*
18. *Bere Regis*
19. *Portsmouth*

Royal Castles, including those granted to the Lord Edward, 1254
Castles alienated by Henry III
Royal Houses, including those granted to the Lord Edward, 1254
Houses alienated by Henry III

20   0   125
Scale of Miles

50   0   150
Scale of Kilometres

32 The residences inherited by Henry III in 1216 showing the spread of locations the king might be expected to visit. From James 1990; drawn by Alex Turner variety of residences he used. Clarendon, often seen as a favourite palace and certainly a major focus of expenditure, was first visited in 1225 (six days in total) and in most years during the 1230s, with a high-point of 31 days in 1239. In many subsequent years the king could not make time for Clarendon, but he managed several longer stays there including several in a year, as in 1249 when his three stays totalled more than 60 days. Even when the king did go further afield to places like Norwich, York and Newcastle, the length of time spent there in any year was kept to 17 days or less. He never went further north-west than Chester, and he never strayed into Cornwall.

Decade	Westminster	Thames Valley/Wessex region
1217-19	95 (no time spent there in 1216)	
1220-29	169	40
1230-39	76	139
1240-49	82	123
1250-59	110	124
1260-69	108	75
1270-72	214	

Table 1: Average number of days per annum spent at Westminster and in the Thames Valley/Wessex region by Henry III. The time spent in the latter region is probably an underestimate.

The completeness of our knowledge regarding Henry III's movements is rare indeed, even for the English kings, and it is far more difficult to trace the progresses of the Gywnedd princes in the eleventh to thirteenth centuries. This is mainly due to the lack of direct historical evidence, though it is possible to establish a royal presence on a given site when official documents were written and issued from there. Commotal centres (*maerdrefi*) were used in this way during the reigns of Llewelyn ap Iorwerth (1190-1240) and Llewelyn ap Gruffudd (1255-82). This kind of information has allowed a partial reconstruction of the court's journeys and stays at *llysoedd* such as Aber and Tal-y-bont from July 1273 to January 1277 (Stephenson 1984). Interestingly we know more of Edward I's tour through the newly conquered domain after ap Gruffudd's defeat in 1282, when he visited most of the Gwynedd *maerdrefi*.

Bishops would have just as much need to travel as the monarch, though the area involved would usually be restricted to the diocese except for journeys to court in London. As with royalty there are some exceptionally well-documented examples of episcopal progresses because of the detailed expenditure and other records kept by diocese such as Lincoln and Winchester. Nothing like the long itinerary of Henry III has yet come to light for a bishop, although there are some good examples of annual or part-year accounts which can be used in a similar way. The activities of Richard de Swinfield, Bishop of Hereford from 1282-1317, are known for the period from the start of the accounting year at Michaelmas (29 September) 1289 to July of the following year because his household roll for these months give has survived (James 1990, 101-5). As with Henry III we see a man travelling for much of the time, in this case to carry out parochial visitations and similar duties. Surprisingly the roll does not record any episcopal visit to the cathedral at Hereford itself except for Palm Sunday, but this may reflect no more than the particular circumstances and needs of the year in question. A great deal of time was certainly spent attending to business within the diocese, with stays of several weeks at residences such as Sugwas near Hereford itself and Bosbury near Ledbury occupying most of the time up to Christmas. Just before New Year the bishop set out for London, stopping overnight at Coln St Aldwin near Fairford (Glos), Faringdon and Wantage (both Oxon) on the 28th, 29th and 30th December before arriving at Reading Abbey (which was evidently well used to hosting such parties). The progress into London continued on 4 January 1290 with a stop from then until the 7th at Bedfont, after which the entourage arrived at the Queenhithe inn belonging to the see. The bishop only remained in London until 13 January, returning thence to Hereford by a similar route to the outward journey (but avoiding Reading Abbey) and arriving back in late February. The next three months were spent within the diocese on the regular round of visitations: in April alone de Swinford stayed at 17 places (moreover the first 10 days had been spent at just one, Colwall), quite apart from those he actually went to on any given day (**33**).

The palace as residence: hall and chamber

A substantial group of people would have travelled with the monarch or prelate on most journeys, consisting of family (where relevant), court officials, guards and a variety of servants. This, along with the need to hold audiences, often with large numbers of people, and other formal ceremonies led to the construction of many very large palaces throughout the medieval period. The plan form and elevational detailing of buildings developed greatly from the late eleventh to the middle of the sixteenth centuries, but the reliance on private chambers and public halls remained remarkably constant during this time — as indeed did analogous building types for other social groups, whether secular or ecclesiastical. It is neither necessary nor desirable to look for a single scheme in the provision and layout of rooms, but recent research points to a model of a hall with associated (sometimes partially attached) chamber block providing the complementary public and private spaces at many sites during the eleventh to thirteenth centuries and beyond. This model may have originated in Anglo-Saxon timber building traditions (see chapter 1) but it seems to have been developed in stone in Normandy a generation or so before its widespread introduction to Britain. Similar accommodation could be encapsulated within an alternative arrangement such as a single structure, the *donjon* or keep, but in practice even here separate ranges were soon erected to provide some of the necessary facilities, especially the public hall. Seigneurial hall and chamber-block groups can be seen in Normandy at Beaumont-le-Richard, Creully, Briquebec and Barneville-la-Bertran, while the ground-floor hall at the Echiquier (Caen) with its traditional ascription to Henry I, is a reminder of the close ties between Normandy and England through much of the medieval period (**colour plate 10**). In England fine twelfth- to fourteenth-century medieval halls survive largely intact at Farnham and Hereford (episcopal), and Winchester Castle Great Hall, Eltham Palace and Westminster (royal), while Clarendon, Bishop's Waltham, Old Sarum, Sherborne and the Lincoln Bishop's Palace provide a good selection

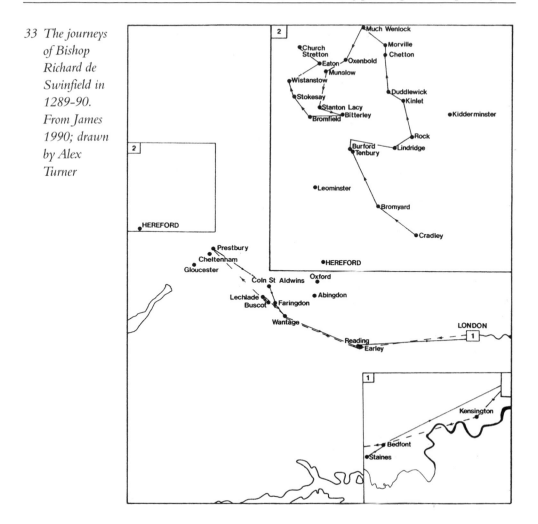

33 The journeys of Bishop Richard de Swinfield in 1289-90. From James 1990; drawn by Alex Turner

of the greater number of ruinous ones (**34**). The latter group also retain substantial traces of the chamber ranges which provided private accommodation, but ironically these have not survived at the first group.

At Old Sarum the hall and chamber arrangement of the original palace within the Inner Bailey is difficult to appreciate on the ground because of the terracing of the courtyard plan (**35**) associated with the upcast defensive bank but the later hall in the outer bailey can still be seen (especially its north gable fragment) and is of impressive scale (around 130ft/40m long and 65ft/20m wide). The hall's aisled plan is known from excavations in the early 1900s but is not marked out on the ground, in contrast to the cathedral itself. There is a clear case for improved presentation here. More of the medieval masonry can be seen at Sherborne, though here again the hall has largely been reduced to foundation level. The domestic rooms to the west and north are ranged around a central courtyard, as at Sarum, and a garderobe block was provided to the north-west. The great keep at the south-west corner of the courtyard was clearly the dominant structure linking the hall and domestic ranges, although the architecture and

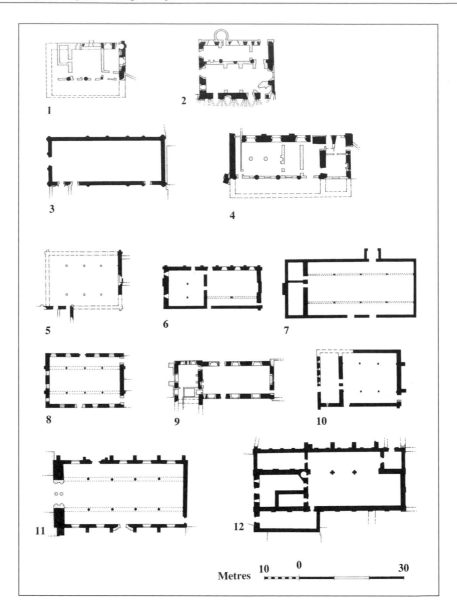

34 Comparative plans of selected French and English halls. Drawing by Dr E. Impey

1 Beaumont-le-Richard (Calvados), *c*.1150.
2 Creully (Calvados), *c*.1160.
3 Caen (Calvados), *c*.1125. As rebuilt after 1944. After L. Froidevaux, 1972
4 Bricquebec (Manche), *c*.1190.
5 Douvres-la-Delivrande (Calvados), *c*.1300.
6 Rumesnil (Calvados), *c*.1260. Reconstruction.
7 Hereford, *c*.1190. Reconstruction. After Blair, 1987

8 Oakham Castle (Rutland), *c*.1190. After VCH *Rutland*
9 Minster-in-Thanet (Kent), *c*.1150.
10 Warnford (Hants), *c*.1200. After VCH *Hants*
11 Winchester, castle (Hants), 1222-35. After VCH *Hants*
12 Winchester, Wolvesey Palace, 'east hall' as rebuilt 1135-8. After Biddle, 1986

35 The courtyard of the bishop's palace within the Inner Bailey of Old Sarum

decoration of the north (chapel) range provided an important counterpoint to the keep's height and sheer mass (*see* **27**). Though much altered in the fourteenth century, the juxtaposition of hall and chambers can also be seen at Bishop's Waltham, where again the two ranges find a common central focus in the tower at the south-west corner of the Inner Court.

These (and many other) examples conform broadly to the hall and chamber-block model, whether the hall was on the ground floor or raised to first-floor level either over an undercroft or through terracing/earthworking. A number of early Winchester palaces offer a somewhat contrasting form: the palace or manor at Witney is a good example of this. Here the see owned substantial tracts of land a little over 50 miles due north from the cathedral itself, and obviously this was far too great a distance for direct management. Accordingly an estate centre was established here in the early twelfth century to administer the properties and to provide episcopal accommodation at need. It is not certain that the Witney complex should be seen as a palace, and the authors of the final report into the excavations at the site in the 1980s and 1990s tend to believe that it was not. What cannot be in doubt is the very high quality of much of the building work on the site, with fine ashlar work and all the elements of accommodation one would expect of a high-status residence. The centrepiece was a massively built solar tower measuring 36ft by 19ft 8in (11.5m x 6m) internally with walls almost 9ft 9in (3m) thick. The undercroft of this survives and is displayed on site, allowing one to see the deep internal splays of the windows into the basement and the splendid ashlar of the central rectangular column base which was added shortly after the tower had been built; the function of this feature is by no means clear (**36; colour plate 11**). From the beginning there appears to have been a range with an external chimney stack running

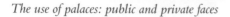

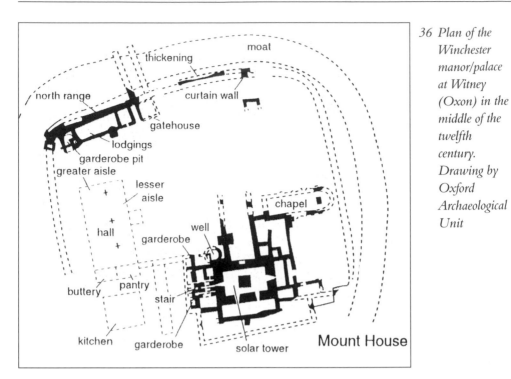

36 *Plan of the Winchester manor/palace at Witney (Oxon) in the middle of the twelfth century. Drawing by Oxford Archaeological Unit*

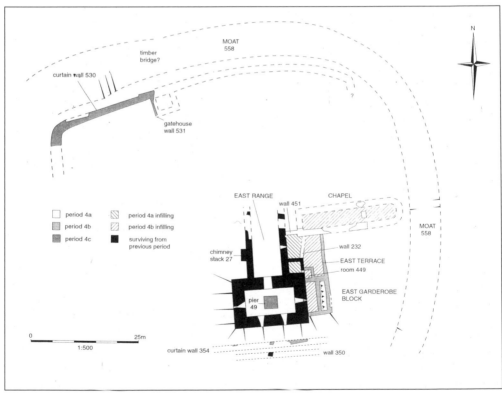

north from the tower, and this may have provided hall accommodation but it is otherwise hard to see how the complex fits in with the 'usual' model either at this stage or in later phases. Subsequently a substantial garderobe block and chapel were added to the east of the original buildings in the middle of the twelfth century, with further partially detached garderobes built to the west in the latter half of the century. A curious feature of the complex at this time was the deliberate raising of the ground level around the outside of the buildings to first-floor height by dumping soil against the outer walls and even within some of the recently completed rooms. Something similar occurred at Castle Acre (Norfolk) at about the same time, and also at the home palace in Winchester.

Back at Wolvesey the vast and complex so-called West Hall built around 1110 by Bishop William Giffard (1107-29) seems to have both hall and chamber elements within the one structure (*see* **1**), perhaps looking more towards French and German palaces than the Anglo-Norman hall and chamber-block tradition (Impey 1999, note 8). Once again a great tower was present, this time attached to the range at its south-west corner and with a walled garden running to its north (ie. along the west side of the 'hall'). As we have already seen (chapter 1), elements of the Anglo-Saxon palace may have continued in use at this time, but Giffard's main rooms were undoubtedly within this range. The three western rooms provided his principal chambers, raised to first-floor level on solid chalk packing, while the near-continuous ground-floor eastern room provided an undercroft for clerks' rooms above. The western rooms were the ones habitually used by royalty when they visited Wolvesey, which they did regularly — indeed the northern chamber was often referred to as the queen's, as was the walled garden immediately to the west. The tower, meanwhile, provided offices (the exchequer and treasury) on the ground floor, a private chapel above (separate from the main chapel to the east — see below) and what must have amounted to the bishop's main private chamber on the upper floor. The whole range was fully 164ft (50m) long and 52ft 6in (16m) wide (excluding the walled garden), while the tower was 33ft (10m) square excluding a narrow garderobe (latrine) block on its west side. The monumental scale of the building was allied to austerely impressive architecture, with great pilaster buttresses around all the exterior faces; those on the long sides (eg. the east and west walls) do not match up, perhaps because of the differential stresses across the building (the western rooms are wider than clerks' range, and the east external wall is much the narrowest of the three long walls).

Such a vast building was clearly designed to impress, as well as to provide spacious and no doubt stylish accommodation commensurate with the status of its builder. Remarkably, however, a second hall was built at Wolvesey in the late 1130s by Giffard's successor to the diocese, the great bishop-builder Henry de Blois (1129-71). Though his block (the East Hall) was slightly smaller than Giffard's overall, it did contain a much larger 'true' hall measuring 88ft (26.8m) in length and 29ft (8.8m) in width, fully open to the roof and with a separate porch and gallery along the west side (**colour plate 12**). These were probably single-storeyed, allowing the provision of a clerestory to light the hall. The gallery continued southwards alongside a two-storey chamber-block attached to the end of the hall. Despite later alterations and ruination this block provides an exceptionally good impression of the scale and character of the mid-twelfth century palace, whether viewed from the south (ie. outside) or north. The hall is not quite so easy to appreciate because the west side has been reduced to foundation level over the years, but the flint core of the east wall survives in part to something like full height alongside a passage between the hall and the palace's 'keep' (actually a kitchen block, built shortly after the hall and chamber-block had been completed). Two courses of original ashlar stonework facing the flint core survive along the bottom of the wall, the upper with a chamfer (45° cutback on the upper surface) showing that the next course up would have been set back slightly. This course, and all the remaining flint facework, has fallen or been robbed away in the post-medieval period: the surviving ashlar was only (re-)exposed during excavation of the East Hall in 1970 (*see* **colour plate 12**).

The north gable of the East Hall also survives very well, showing how de Blois raised the whole of the hall by the equivalent of a storey above a prominent horizontal string course, with the interior remaining open to the roof. The new masonry was significantly wider than the original build because it had to incorporate a new passage within the thickness of the wall. This can be seen most clearly where the passage turns through a right-angle at the north-east corner of the hall. The new thicker wall was supported on impressive blind arcading springing from corbels inserted into the existing masonry (**37**). The pointed arches of the arcading and the round arches of the passage above retain fine ball ornament showing a lightness of touch in marked contrast to the austerity of the West Hall. The blind arcade would also have provided a fitting backdrop for the bishop when he sat enthroned on a dais during ceremonial events. Similar arcading can be seen in the hall at Bishop's Waltham where it can also be taken as evidence for the position of a dais. The location of such a dais at the Lincoln bishop's palace of Lyddington has had to be inferred from below-ground archaeological evidence as none of the hall survives above ground.

The Tower of London

London, of course, has one of the greatest of all early Norman buildings in Europe: the White Tower (**colour plates 5 & 6**). It is difficult to determine the extent to which this was intended as a royal residence: it (and indeed the Tower as a whole) has been seen as purely defensive by some, and purely ceremonial by others. It is likely that the truth lies somewhere in between such polar opposites: the Tower was undoubtedly an impressive symbol of defence and control (see chapter 3) where major ceremonial events could be staged (see below), but most monarchs up to and including Henry VIII also used the castle for their own or their family's residence at some time. By no stretch of the imagination could it be called one of the most important palaces, however, and this applies as much to the great stone keep as to any other part of the castle.

The White Tower contains a great deal of physical space, and some of it such as the Chapel of St John or the storage space in the basement is easy enough to understand (see below). The remainder is not so readily interpretable, largely because there are relatively few clues as to the specific function of individual chambers beyond obvious features such as fireplaces and garderobes which offer no more than general evidence of domestic activity. Neither are the documentary sources a great deal of help at this early date,

37 Detail of the blind arcading and high-level wall passage at the north end of Wolvesey's East Hall

although Henry I's imprisonment of Rannulf Flambard, bishop of Durham, within the White Tower in 1100-1 speaks volumes: Flambard was one of the most important and powerful men of the realm, scarcely much behind the king himself, and his temporary involuntary home (from which he escaped) had to be fitting for his rank. Even the means of his escape is significant, for he was allowed to hold a sumptuous feast to which his guards were invited; once they were paralytic with wine he used a rope — which had been smuggled in with the wine — to climb down the walls. We are not told in which room, or even on which floor the revelries took place, but that scarcely matters: a great (if not entirely ceremonial) banquet evidently did take place, and the food had to be cooked elsewhere. The lack of kitchens within the White Tower has often been held against its domestic potential, though of course kitchens were always separate to and often detached from the principal accommodation in the first-floor hall and chamber model.

Clearly cooking took place somewhere very close by in 1101, and later in the same century we begin to read of other buildings at the castle as the frequency of documentary references increases. Unfortunately it tends to be difficult to establish what the buildings were, still more so where they were. Returning to the White Tower, however, we must consider how the two principal floors (eg. excluding the basement) functioned. As we have seen the most recent archaeological research has shown that the upper walls provided a screen hiding the roofs. Previous descriptions of the upper floor as being tall and open to its lofty ceiling must now be re-assessed, for the whole space was much lower; the ceiling level on the middle floor as we see it today probably equates quite well to the eaves height of the original upper chambers. This means that the upper rooms would not have provided much of a contrast in height and volume to those on the entrance level, as had previously been thought, and to that extent there was little to differentiate between the spaces involved. Nevertheless they must have had a degree of functional separation, implicit in the provision of entry through one level only: moreover access throughout the rest of the building depended on and was controllable from this level, principally by means of the spiral staircase in the north-east corner turret opposite the entrance itself which was in the south wall close to its west end (**38**).

It has become somewhat conventional to see the upper floor as the king's apartments and the entrance level enjoying lower status, but with both containing identical suites of a hall, chamber and chapel. An alternative model has been developed as a result of the recent campaign of archaeological and historical research into the White Tower, placing emphasis on a virtually processional use of the space within and between the two floors by a single group, not two households. The residential shortcomings of the entrance level are clear enough, not only through its very use for entry through the western chamber and passage to the floor above via the eastern room, but also because the latter is devoid of garderobes, those everyday essential smallest rooms of the medieval household. Furthermore this chamber also has a deep recess in its south wall with a door giving the only access into the chapel sub-crypt behind it. The western chamber can be interpreted as a guardroom cum congregation and waiting point readily enough, and we may note that the garderobes lie at the north end of the room. There are good practical reasons for this (see chapter 5) but it does also place them at the furthest possible point from the entrance and immediately in front of the doorway through the keep's central spine wall into the eastern chamber. The latter would work well as a ceremonial reception room, with a dais or throne in the recess and a retiring room for the monarch in the chapel sub-crypt. The rooms in the upper floor would work well as hall (west) and chamber (east), especially if there was a screened passage across the north end of the eastern room to direct people through into the 'hall'. There is in fact some circumstantial evidence for this (see page 153). St John's Chapel at the south-east corner of the floor was accessible from both rooms. The main problem with this model lies in the king's routes out of the 'reception' chamber on the entrance floor from his recess: the chapel sub-crypt is a literal dead end trap, but equally access to the upper rooms necessitated passage through the press of his audience — or that it should have been cleared in advance. Neither seems attractive, but in truth we may never come to a full understanding of how the White Tower was intended to work.

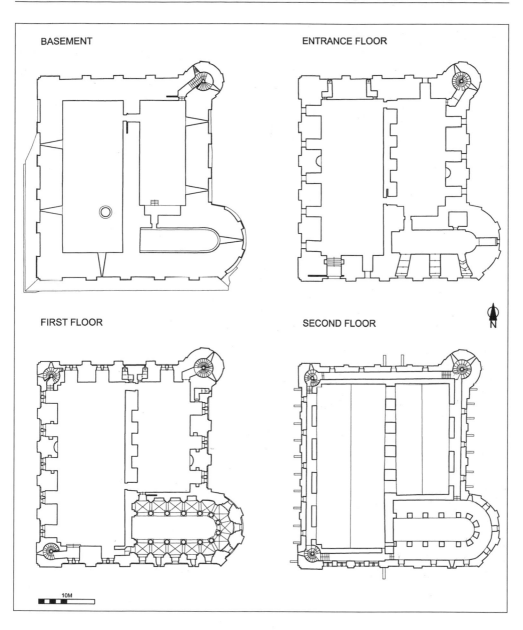

38 *Floor plans of the White Tower, Tower of London, as completed c.1100. The 'second floor' plan shows the ridges of the roof now known to have occupied this position; the intramural walkway thus overlooked the roof, not the interior of the building as previously thought. Drains took water off the roof through the upper walls. Note the garderobes and drawbar sockets inside the building, and the well in the basement. Drawings by R. Harris*

Regardless of the way (or ways) in which the White Tower was used, we know that the medieval palace within the castle was transformed during the thirteenth century under Henry III and Edward I at the same time as the defences were being massively extended (see below; also Impey and Parnell 2000, Lapper and Parnell 2000). The new royal and court accommodation was concentrated to the south of the White Tower, between it and the river Thames in the area known as the Inmost Ward. Henry III in particular created an extensive and elaborate suite of apartments, and these were further enhanced by his son before the century was out. The father's interest in building such fine and expensive accommodation seems surprising in the light of the very limited amount of time he resided at the Tower during his reign (see above), but it is clear enough from the records and accounts of the period that he put up new towers, chambers, a great hall, a kitchen and various other ancillary buildings. Such work was not for the king's use alone, of course, and in 1235 his sister, Princess Isabella was resident at the Tower. In the following year the king married Eleanor of Provence, and he set about converting or building new accommodation for her. Sadly little of Henry III's palace survives either above or below ground with the important exception of the mural Wakefield and Lanthorn Towers (the latter a late Victorian rebuild — the original tower had been demolished in the late 1770s) on the inner curtain, but archaeological work and historical research have shed considerable light on the disposition of the king's works.

The centrepiece, as usual, was the Great Hall, of which virtually nothing survives archaeologically. Fortunately there are a few late- and post-medieval depictions of it, notably the Haiward and Gascoyne survey of 1597 which shows that the hall was roofless and 'decay'd' by then. Indeed there are documentary references to its use for storage in 1387, while repairs had to be carried out to make it ready for Anne Boleyn's coronation in 1533. Sources from later in the same century suggest that no further attempt had been made to halt its gradual decline into ruination: in January 1558, for instance, a ceremony for the Knights of the Bath had to be moved into the White Tower. Matters were evidently so bad that a canvas roof had to be put up within the shell of the hall for James I's coronation in 1603 — a sad reflection on a once-great building. The canvas covered an area of 70ft (21.34m) by 25ft (7.62m) and it is clear from other works at the time that this did not cover the whole area of the hall; the latter would probably have run to a length of about 80ft (24.38m) and width of 50ft (15.24m). Certainly the building was aisled (a survey of 1335 specifically refers to 'postes' and 'pylers'), and such a length would allow four bays of around 20ft (6.1m) each, as in the contemporary great halls at Winchester Castle, Clarendon Palace (see below) and that built by Archbishop Langton at Canterbury. The 1335 survey led to an extensive campaign of repair, and in the following year significant alterations took place along the north wall of the hall. This involved taking down the roofs of lateral gables, each of which would contain a window although the south wall was probably plain and windowless, and heightening the walls, thus creating a flat wall face in contrast to the rhythmic interruptions which the gables had formerly provided. The heightening of Winchester's Great Hall provides an exact analogy for this process at about the same time, and the blocked-in gables can still be seen there (**39**). Henry's halls at the Tower and Winchester are direct contemporaries completed in the mid-late 1230s, but the king seems to have drawn his inspiration from Langton's work at

Front Cover

Bishop William Waynflete's magnificent entrance tower of 1470-5 at the west end of the medieval hall range at Farnham Castle

1   The brick entrance tower at Farnham Castle (Surrey), built in 1470-5

False colour plot of gaussian filtered 1m interval resistivity data

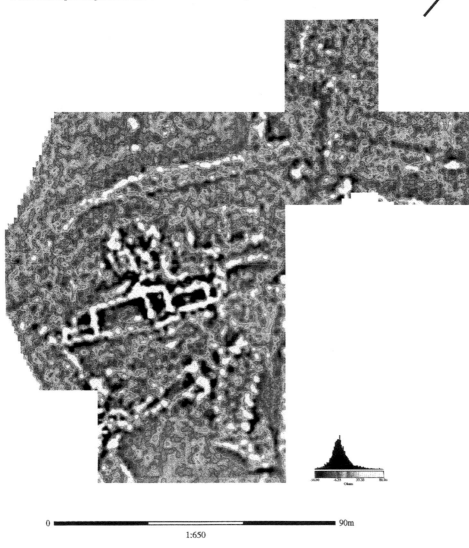

0 ▬▬▬▬▬▬▬▬▬▬▬▬ 90m
1:650

2   *Geophysical surveying on a possible palace site: this plot of resistivity information shows a wealth of detail for several buildings and the enclosure they occupy at Freens Court (Herefordshire). © Crown copyright: English Heritage*

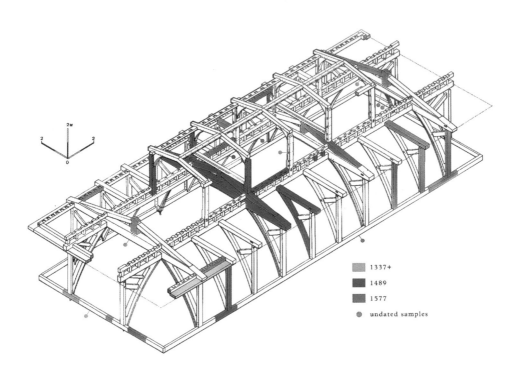

1337+

1489

1577

undated samples

3 Results of dendrochronology work on timbers from the Great Kitchen roof damaged by the fire at Windsor Castle on 20 November 1992. The different dates from the samples can be related to historically documented works.
© Crown copyright: English Heritage

4 St Mary's Guildhall, Lincoln, seen from the south-west. Photograph by J. Ashbee

5 The Tower of London as it might have looked during Henry III's extension of the defences in the 1230s and '40s. The painting takes account of historical evidence and the latest archaeological research. Painting by Ivan Lapper. © Crown copyright: Historic Royal Palaces

6 *A view across the Tower of London today from the west, with the White Tower prominent. Henry III's inner curtain wall with the Beauchamp Tower runs in front of the keep, and Edward I's outer curtain lies further forward still. Edward's entrance to the castle can be seen at the bottom right, with the Middle Tower in front and the Byward Tower behind*

7 *Hampton Court Palace (Surrey) where millions of bricks were made and used from 1529-38 along with many more in subsequent building campaigns. This view shows the great gatehouse in the west front, with the top of the Great Hall visible in the background*

8 The Henry III masonry and oak timbers in the west moat at the Tower of London being excavated in 1996, seen here from the north. Photograph by Oxford Archaeological Unit/Historic Royal Palaces

9 Edward I's Postern Gate at the Tower of London, rediscovered and displayed when a subway was built in the late 1970s

10 *L'Echequier, Caen, Normandy (France). Photograph by Dr E. Impey*

11 *View of the massive solar tower at the Witney manor house or palace of the bishops of Winchester during excavations in 1984. Note the garderobe block to the left. Photograph by Oxford Archaeological Unit*

12   Henry de Blois's East Hall at Wolvesey Palace, Winchester (Hants), viewed from the southern (chamber block) end

13   The Jewel Tower, Palace of Westminster, with the Abbey in the background

IMAGE 4, ST.GEORGE'S HALL, WEST ELEVATION,
SHOWING ROOFLINES OF VARIOUS DATES

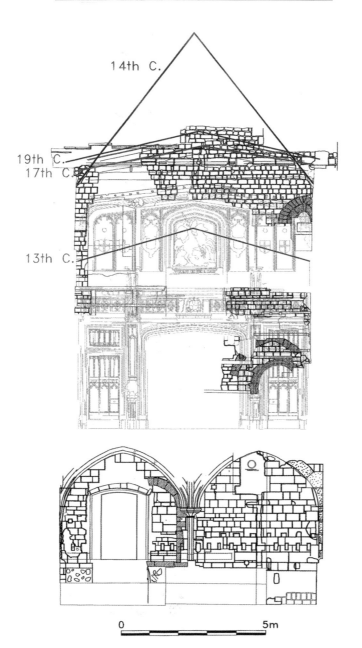

14th C.

19th C.
17th C.

13th C.

0   5m

14   Elevation of the west
end of St George's
Hall, Windsor Castle
with medieval and
later features revealed
during post-fire
restoration in the
1990s. © Crown
copyright: English
Heritage

15   Clarendon Palace today

16   The medieval llys at Aber under excavation, looking north along the palace building with the motte in the background.
     Photograph by N. Johnstone

17   *The Great Hall at Hampton Court Palace. © Crown copyright: Historic Royal Palaces*

18   *The Tudor Chapel at Hampton Court Palace. © Crown copyright: Historic Royal Palaces*

19 Edward I's Gloriette at Leeds Castle (Kent). Photograph by J. Ashbee

20   *Oven range in the fourteenth-century kitchen at Bishop's Waltham Palace*

21   *The moat at Hampton Court Palace in front of the great west front. This photograph is taken from the House of Ease looking northwards towards the entrance to the kitchen court*

22   The 'keep' and palace at Sherborne (Dorset)

23   Fete day at Bishop's Waltham Palace, July 1997. How often are ancient monuments this full?

39 The south face of the Great Hall at Winchester Castle (Hants), built by Henry III in the 1230s. Note the bottoms of the circular windows and the vertical edges of the gables below them (both blocked up) over the middle windows. Photograph by J. Ashbee

Canterbury: his hall there was built between 1200-20, and in 1243 the king issued specific instructions that the windows of his new hall at Dublin Castle should emulate those at Canterbury. Elements of Langton's hall, including parts of his original window arrangement, survive within the modern palace at Canterbury (Tatton-Brown 1982, fig 2 and plates XXXa-b).

If the hall was at the literal and metaphorical heart of the new palace then the king's chambers, and subsequently those for his queen, were scarcely any less important. Unfortunately these have suffered especially badly from later developments, and the various ranges dedicated to the queen which can be seen on the 1597 survey have long since disappeared. Equally the destruction of the Lanthorn Tower in the late 1770s removed vital chambers at a stroke, and no amount of subsequent reconstruction can compensate for this. The Wakefield Tower does survive, and this was clearly part of the royal accommodation; indeed the king's own chambers seem to have been in this area (though not necessarily within the tower itself) after his marriage, and certainly by 1250. Further support for the importance of this area came with the rediscovery of Henry III's private watergate on the east side of the Wakefield Tower during an important archaeological excavation in 1957-8. There is a reference to the construction of a quay for the king in 1228 which must surely describe this location, and the excavations duly exposed the remains of a timber jetty or landing stage. The upper jambs and arch of the

40 Henry III's privy (private) watergate and the base of his chamber block to the east of the Wakefield Tower, Tower of London. These were revealed by excavation in 1958

door have long since disappeared, but the lower elements have been left exposed and form an impressive sight. Small holes were provided in the sill of the door to allow for the escape of any tidal waters which lapped into the threshold. Such water was prevented from washing into the basement of the Wakefield Tower by a two-step landing which gave access either down into the Wakefield or to a spiral staircase leading up into a rectangular chamber block which spreadeagled the inner curtain and attached to the east face of the tower; the surviving lower courses of this block were also exposed during the 1957-8 excavation. The spaciousness of the stairway (it is 10ft/3m in diameter) is testament enough to the importance of the block it provided access to, and this must have formed part of the king's own apartments (**40**).

Henry III's private landing stage lost its function, of course, when Edward I built the outer curtain wall further out into the Thames and St Thomas's Tower with it, his ceremonial water entrance and impressive extension of the castle's royal accommodation. The new tower was linked back to the Lanthorn by a flying bridge between the two structures; the existing bridge dates to the 1860s, the medieval one having been removed in the eighteenth century, but documents of 1324-5 referring to the high walkway (*alura*) over a gate between the towers must describe the original build. Restoration of the interior of St Thomas's Tower during the early 1990s revealed a number of important primary features, most notably two substantial fireplaces in the south wall (ie. on the Thames side) and a garderobe in the west wall. It seems likely, therefore, that the great chamber and hall referred to in the contemporary building accounts lay on the west and east sides respectively of the tower. Below them lay the apron within the tower where the Thames flowed in though Traitors' Gate, providing a grand processional entrance (though not necessarily a welcoming one, as the name of the entrance makes clear).

The Palace of Westminster

The medieval palace at Westminster was the mirror of the Tower of London while also being complimentary to it. Westminster was on the opposite side of the city on a riverside site, though unlike the Tower it lay outside of the old Roman walls. Where the castle and its great keep were ideally sited to loom over the city and its populace, however, the western palace was not on a good defensive location: it was tightly constrained between the river and the abbey (**41**), and it had no ready-made curtain wall as the Tower did. On the other hand Westminster provided a grand ceremonial foil to the castle — especially in its great hall — and it was the older site by some years, having already been the scene of important building works under Edward the Confessor for whom it was evidently a favourite site. It continued to be so for subsequent kings through to the very end of our period, when a major fire in 1512 finally encouraged Henry VIII to develop other inner London palaces to replace it. Under Henry III, at the very heart of the Middle Ages, Westminster came as close as one could imagine within the period to being a permanent home for the king (see pages 83-5).

Despite this medieval popularity there is a sense in which Westminster, like the Tower, is a frustrating site because so much of the medieval palace has been lost to us. To be sure, the Great Hall lives up to its name like few others and retains the power to impress not only on a first visit but also ever after. Despite this we have lost much of the former royal accommodation, including major treasures such as the Painted Chamber of which we can now catch little more than fleeting glimpses through record drawings made in the early nineteenth century before fire ravaged what was left of the medieval palace. What remains is difficult to 'read', contained as it is within the Victorian parliamentary complex which is of course impressive enough in its own right even if the conscious medievalism of its architecture may confuse the unwary. The abbey with its precincts and the river Thames continue to provide important bearings in what is left of the medieval geography, but the almost forlorn way in which the fourteenth-century Jewel Tower sits in isolation under the shadow of the abbey on the other side of a busy road from Parliament (and the medieval palace) typifies the interpretative problems of the site (**colour plate 13**). This little tower with its doubly apt name — it functioned as the repository for late medieval monarchs' personal treasure and it is a little gem of medieval architecture — sits at one corner of the former palace precinct and should, therefore, provide a useful orientation point for the rest of it. There can be little doubt, though, that it is all but ignored by the vast majority of visitors to the area.

Like the Tower there is a long and venerable tradition of antiquarian interest in the Palace of Westminster, though archaeological research has often been restricted to small-scale 'keyhole' excavations and watching briefs. The enduring national disgrace of the destruction of what appears to (and undoubtedly should have) been very important remains during the (non-archaeological) excavation and construction of the New Palace

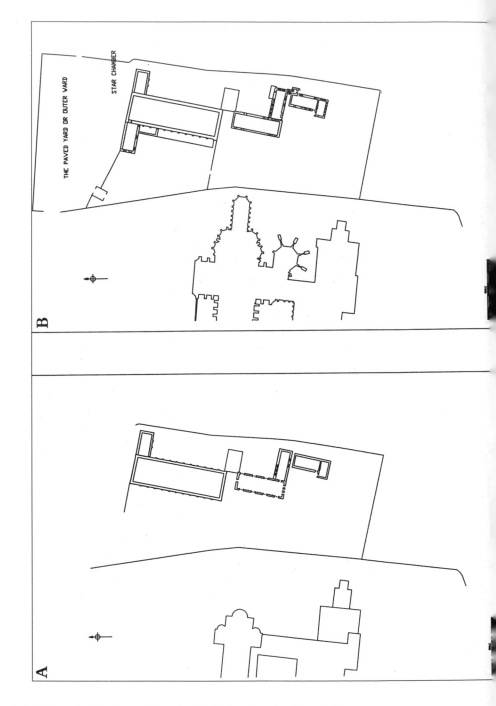

41 Plans of the Palace of Westminster. Drawing by R. Harris, after H. Colvin

A The Norman and Angevin palace, 1087-1199
B The palace of Henry III, 1216-72
C The palace of Edward I to Richard II, 1272-1399
D The surviving medieval buildings of the Palace of Westminster shown in black

Yard car park at the heart of the medieval palace must be seen in this context (Jones 1984, 57-61). Nevertheless there is still great potential for the re-assessment of existing information and future excavations (if allowed). Just such an enquiry into existing material is currently under way, and so far has focused on the Great Hall itself along with highly accurate and detailed mapping of extant and archaeologically documented buildings and features, an exercise which, surprisingly, had not been undertaken previously. The hall built by William Rufus and finished at the very close of the eleventh century was vast (240ft/73.2m long and 67ft 6in/20.6m wide), on a scale unsurpassed at the time in Europe, or indeed subsequently in medieval England. The hall was divided into twelve bays each with a high-level gallery window, and the long east and west sides ran parallel with the Thames. The bay arrangement was uneven across the sides, presenting a rather staggered effect in plan, though we may doubt whether this would have been apparent to a contemporary observer taking in the sheer expanse of the interior. This may have been caused by the difficulty of surveying and building around existing structures of Edward the Confessor's time, though we know little of these from any source. Though altered subsequently, especially when Richard II had the great hammerbeam roof erected in the 1390s, the impression created by Rufus's hall can still be appreciated today (**42**). Sadly the same cannot be said of most other elements of the medieval palace, lost in successive fires during the sixteenth and nineteenth centuries.

Windsor

Windsor, like Westminster, had important pre-Conquest antecedents. Edward the Confessor had established a palace at Old Windsor, and despite the castle's foundation in *c*.1070 the former continued to be the favoured royal residence here until the early twelfth century. At Easter 1110 Henry I signalled a shift towards the castle by holding court there, and from then on it became the dominant royal seat on the route out west from London, while Old Windsor faded away. The great motte at the centre of the castle was the focus for all early activity, providing both a massive defence and royal accommodation. The masonry shell keep of the Round Tower seems to have been built later in the century by Henry II, who probably erected the masonry defences of the Upper and Lower Wards or at least started the latter — the defences were not complete when the castle was besieged in 1216 by the enemies of King John. Henry II may also have been responsible for the basic layout of the King's House in the Upper Ward, but it was John's son Henry III who provided the greatest impetus yet; he spent more than £10,000 on the castle and especially its royal apartments between 1236-60 and, as his Itinerary again demonstrates, it was undoubtedly a favoured residence.

Once again Henry's work at Windsor displayed little formal planning; the accommodation was asymmetrically arranged and must have been determined at least as much by the existing defences as by anything else. Even so there was a central courtyard or cloister (some contemporary documents specifically use that term) with the usual hall and chamber ranges around it, and a kitchen was provided to the east. Very little was known archaeologically of Henry III's buildings at Windsor before the early 1990s, but many details of his work were exposed and recorded during the restoration work after the fire in 1992. The removal of nineteenth-century plasterwork from the west end of St

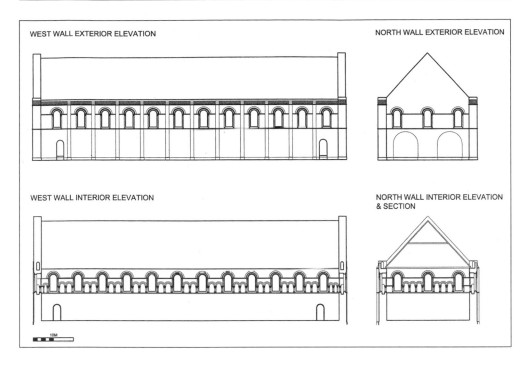

WEST WALL EXTERIOR ELEVATION

NORTH WALL EXTERIOR ELEVATION

WEST WALL INTERIOR ELEVATION

NORTH WALL INTERIOR ELEVATION & SECTION

10M

42 Elevations of William Rufus's Great Hall at the Palace of Westminster reconstructed from archaeological, historical and architectural information. Drawing by R. Harris

George's Hall, for instance, revealed that this wall had formed the east face of a tower with a two-storey range running eastwards from it (**colour plate 14**). The masonry of Henry III's day was largely intact, and the low pitch of the thirteenth-century roof line could be seen with a door above it giving access from the tower out onto the roof itself. Further doors from the tower into each of the two storeys could also be seen. Henry's work of the middle 1200s survived with little apparent alteration for the best part of 100 years, but unfortunately it is still difficult to assess how his buildings functioned because much of his work was then engulfed in or swept away by the enormously expensive redevelopment of the castle by Edward III (see pages 28-9). In the Upper Ward this centred on the grand architectural statement of St George's Hall and chapel, the largest state rooms of any English royal palace; the hall itself was second only to that at Westminster (**43**).

Here again many details previously hidden under nineteenth-century wall coverings were laid bare by the fire and could be appreciated far better after it than before. This even applied to the 18 bays of the vaulted undercroft, which had been divided into a series of individual compartments in the seventeenth century. Many of the later walls were stripped out as part of the restoration work, allowing the open space to be appreciated once more. The west end of the hall, meanwhile, also provided important evidence for Edward III's roof line. This had been rebuilt successively in the seventeenth and nineteenth century from a slightly higher eaves height but at the pitch of around 17°which was typical of most of the castle's medieval roofs; remarkably, the fourteenth-

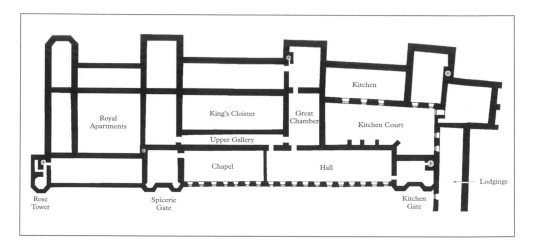

43 Ground and upper floor plans of Edward III's royal apartments in the Upper Ward at Windsor Castle. © Crown copyright: English Heritage

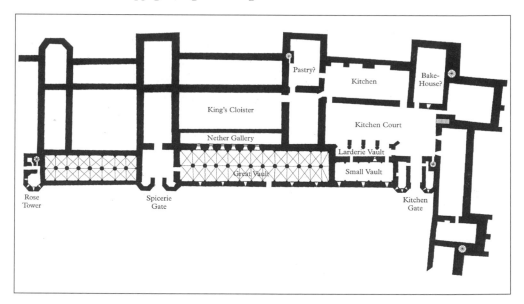

century roof had been given a pitch of 55° (**colour plate 14**), making it very tall and thus increasing the effect of the sheer scale of Edward's rebuilding. Most of his other interiors were more modest in scale, but with a typical width of around 7.2m and height of 7m they were still impressive enough. Moreover all the principal apartments were interconnected and at first-floor level, while the hall, kitchen and entrance were widely separated. In other words, the king and his design team had moved well away from the traditional hall and chamber block layout towards something more akin to the careful succession of spaces found in the great houses of the seventeenth and eighteenth centuries.

Clarendon

If Windsor was a favourite residence on the route west out of London, Clarendon Palace in Wiltshire was one of the most popular ends to journeys in that direction (**44**). As we have seen the royal residence here probably had pre-Conquest origins and its initial success largely rested on its location within excellent hunting estates. This continued to be an important reason for its popularity, but the establishment of a vital royal castle and diocesan centre at Old Sarum, and the transfer of the cathedral to Salisbury itself in the 1220s, undoubtedly enhanced its value for the monarchy. The hilltop (indeed hillfort) site at Old Sarum was scarcely fit for a king, and the privations of its situation were major contributory factors in the bishops' decision to move to a new site. The existing hunting lodge at Clarendon must have been an obvious choice for more commodious accommodation. Although we know little of the scale and quality of the old lodge it is abundantly clear both from documentary sources and the results of archaeological work that it underwent massive expansion during the twelfth and thirteenth centuries when Clarendon's popularity was at its height.

The overall extent of the palace site, to say nothing of the royal hunting park around it, is one of its most impressive aspects, both on plan and on site. The unkempt and overgrown nature of the site can make appreciation difficult (though see chapter 6), but from the western entrance one can still see the standing fragment of the Great Hall's eastern gable (**45; colour plate 15**). It is then a salutary experience to realise that there are buildings not only over most of the space between you and the hall, but also for more than 400ft (122 m) beyond it as well. The fully-developed palace complex was surrounded by a perimeter wall, parts of which survive, enclosing an area of around 7.65 acres (3.1ha). The ground is generally quite level, but then slopes away steeply to the north of the buildings to provide a splendid view of the cathedral and city to the north-west. An artificial terrace along the edge of the slope was probably the site of formal gardens: there are documentary references to these in the middle of the thirteenth century. The site, perhaps unsurprisingly, has attracted several excavators from the 1820s onwards, though the early techniques would have been rudimentary in the extreme by modern standards. Work carried out during the 1930s was especially valuable in elucidating important elements of the plan, while also demonstrating the considerable complexity of stratigraphic phasing. The twelfth-century Great Hall, for instance, overlies a substantial flint wall found in 1935 some 4ft (1.22m) below the hall's uppermost floor, which was of fourteenth- or fifteenth-century date. The earlier wall may date to the decades around 1100 and its function is unknown, but the excavations also demonstrated that there was 5ft 2in (1.57 m) of stratigraphy between the natural ground surface and the latest floor (see James 1988, 90-6 and figs 23-4). The site has not been 'mined out' by any stretch of the imagination, however, as most of the deeper excavations to date have been very limited 'keyholes' into the site; much more could be done with the will, and the money.

As usual the main apartments were the aforementioned hall and the chambers to its east (**44**). The four-bay aisled hall measured 82ft (25m) by 52ft (15.9m) internally, with a service area separating it from the kitchens to the west (see pages 144-5). There was an entrance at the south-west corner (later supplied with a porch) giving access from what appears to have been a vast open yard (though buildings may lie undiscovered here), while the more important entry was that from the royal apartments, provided through a door at the south

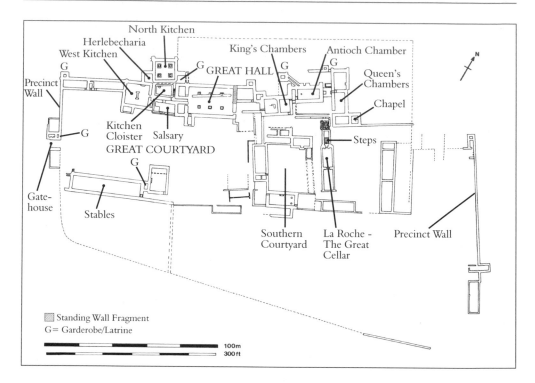

44 Plan of Clarendon Palace (Wilts). After James and Robinson 1988, 11

end of the east gable. The latter was fronted internally by a kerbed platform or dais, 33ft (10.11m) long and 11ft (3.35m) wide which must have ended before the threshold of the door was reached.

We can get little impression today of how the hall once looked, although documentary references provide some evidence; in 1249, for instance, Henry III ordered that it should be 'whitened' (painted or whitewashed). This was one of Henry's most-favoured residences, though as we have seen he had to spend longer than he might have liked away from it, including stretches of consecutive years in several decades. He was meticulous in his attention to detail on the interior decoration of the royal rooms, notably the famous Antioch chamber, and both historical and archaeological information shows just how splendid they must have been (see chapter 2, page 54). The private royal rooms lay to either side of this chamber, the king's to the west (eg. between Antioch and the Great Hall) and the queen's to the east. The south end of the queen's chambers connected directly with a chapel, while there was a covered pentice (lean-to) walkway between it and the king's rooms. Several privy garderobes were provided directly off the royal suites, and there was a further one connected to Antioch by a walled passage. The exterior surfaces were not ignored either: when the north wall of Antioch chamber was excavated in the 1930s a fine coat of plaster was found over the external face of the flint rubble masonry. The chamfered weathering courses at the base of the wall and the attached buttresses needed to support the weight of the upper room were in top-quality ashlar.

45 Clarendon Palace under excavation in the 1930s. The remaining fragment of the Great Hall stands in the background, with the kitchen courtyard in the foreground. Compare this view with **colour plate 15**. *Photograph by J. Charlton*

These still survive, but sadly the plaster surface does not (contrast **46a** and **46b**).

Clarendon never quite seems to have regained the favour it found under Henry III, though it was to be a long time before it was allowed to slip into quiet decay. His son and successor Edward I turned his attention more towards palaces in and close to London than to rural seats like this, but there was a steady programme of repair work and the king stayed at the palace as needed. It also continued to be an invaluable collection point for royal revenues from the surrounding area. Edward II and III maintained interest in Clarendon, and all three commissioned surveys of the property, which showed a remarkable propensity to deteriorate if maintenance was neglected for any length of time. Gradually, and despite the regular rounds of upkeep, royal interest dwindled: Richard II rarely used the palace despite his frequent presence in Salisbury (though he seems to have built a dance room), while Henry V may not have so much as visited. By the end of the medieval period the site had been all but abandoned by the monarchy, though the last recorded royal visit did not occur until 1574 when Elizabeth I used the decrepit remains during a day's hunting (she stayed at Wilton, not Clarendon).

The *llysoedd* of medieval Gwynedd

During the 1990s archaeologists in Gwynedd set about locating some of the principality's medieval *llysoedd*. These, and their parent *maerdrefi*, were well enough known historically but the desertion of the palaces after the English victory over Llewelyn ap Grufudd in 1282 meant that their former positions had largely passed out of common knowledge. Local

46 *Clarendon Palace.*

*a   The fine ashlar weathering courses and buttress on the outside of the Antioch Chamber's north
     wall, with the medieval plaster coat still intact during excavation in the 1930s. Photograph by J.
     Charlton.*

b   A similar view today, with the plaster missing

place (and especially field) names occasionally carried echoes of former glories, as in the case of Rhosyr (see below), but their true significance had been lost. The recent work has begun to reclaim these important sites, or those which have survived: unfortunately several have been damaged or lost already under modern developments (Johnstone 1997, 62).

The best archaeological evidence so far has come from Aber, on the mainland side of the Menai Strait, and Rhosyr on Anglesey. Aber was a favoured royal residence in the thirteenth century, and interest has centred around a motte at Tyn-y-Mwd since Leland's account of it in 1530. Excavations in 1993 duly uncovered the greater part of a substantial stone building, 85ft 4in (26m) long and 33ft 6in (10.2m) wide in all and divided into three separate rooms (**47; colour plate 16**). The central chamber, tentatively identified as the hall, measured 36ft 9in (11.2m) by 26ft 3in (8m) internally and was flanked to north and south by wings projecting eastward. The plan is astonishingly similar to that of a Romano-British winged corridor villa in its simplified form, but the finds included more than 30 potsherds and a decorated bronze ring brooch of thirteenth- to fourteenth-century date (Johnstone 1997, 63-5).

The excavations so far at Aber have been quite restricted, but much more has been done at Rhosyr along with extensive geophysical surveys (Johnstone 1999). The site lies to the south of the present parish church which may have originated as a royal chapel, and has commanding views of the Menai Strait and Snowdonia beyond. The field where archaeological endeavour was concentrated during 1993-6 is still known as *Cae Llys*, a classic case of local memory preserving ancient traditions. The geophysical survey and excavations identified a rectangular enclosure about 262ft 6in (80m) long from east to west and 196ft 10in (60m) wide, encompassing an area of roughly 1.3 acres (0.52ha) defined by a stone perimeter wall. Just under one-third of the interior was excavated, and at least five buildings have been identified so far (**48**). The most important buildings seem to have occupied the centre and south-eastern corner of the enclosure, though one of the three structures involved has only received very limited excavation so far. The others, however, seem to equate well with the hall and chamber block model (buildings A and B respectively). The third building (G) might be a second hall, one being for royal use and the other for the court, but this remains to be proved. The finds were predominantly of thirteenth-century date, and the *llys* is known to have been abandoned by the 1330s. Its fate was probably sealed, literally and metaphorically, by its coastal location, for blown sand is a perennial problem in such places. A great storm in 1332, for instance, covered and destroyed eleven cottages and large areas of land at Rhosyr with sand.

The structures (especially the hall) at Rhosyr had suffered from extensive stone robbing after abandonment, but much structural and internal detail survived despite this. Building A, for instance, had probably been built in two stages, the first being a single chamber 55ft 9in (17m) long and 36ft (11m) wide which then had narrow southern and western ranges added on. These took the total size to 65ft 4in (20m) by 46ft (14m), somewhat smaller than contemporary English royal halls but equal with the bishop of Bangor's at Gogarth (Llandudno). The latter is otherwise the largest of the period in north Wales. At Rhosyr internal details included two hearths, a fire pit, and a row of post-holes across the west end which may have related to a dais position. Building B (perhaps a chamber block) lay parallel to and immediately south of the hall and also seems to have developed through time,

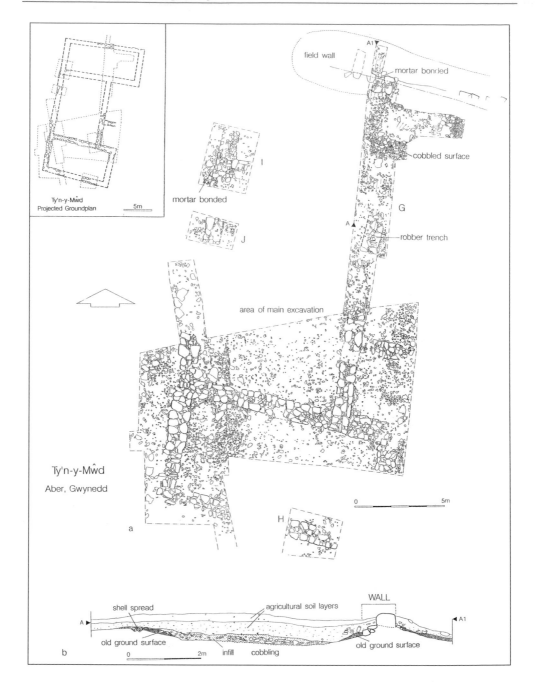

Ty'n-y-Mŵd
Projected Groundplan   5m

mortar bonded

I

J

field wall

mortar bonded

cobbled surface

A

G

robber trench

area of main excavation

Ty'n-y-Mŵd

Aber, Gwynedd

0   5m

a

H

WALL

shell spread   agricultural soil layers

A   A1

old ground surface   infill   cobbling   old ground surface

b   0   2m

47 Plan of the medieval llys *at Aber (Gwynedd). Drawing by Gwynedd Archaeological Trust*

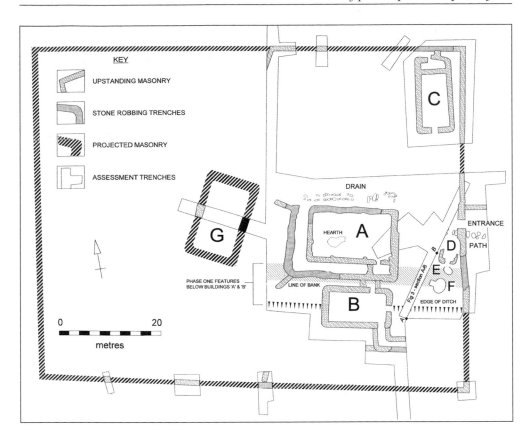

48 Overall groundplan of Cae Llys *(Anglesey). Drawing by Gwynedd Archaeological Trust*

though here the size stayed constant at 42ft 8in (13m) by 24ft 7in (7.5m). The main alterations related to the blocking of old and opening of new doors, and the construction of a short passage linking it with the southern range of the extended hall. Finally a stone corridor was added to the south-east corner of building B (**49**).

Late medieval Scottish royal palaces

Unlike twelfth and thirteenth-century Gwynedd, and England with its wealth of surviving royal apartments from throughout the medieval period, virtually no equivalents pre-dating the late fourteenth century remain in Scotland. The surviving portions of David's Tower at Edinburgh Castle belong to the late 1360s and early 1370s and seem to represent 'the earliest surviving royal lodgings' in the country (Dunbar 1999, 75). From the early fifteenth century (and especially the reign of Scotland's James I) onwards, however, we see an extraordinary flowering of activity from royal builders which continued with few checks through to the very beginning of the seventeenth century. Palaces such as Falkland, Holyrood and Linlithgow are justly famed, while new suites at castles such as Edinburgh itself and Stirling are equally impressive.

What makes these and other cognate sites particularly remarkable, especially, perhaps,

49 Cae Llys *during excavation, with Building B in the foreground and the partly-robbed Building A (the hall) in the background. Photograph by N. Johnstone*

from an English viewpoint, is their very completeness: the death of Elizabeth I saw the unification of the two crowns under James VI of Scotland or I of England. The former's court and many of the functions attendant upon it transferred to London thereafter, and many of the 'old' Scottish palaces simply ceased to function as such, which is not to say that they were completely deserted. They can therefore seem like veritable time capsules, standing now largely as they were left, when compared to English palaces such as Hampton Court which suffered (if that is the right word) extensive redevelopment as Tudor lodgings became outmoded. There is no need to enter into lengthy descriptions of the Scottish palaces here, largely because an excellent survey of the subject has only just been published (Dunbar 1999). It is worth extracting a few salient points from his work, however, before we progress on to the final flourishing of England's medieval palaces.

Scottish palaces usually provided the same components of hall, chambers (with separate apartments for king and queen) and chapel along with a variety of service buildings and others for the pursuit of leisure. This is not surprising given the European rather than insular context of such traditions and the wide contacts between late medieval courts across the continent. Many of the Scottish halls are of impressive scale. James IV built three great halls in the opening decade of the sixteenth century and just after, of which Edinburgh was the smallest at 82ft 4in (25.1m) by 66ft (20.1m). This would be a respectable size by any standards, especially when the castle's status relative to Holyrood at the time is taken into account (see below), and it is similar in scale to the hall at Linlithgow of around 70 years earlier. The hall at Falkland Palace was significantly longer (99ft or 30.2m) but also narrower (26ft or 7.9m), and must have been modelled on the slightly earlier one at Stirling Castle (*c*.1498-1503). This was simply enormous, with few peers in England or Europe; it was 126ft 8in (38.6m) long and 36ft 5in (11.1m) wide (the measurements are internal, as usual), with a height of around 54ft 2in (16.5m). It was far bigger than Henry VIII's hall at Hampton Court Palace, for instance (Henry and James were brothers-in-law), and slightly larger than Edward IV's one at Eltham Palace which had been completed in 1480 and may well have provided the model for James. Such a vast space required exceptional measures in other ways: there were paired and externally splayed windows at high level in all four walls, with large bay windows providing additional (and no doubt deliberately impressive) lighting for the dais at the upper end of the hall. No less than five fireplaces had to be provided to heat the interior, and again one of these was directly behind the dais for the comfort of the king and his closest cohorts at their meals.

Eltham offers another parallel for an obvious factor which is common to the majority of Scotland's late medieval palaces: the arrangement of accommodation around a central courtyard. As we have already seen, courtyards had been a feature of palace planning for many centuries, but they tended to arise almost by accident because of the way a site developed rather than through any particular plan. The 'courtyard' between the West and East Halls at Wolvesey, or the various enclosed spaces at Clarendon or Windsor offer good examples of what might very loosely be termed organically-developed courtyards. Even to contemporary eyes, though, these would have stood in marked contrast to the carefully planned layout of the monastic cloister which was repeated time after time throughout Europe. The example of Eltham shows that English thinking was moving towards a more regularised arrangement of accommodation as the end of the fifteenth century approached, although even here existing features constrained or influenced what was possible. The same interplay of influences can be seen in most of Scotland's late medieval palaces, with a few very distinctive touches of their own.

The disposition of related suites of apartments around a central courtyard was adopted generally in the Scottish palaces (the unique hall-house at Kindrochit seems to have been the sole exception). In some cases the term 'courtyard plan', with the emphasis on the latter word, might be going too far: the layout of some of the lesser palaces had as much in common with uncoordinated approach seen at many English residences, even great ones. The more important houses such as Linlithgow, Falkland, Edinburgh and Holyrood, however, show a greater degree of control in their layout, even if the fully-developed plan was often the result not of a single king's works but several, as at Linlithgow, and therefore cannot be ascribed to a master plan, as at Henry VIII's Nonsuch (see below). Holyrood displays a particularly rigorous formality on its plan layout, reflecting the monastic background which provides such a fascinating backdrop to the history of this site. The lack of similar rigour at Dunfermline, where the palace also grew off the west side of the monastic cloister, is doubtless largely due to the topographic constraints of the steeply-sloping Pittencrieff Glen which runs from north-west to south-east past the lower side of the cloister. It is curious that similar dedicated palatial apartments did not grow up at any English abbeys, despite the well-known propensity of many kings (eg. Henry III) to avail themselves of monastic hospitality (eg. at Reading and Chertsey Abbeys) when it suited their itineraries.

A further aspect of Scottish planning, evidently seen but rarely south of the border, was the use of superimposed corridors or galleries on several storeys around the inside of a courtyard or along one side of a range. These provided the equivalent of cloister walks, or the covered pentice walkways sometimes seen within or between courtyards and/or buildings at other palaces (see Clarendon). The major difference was that the Scottish corridors were more integral to the overall planning of the accommodation: they usually rose through the full height of the range(s) of apartments, giving access to each storey. The corridor levels themselves were entered by newel (turnpike) staircases, generally located at the corners where ranges conjoined. At Linlithgow the corridors ran around two, the primary east range and the secondary southern one, or perhaps three sides of the courtyard. At Falkland there was a gallery along the east side of the extremely long (187ft or 57m) royal lodging block and again rising through its full height, but in this instance on the external face away from the courtyard.

The possible influence of some English sites (notably Eltham) on Scottish palace design has already been mentioned. Given the relative histories of the neighbouring countries, though, it is scarcely surprising that the Scottish residences show at least as much (arguably more) Continental influence. France was certainly the most important centre of ideas from this point of view, for the French and Scottish courts were intimately linked both politically and by marriage, but Italy and the Netherlands were significant as well. Sometimes the influence seems to have come in the hands of a particular craftsman or designer, including French master masons such as Moyse Martin and Nicholas Roy (both did important work for James V at Falkland Palace) or Cressent, an Italian who worked on James IV's Great Hall at Edinburgh Castle. In other instances specific European buildings can be seen as the progenitors of features appearing in Scottish architecture, presumably because they were seen either by a member of the royal family, a senior courtier or a trusted member of the court's workshops. Parts of the late fifteenth- and early sixteenth-century work at Linlithgow may have been influenced by fourteenth-century features at Saumur or, in the case of the hall's triple chimneypiece, examples at Poitiers, Angers, Bourges and Coucy. The elevational detailing of the James V courtyard at Falkland Palace, meanwhile, represented 'up to the minute essays in the style of the Parisian region, . . . among the earliest examples of coherent Renaissance design in Britain' (Dunbar 1999, 36 and figs 1.17a/b).

One final aspect of the Scottish palaces deserves to be considered here — or to be more specific, the relationship between two of them: Holyrood and Edinburgh Castle. As we have seen, the former grew out of the royal apartments which had been a feature of the abbey, while the latter had been an important residence from much earlier in the medieval period. The growing value so evidently placed in Holyrood from the time of James IV onwards (in 1503 it was specifically described as 'the king's palace near the abbey of Holyrood'), however, saw the great castle's eclipse as Edinburgh's premier royal house. Thereafter it functioned predominantly as a fortress and arsenal as well as a repository of state records. There are interesting parallels here with the fate of the

Tower of London during and after the time of Henry VIII, when any lingering pretence of using the castle as a palace finally disappeared. The relationship between Edinburgh Castle and Holyrood, moreover, has telling overtones of the much earlier duality at London of Westminster and the Tower. Edinburgh, of course, had only become capital of Scotland in the fifteenth century, but the contrast thereafter between the cold and windswept hilltop location of the castle and the pleasantly secluded atmosphere of the abbey with its gardens and orchards must have made the long-term choice between the two seem quite easy.

The palaces of Henry VIII

The royal accommodation of Henry VIII has been very fully covered by several authors, and Thurley's exhaustive survey (1993) of the Tudor palaces should be consulted for a detailed overview of his works. Space dictates that only a few of his houses can be considered here, the principal of which, if only because of its exceptional survival, must be Hampton Court Palace. Here Henry inherited a site that the disgraced Thomas Wolsey had already begun to develop before 1530, and to some extent the king's work can be seen as the logical extension and completion of what the Cardinal had started. Though much altered by subsequent monarchs and their builders, especially William III who replaced the Tudor royal apartments with new ranges designed by Wren, it is still quite easy to understand and be impressed by Henry VIII's palace. The immediate impression of space which one gets when approaching the main entrance in the west front is perhaps slightly false because buildings to the south of the pathway from the Trophy Gate have long since disappeared, but even with large numbers of visitors there is little of the cramped, almost claustrophobic atmosphere of (say) the Tower of London. Instead, as one stands before the great entrance itself and looks within, there is an impression of order and staged progression which is carried through when one passes under the gatehouse (**50**).

Firstly one enters the Base Court, with offices, services and the great kitchens with their complex of minor courts to the left (north) and court lodgings around the remainder. The next courtyard (now Clock Court) formerly held a central fountain, perhaps similar to the (reconstructed) one at Linlithgow Palace in Scotland. Court accommodation continued here but the architecture was much more grand, largely because the great royal chambers began with the Great Hall (**colour plate 17**), like the kitchens on the north side of the court. The hall was entered via a grand staircase in the northern tower of the gatehouse between the Base and Clock (fountain) Courts, and from it begins the suite of surviving Tudor royal chambers which starts with the Great Watching Chamber and progresses along galleries to the magnificent chapel. The bulk of Henry's royal lodgings were lost in the William and Mary redevelopment, but we know that they would have been impressively proportioned and decorated (eg. with terracotta panels and figures). As usual separate suites of chambers were provided for the king and queen, each with their privy households.

It seems ironic that lavish halls should be built in both England and Scotland at just the time when communal dining of king and court was passing out of fashion (though Hampton Court was the venue for the only true Great Hall built by Henry VIII; Thurley 1993, 114). The wider court would still dine in hall, and there can be little doubt that the

50 Hampton Court Palace. A view into the Clock Court and Base Court beyond. Henry VIII's Great Hall lies to the right in Clock Court, through the first arch

numbers involved had grown very considerably to as many as 500 in Henry's day. The king and queen, however, would dine in their own chambers, and the most favoured courtiers might be allowed to join them or even take meals in their own private rooms. The provision of such chambers is exemplified at what was intended to be Henry VIII's greatest palace, his nonpareil — Nonsuch. This was unquestionably one of the most important buildings in progress as the medieval period in England passed on towards modern times, and indeed the palace looked forwards in many ways. One of these was in its deliberate and single-phase planning. Even such important Henrician palaces as Bridewell, Hampton Court and Oatlands could not boast as much despite their overall similarities of plan form and their reliance on a succession of courtyards as the basis for the accommodation, for they had all evolved out of existing building complexes started by former owners.

At Nonsuch, however, the king and his builders were able to start from scratch once the old church and other buildings of Cuddington had been swept away. Two conjoined

Outer and Inner Courts were established, equally sized at around 132ft (40.23m) long and 115ft (35.05m) wide internally (**51**). The whole complex was oriented roughly north-south to suit the site's topography (see chapter 5, page 138), and there was a great twin-towered entrance into the Outer Court in the middle of its north range. This courtyard contained a series of collegiate-style apartments opening directly off the cobbled yard. As at Hampton Court there was a further twin-towered gatehouse between the Outer and Inner Courts, the latter again housing the king's and queen's chambers. The southern range of the Inner Court provided the principal rooms and also the main façade of the whole palace facing out over the gardens and park. The inner façades of the royal apartments around the Inner Court and the great southern face were elaborately decorated with ornate Renaissance designs in carved slate and plasterwork. The many thousands of fragments recovered during the excavation of the site in 1959 showed that both the overall schemes and the craftsmanship were of the very finest quality. It was this decoration above all which earned the palace its title, virtually a nickname. The groundplan, meanwhile, was completed by the more prosaic utilitarianism of the kitchen complex, to the east and straddling the outside of the two main courtyards. Sadly, nothing can be seen of the great palace at Nonsuch above ground today, though for a few brief months in 1958 the splendours of the site re-emerged during its excavation.

Religion

Religion was an important part of daily life for the monarch and theoretically at least it was absolutely central to that of the episcopate. The religious and ceremonial implications of death and burial were rarely of more than passing significance at palaces, though several monarchs and bishops did pass away in their favoured residences. Therefore funerary archaeology is not a major part of palatial studies, except in the unusual parochial circumstances which occurred at sites like the Tower of London. The routine observance of daily offices and regular masses did have important implications for royal and episcopal sites alike, however, and chapels, or buildings which have been interpreted as such, are common features at palaces even before the Conquest (Paulinus may have preached to the Northumbrians at Yeavering back in the early seventh century) and certainly after it. At Cheddar a succession of late-Saxon and early-Norman chapels have been excavated (**52**); the earliest in the sequence belonged to the first phase of rebuilding after 930, and was actually erected over the site of the original long hall. The new chapel was a rectangular structure certainly of one and possibly of two cells. The first was just under 23ft (7m) long by 13ft 2in (4m) wide externally and it would scarcely have accommodated a large congregation; no more than the stub of the possible second cell was found on the south-east corner of the first. It should be seen as an essentially private chapel (it is likely that most which were built within palaces or their precincts would have functioned in this way) rather than as a place of public worship or ceremony. The same could be said of each of the two succeeding chapels at Cheddar, one built in the eleventh century over the original structure and the other a rebuilding in the thirteenth century: both quite definitely had the two-cell plan of nave and chancel which typifies so many Saxo-Norman

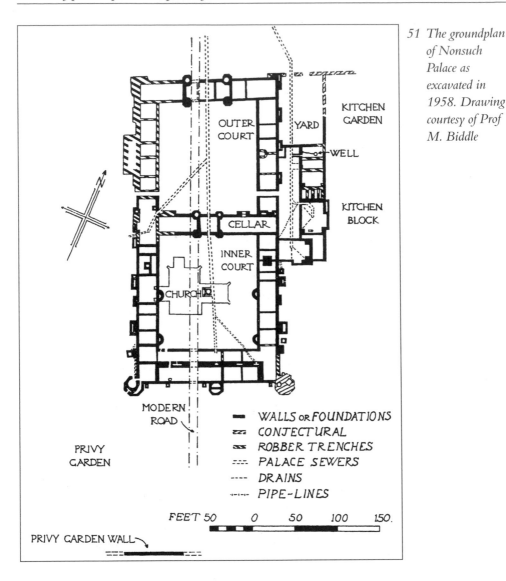

51 The groundplan of Nonsuch Palace as excavated in 1958. Drawing courtesy of Prof M. Biddle

churches, but they were still no more than the basic buildings one would expect to find in a village, let alone at a royal site. The later one was only fractionally larger than its predecessor, being about 60ft 9in (18.5 m) long and 23ft wide (7m — again both measurements are external).

Wolvesey also seems to have had a chapel in the late Saxon period, if the structure originally built with apses at both its west and east ends is correctly identified as such. This was 37ft (11.3m) long, and the eastern apse had been replaced with a rectangular 'chancel', though date of this change is not clear. The chapel was probably still in use while William Giffard was developing his new West Hall in the early decades of the twelfth century, but is likely to have been abandoned under Giffard's successor Henry de Blois who added a new rectangular chapel. This much larger building, about 40ft or 12.6m long internally, survives in its fifteenth-century form at the south-east corner of the West Hall and is still

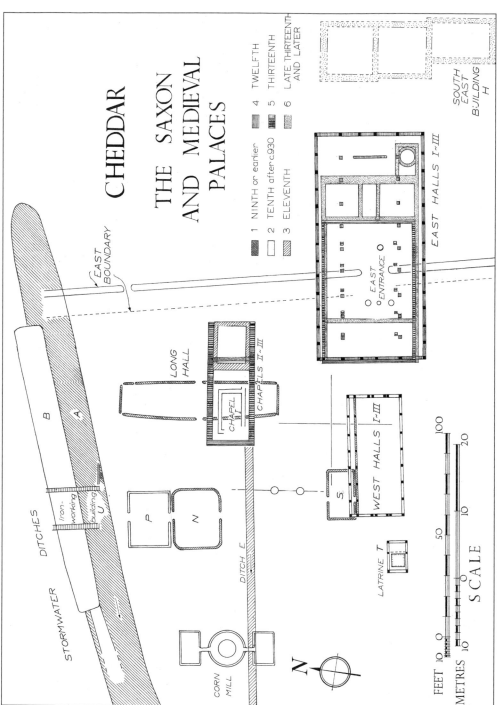

CHEDDAR

THE SAXON AND MEDIEVAL PALACES

1 NINTH or earlier
2 TENTH after c.930
3 ELEVENTH
4 TWELFTH
5 THIRTEENTH
6 LATE THIRTEENTH AND LATER

52 Plan of the medieval palace complex at Cheddar. After Rahtz 1979

used as part of the present Bishop's Palace. It was the only element of the old buildings retained when Bishop Morley built a new Baroque residence in the 1680s. Henry's chapel probably lay at first-floor level (like the principal rooms in the West Hall) but it was probably raised on a vaulted ground-floor undercroft (later filled in). A similar but apsed feature was built by de Blois at Bishop's Waltham, though here the undercroft was more properly a crypt partially or wholly below ground (the sloping splays at the bottom of the windows demonstrate this quite clearly). The fine ashlar masonry of the crypt's interior and two bases of the central piers which supported the vault were revealed by excavation after the site was taken into state guardianship in 1952. At least one more bay of the crypt was left unexcavated, so we do not know how long it was; this chapel was probably much smaller than at Wolvesey, which was almost twice as wide. Both buildings may have had chapels in the undercrofts as well as at first-floor level, but irrespective of this it is very difficult to gain a true impression of the original Norman work because of the later rebuilding at Wolvesey and the ruination at Waltham. More of the earlier medieval work survives at the Winchester palace at Farnham (Surrey) where a fine twelfth-century arcade for an aisle (later blocked in brick) can still be seen from outside on the approach to the broadly contemporary shell keep (**53**).

Similar chapels or the remains of them can be seen at the Salisbury palaces of Old Sarum and Sherborne. In the former case the flint walls of the ground-floor room survive to head height or more because the central courtyard of Bishop Roger de Caen's early twelfth-century palace was built up above the general level of the Inner Bailey. This created a terracing effect, with the ground floors of the east and south ranges becoming undercrofts by default. The chapel was placed in the south range so that it could be oriented east-west, and there may actually have been chapels at both the undercroft and first-floor or courtyard levels. Part of the altar survives at the east end of the ground floor, where the dedication may have been that to St Margaret documented in 1246. At Sherborne the palace accommodation was again disposed around a central courtyard; the chapel was on the first floor of the north range, supported on three groin-vaulted bays and a barrel-vaulted fourth at the west end. Part of the paving of the upper floor is preserved in the south-west corner of the chapel, while finely decorated original windows and fine external blind arcading survive at the north-east corner and on the south wall respectively (**54**).

The Chapel of St John on the upper floor of the White Tower at the Tower of London is one of the finest Norman examples to have survived. It is supported by a massive double crypt on the basement and entrance floor levels, each carried on barrel vaults. The apse which is carried through each of these levels protrudes beyond the east side of the keep at its south-east corner, and the external pilaster buttresses follow all round the apse. Entrance could be achieved from either of the western and eastern chambers of the upper floor (as built), and if the recently-proposed model for the use of the White Tower is accepted the door from the eastern chamber into the north-western corner of the chapel would have been principally for the king's use. A shallow recess under a tall round-headed arch in the west wall (ie. opposite the high altar), meanwhile, may have housed the king's own seat. The simple boldness of the columns and their capitals within the chapel bears powerful witness to the architecture of the post-Conquest period, and the lack of colour

53 *Farnham Castle (Surrey). Twelfth-century arcading and a pier of the medieval chapel can be seen to the left of the corner*

54 *The chapel range at Sherborne Castle, showing the blind arcading on the courtyard face*

121

is striking. Indeed many have suspected that this plainness is rather false, and that the interior would originally have been brightly coloured (perhaps even gaudy to our eyes). Detailed survey and research in the late 1990s failed to find compelling evidence for such a scheme, however, despite the fact that there are several areas, notably the high-level ambulatory which is not generally accessible, where traces of pigments should have survived if they had been present in the first place. This work has also provided evidence for what seems to have been a brief halt during the building campaign in the 1080s (Impey and Parnell 2000, 17). The stone used changes towards the top of several columns, especially those towards the west end, and the decoration on the capitals is not uniform, either. The walls of the White Tower as a whole display similar evidence for a short building break, probably reflecting the sheer expense of carrying through such a major project at a time when, after all, the conquerors were still striving to impose themselves on the conquered (**55**).

The Chapel of St John is substantial and its relationship with the remaining accommodation within the keep, regardless of how we interpret this, shows that it could provide for public ceremony as well as private worship. More private chapels could be required, however, and in the thirteenth century Henry III had a small and very personal one (often known as the Oratory) built within the upper chamber of his new Wakefield Tower. This little gem is scarcely more than a slightly enlarged window embrasure in the south-east face of the round tower, immediately to the south of the chamber's entrance off the spiral stair from the king's private water gate (see above). This meant that the oratory faced east, which was not only liturgically appropriate (a small altar could be placed directly under the window itself) but also provided excellent early morning sunlight into it. It is notable that the little chapel has the largest window in either level of the tower, and contemporary references to stained glass within it show that the potential value of the light source was not lost on patron or builders. There are also references to the provision of a wooden screen between the oratory itself and the main chamber in 1238, confirming the very private nature of this tiny space. Both the glass and the screen were 're-introduced' to the chapel as part of the re-presentation of the medieval palace in the 1990s.

As we have seen the Wolvesey chapel was rebuilt in the fifteenth century on the Norman foundations, perhaps during the episcopate of Henry Beaufort. Certainly he constructed the new chapel at Bishop's Waltham, immediately over the remains of the old one — excavations in 1970 proved that the foundations of the new north wall extended well beyond the point at which they seem to stop today, ie. where the apse of the crypt begins. Once again we do not know exactly how large the new chapel was but it was almost 33ft (about 10m) wide and, with the evidence of the north wall foundation, substantially more than twice this long. Building work started *c*.1416 and progressed well for a season, but then there seems to have been a hiatus of a decade during which the window embrasures — evidently incomplete — were blocked up and roofed over with wattles. The break coincided with the furore which arose when the Beaufort was granted the title of Cardinal without royal approval, and his re-entry into favour was doubtless helped not only by relinquishment of this title but also by his loan of more than £17,500 to the Crown in 1421. The £155 or so spent during this period on Waltham and

break

break

55 *The southern elevation of the White Tower, Tower of London, showing the position of the 'building break' which seems to have occurred in the 1080s. Drawing by R. Harris*

documented in the Winchester accounts undoubtedly underestimate the actual expenditure, but even so the amount pales into insignificance compared to Thomas's loan. In the circumstances it is perhaps surprising that the chapel was finished at all, let alone that this was done in 1427. The structure survived until the eighteenth century, but sadly it had disappeared by the time a map of the Inner Court was drawn in 1785, and only the lower walls survive today.

These chapels might accommodate some open ceremony but they were all essentially private chapels for the close circle of people around the magnate — even the White Tower's Chapel of St John. As such they are reminiscent in many ways of the private chapels often found at manors or on smaller medieval village sites where separate parochial status was out of the question. The Tower of London and Windsor Castle provide interesting comparisons with those circumstances, because both sites were, and indeed still are, extra-parochial; in other words, they fall outside of the normal system of church government which applies virtually everywhere else. We have already looked at the Wakefield Tower's private oratory, and Windsor similarly had a 'private' royal chapel, but both also acquired or developed what amounted to parish churches. At the Tower this was the church of St Peter ad Vincula (St Peter in Chains), taken within the castle in the 1230s when Henry III extended the defences northwards from their previous north-west corner close to where the Beauchamp Tower is today. The chapel we see today is largely a post-medieval remodelling, but burials are occasionally exposed outside it in what had been the Tower's own cemetery; a group of skeletons was excavated in the early 1960s at the south-west corner of the Waterloo Barracks, but it is more common to find individual bones from long-since disturbed graves. The skeletal remains are usually 'reburied' with due ceremony in a small vault inside the chapel, which still has a chaplain and its own Chapel Royal choir.

Circumstances at Windsor were somewhat different, though here again there had been a private chapel since the twelfth century. As with many other aspects of the royal accommodation, Henry III upgraded this in the early to mid-thirteenth century, while Edward III refurbished the private chapel and provided a small separate one in the queen's new apartments in the middle of the following century. Equally importantly, however, Edward also remodelled Henry III's more public chapel in the Lower Ward from 1350-6 to provide an appropriate religious venue for the new Order of the Garter. At the same time he established a college of canons to serve the chapel and order. Edward IV's fifteenth-century Chapel of St George replaced Edward III's building and stands today as one of Windsor's finest structures. These were more public buildings than the private chapels directly attached to or incorporated in royal apartments, and though they would doubtless still be used by the monarch there was an element of display about them which is a long way from the devotional focus of the smaller chapels. In many ways this movement reached its high point at Hampton Court Palace and other Tudor residences under Henry VIII. The former's chapel is substantial by any standards, and its height in particular was emphasized by the exquisitely decorated ceiling with its ribs, bosses and pendants; the richness of this decoration was commented on by several sixteenth-century visitors. It is an interesting irony that, having established such a substantial and richly decorated chapel, Henry chose to provide himself with a private viewing gallery (the Royal

Pew) at its west end. Here the king and queen with their attendants could watch unfolding ceremonies and undertake their religious observances separate from the congregation below (**colour plate 18**). Indeed when the Pew was originally built the king and queen each had their own chamber within it.

Defence

It is often said that palaces were undefended, and to a degree this is true. Many of the royal and episcopal residences were surrounded by a moat or ditch of some sort, but these were as much if not more for enclosure and definition as for any military purpose. There are undoubted exceptions such as the Tower of London and Windsor Castle (in its earlier stages, anyway), but these are not necessarily analogous with the majority of palaces. At the same time we must acknowledge that many residences were provided with a defensive appearance — presumably this was deliberate — even if this might be of minimal practical value. High walls and towers surrounded by a broad ditch might well impress, but that may have been the limit of their function in this direction. There are a number of factors which need to be borne in mind here: firstly that medieval kings and bishops were genuinely very powerful (though not necessarily popular) and for the most part do not seem to have feared for their safety within their kingdom or bishopric. Secondly the very mobility of the monarch or prelate and their courts inevitably meant that only the most favoured sites like Westminster and Windsor could expect long stays; bishops would have equivalents such as Farnham or Bishop's Waltham for Winchester, or Lyddington for Lincoln, quite apart from the home palaces close to cathedrals. Therefore at any one time the vast majority of houses would be occupied by caretaker staff only, and in no wise would they be capable of serious defence. Finally, and related to this point, the very fact that sites would be lightly occupied for long periods of time made it all the more important that they should look secure: wide moats and tall walls might be of little military value but they would deter most brigandage. This is well demonstrated at a site such as the royal hunting lodge built at Writtle in Essex by King John in 1211 (Rahtz 1969).

Having said that there were some sites where defence (or offence) was very clearly in the minds of the builders. Quite apart from places like the Tower of London we need only look as far as the twelfth-century tower and mound at Farnham and its encasement by the massive walls of the shell keep later in the same century. The base of the tower was built up by about 30ft (9m) from the original ground level and then covered with earth to form the mound. The tower then continued for an unknown height; it was demolished, possibly after Henry II came to the throne in 1154, but the mound remained and was later refortified with the shell wall which still impresses visitors today. Farnham Castle is also suitably positioned for military operation, lying on the edge of the hill which dominates the town and the lower ground to the south. The castle certainly would not have been immune to attack, as the ground is quite level to the north, but it is in a strong position even so.

Henry de Blois, the great builder-bishop of Winchester, seems to have been responsible for the tower and mound at Farnham (one of his successors erected the shell keep), and we may look to the circumstances of his age for a main factor in its defensive capacity. Henry had been bishop for six years when his brother Stephen became king in 1135, heralding the Anarchy of his disputed reign. The king could not count on his brother for unqualified support it seems, for de Blois briefly switched allegiance to his rival, the Empress Matilda, in 1141. Later in that year Henry switched sides again and Winchester became the centre of conflict between the two sides. The bishop had two strongholds in the city, one of which was Wolvesey which according to a contemporary account had been 'strengthened so that it was now impregnable like a castle' (Biddle 1986, 10). The chronicler's distinction is interesting, and probably relates to the linking of the East and West Halls with what amounted to curtain walls. Early in August de Blois's forces set fire to the city and soon afterwards he further strengthened his palace by building a keep-like square tower in the middle of the east side (it actually contained the kitchen and seems to have been intended to do so from the start). The junction of the south-east corner of the East Hall with the recently-erected curtain wall was improved at the same time: a garderobe turret had already been built here, but it was now encased in a new and very strong corner tower, subsequently named Wymond's Tower. Stephen eventually carried the day nationally, and his brother became one of the country's most powerful men. The king's death and the accession of Henry II in 1154 spelled trouble for de Blois, however, and as we saw in chapter 1 he had to endure exile in Cluny until 1158. Meanwhile the new king ordered that his castles should be slighted (in effect, torn in half): some such as Farnham seem to have suffered this fate, but little evidence for such dramatic steps has been found at Wolvesey.

The Winchester palaces were not alone in being fortified at this time, and the two principal residences of the bishops of Salisbury display similarly impressive defences. At Old Sarum Bishop Roger de Caen was given permission to replace the existing royal castle in the early twelfth century. He ordered the excavation of a massive dry moat, and the upcast spoil was used to create the Inner Bailey on which his palace was to stand. The new work must have made a tremendous impression on people approaching the site from any direction — it still does today, even in its ruinous state. At about the same time Roger built a new palace at Sherborne. The site was not quite as good for defence as Old Sarum, but it was well above the surrounding land, while the ground to the north and east was also marshy. The new defences comprised an elongated octagonal curtain wall with towers on four of the corners, those at the opposed north-east and south-west angles incorporating gatehouses. The deep ditch and external counterscarp bank could be crossed from these entrances or a third on the north side of the defences. The bishop's accommodation sat centrally within the enclosed area; today they sit in apparent isolation but it is likely that the area would have been more extensively covered by buildings in Roger's day.

It is intriguing to note the extent to which defended sites were established or existing ones fortified in response to the internal threat of unrest which became outright civil war in the early twelfth century, rather than against any 'foreign' problems. Roger's work at Sherborne did not save the palace from being seized by king Steven in 1135 — the bishopric did not regain control of the site until 1354 — but as we have seen other sites fared better during the conflict if not subsequently. It is worth noting that the refortified castle at Farnham was captured by the Dauphin Louis VIII of France in 1216 during his rapid advance through south-east England. Henry III was crowned king at Gloucester later in the year as a minor, and in March 1217 the French garrison surrendered Farnham to the Earl of Pembroke who was acting on the young king's behalf. On neither occasion does there appear to have been much of a fight, if any at all, by the castle's defenders, and the French had been content to negotiate safe passage home (Thompson 1987, 15). Siege was clearly a powerful weapon, especially against an adversary who was not on home soil, but it seems equally clear that battle would only be joined as a last resort (especially if the owner was not at home, and as we have seen this would be the majority of the time).

The Tower of London had also succumbed to the Dauphin in 1216, and this lesson seemed to be well learned if the massive refortification put in hand by Henry III is anything to go by. Almost £10,000 was spent on the castle during his long reign, only exceeded by the £15,000 expenditure at Windsor. As we saw in chapter 3 Henry and his son Edward I transformed the Tower both in extent and strength, and both defended the river edge just as much as the landward approaches. Henry's Bloody Tower gateway was dominated by the Wakefield Tower and the inner curtain wall to either side, while Edward's St Thomas's Tower jutted out well forwards into the river. The greatest strength and expense of the landward defences, however, was concentrated on the west side of the castle, ie. looking inwards toward the city of London rather than outwards to the relatively undeveloped suburbs and the lower reaches of the Thames. Thus Henry III established his great gateway at the Beauchamp Tower with what we now know to have been a complex approach over a moat which was much wider than previously believed, on this side of the castle anyway; unfortunately we know very little about the eastern side of Henry's moat, or even whether he provided a land entrance over it, though this might be implied by the postern gate still to be seen in the eastern inner curtain wall (**56**).

This sense of effect was carried through into or even strengthened during Edward I's reign, when the massively impressive half-moon barbican which came to be known as the Lion Tower and its associated defences and causeways were built at the south-west corner of the castle, again to face the city. Anyone approaching the castle from the city along Great Tower Street now had to deflect from the old direct route (which may have been abandoned anyway after the collapse of Henry's masonry in 1240/1), and turn south down Tower Hill. At the latter's foot they passed across a stone causeway protected by an outer gate and drawbridge (the causeway with its counterweight pits was buried in the seventeenth century but was re-excavated in 1936/7) and thus entered the barbican. Initially this probably amounted to a forecourt overlooked from the half-moon walls and the Middle Tower where people would have to wait for their audience, but it soon seems to have become the main home of the royal menagerie at the Tower (Parnell 1999). Sadly the Lion Tower was demolished in the 1850s after the royal animals had finally left the Tower, but the remainder of the approach route through the Middle Tower and across a further causeway to the Byward Tower still survives. We have already noted that the building materials were carefully chosen throughout this progress to contrast with the curtain walls, and little expense was spared on the approach from the city (**colour plate 6**).

By contrast a much more modest landward entrance was built at the same time at the south-east corner of Edward's new moat. This faced outwards to the suburbs and was thus on a likely approach route for any external enemy coming in from the east by land or river. Despite this the first causeway seems to have been built in timber (see chapter 3 for

56 The postern gate in Henry III's inner curtain wall at the Tower of London, left stranded 'in mid-air' when the earthen berm in front was cut away in later years

archaeological evidence for this), and it evidently supported a tidal mill. It was defended by a gate tower on the eastern side, ie. outside the castle, and this defence (the Iron Gate) gave its name to the causeway itself. We do not know a great deal about the gate, although it is depicted on a number of post-medieval illustrations of the Tower from the Thames. Unfortunately the gate tower and the entire outer edge of the east moat was oversailed by the approach to Tower Bridge built at the end of the nineteenth century. It is possible that some part of the gate was retained in the construction of the approach — certainly the arched bays on the inner (ie. moat) side of the bridge get progressively deeper towards the river, mirroring the former line of the moat edge here.

Both the curtain walls of Henry III and Edward I provided lofty protection to the castle and, of course, dominance over the city. Henry's inner curtain seems to have been of a single construction, ignoring the section which had to be rebuilt by Edward I, but his son's outer curtain was apparently erected in two stages. The first was a relatively low wall terminating in a parapet just above the grass level in today's moat. The inner circuit with its regularly spaced mural towers standing tall and severe behind it must have continued to provide not only the main visual effect but also the defensive firing platform. The outer wall became an advanced position, strengthened at its north-west corner by Legge's Mount, a large and originally open-backed bastion built integrally with the battered lower part of the curtain. It is interesting to note that the Brass Mount on the north-east corner (ie. away from the city) was not primary but was built at the same time as the wall was heightened. Instead the east side of the moat had three turrets built out from the curtain; one of these stands intact, but the other two only survive below grass level. All three were examined archaeologically in 1960, with further work on the northern and southern ones in 1981 and 1997 respectively. They extend out almost to the middle of the moat (as it now survives after the building of Tower Bridge) and the below-ground part slopes down to the east. Presumably these turrets supported artillery facing out into the suburbs to cast stones down on any attackers.

We do not know exactly when the outer curtain was raised to the full height we see today, but it probably followed on very soon after the original building work. Certainly by 1300 the royal mint at the Tower had been ordered to erect a new 400ft-long (122m) building which can only have been in the Outer Ward between the two curtains. Such an order only makes sense if the outer wall had already been heightened. The wall tops were rebuilt in the nineteenth century (a triangular-sectioned coping stone, possibly original, was found during the west moat excavation in 1996), but the positions of the original battlement crenellations can still be seen towards the top of the wall. They are not easy to pick out on the front face of the curtain wall where they were blocked with stones, though careful examination of the arrangement and types of stone makes them clearer especially in the stretch of wall immediately to the south of Legge's Mount. They are more obvious on the rear (inner) surface of the wall where the Victorian blocking is in brick, but this part of the Outer Ward, known as the Casemates, is not usually open to the public.

There is little doubt that the many moats dug from the Conquest to the thirteenth century or even later were potentially defensive, though this need not have been the sole or even necessarily the main function. Bishop Antony Bek's massive late thirteenth-century moat at Eltham Palace is a good case in point: undoubtedly of defensive scale and intent, it also provided an impressive surround to what seem to have been sumptuous ranges of accommodation built within it (**57**). There are other moats of the same period, however, which cannot be seen in even remotely military terms, either because of their scale and form or because of the nature of the buildings within or immediately around them. The possibly twelfth-century moat at the bishop of Lincoln's house at Lyddington (Leics) has a churchyard to its south, for instance, while the early thirteenth-century hunting lodge at Writtle noted above can scarcely have warranted true defence — though as suggested above such sites would have benefitted from the protection a moat offered against thievery and even animal movements. We may also note the association of moats with more extensive less defensive water features at for example Bishop's Waltham (Hants), Kenilworth (Warks) and Somersham (Cambs), a theme we will return to shortly.

The multi-functional nature of defences can be seen to good effect at the Tower of

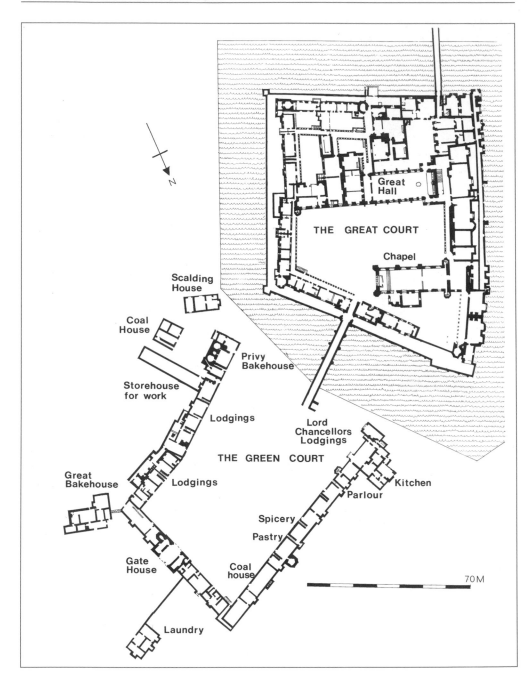

57 Plan of Eltham Palace, Kent. Drawing by J. Steane

*58 An intact medieval fishtrap being excavated in the moat at the Tower of London in 1997.
Photograph by Oxford Archaeological Unit/Historic Royal Palaces*

London. Mural towers such as the Lanthorn and Wakefield Towers of Henry III or Edward I's St Thomas's Tower supported important areas of the thirteenth-century palace accommodation, for instance. The moat, meanwhile, was used not only defensively but also for fish stock (**58**), water power (there were mills associated with the moat, and later it provided power for the Royal Mint as well as for a steam engine), and display. In the latter case the mural defences would have seemed doubled in scale, both conceptually and physically, when seen reflected in the water-filled ditch. Of course this effect would be diminished (as would the moat's value in several other areas) as the feature became clogged with silt, rubbish and foul waste. This seems to have been a perennial problem at the Tower — the moat had to be dredged clean as early as 1294, barely two decades after Edward I had ordered its excavation — and ultimately led to the Duke of Wellington's decision to drain the moat in 1843 and turn it into a dry feature. The problem of cleaning may have been particularly acute at the Tower where the ditch was largely fed by the tidal Thames, but it would have been faced at many other wet moats. It is surprising how quickly leaf-mould alone can accumulate into quite thick layers of rotting matter, and siltation would have to be dealt with in most cases. Defence became less and less a factor in the construction of moats later in the medieval period, and by the fifteenth century most such features were more likely to act as an ornament to a site's buildings while often doubling up as an important element in the drainage system (eg. the moat of *c*.1460 at Oatlands House — see chapter 5). The extraordinary nature of the Tower is nowhere better demonstrated than in the plans drawn up in 1666 by Sir Bernard de Gomme, Chief Engineer at the Board of Ordnance, for remodelling the anachronistic moat so that its military value could be retained. Some of his plans would have involved huge losses of archaeological levels, but fortunately for us he had to be content with inserting a brick revetment wall around the outer edge of the wide ditch.

5   Other buildings and functions
of medieval palaces

Chapter 4 explored the main residential and ceremonial buildings of palatial sites, but they could not have, and did not, exist in a vacuum. Every hall or chamber had to be accompanied by a variety of buildings, along with their occupants and trades, while it also became increasingly common for palaces to be located as much for the potential of their setting as anything else. This was partly about exploitation of estates and resources, but enjoyment of the setting and its components was undoubtedly significant as well. This chapter looks at the evidence for these associated aspects of medieval palaces.

'Pastime with good company'

If palaces had important, even vital, court, defensive and ceremonial functions, we must also recognise their importance as relatively private spaces for the monarchy and episcopate. To some extent they were places of refuge from the very real stresses involved in medieval governance in both the secular and religious worlds, and the palaces themselves often reflect this. The hunting lodges which typically lie towards the lower end of the palatial spectrum in terms of scale and facilities perhaps epitomise this, but in virtually all areas of palace life the importance of recreation and relaxation is evident.

Recreation and diversion from everyday concerns would necessarily begin indoors within the palace itself, where interior schemes of decoration could be remarkably lavish as we have already seen. Once outside, there were different opportunities for pleasure. Some of these were of an altogether earthier kind than the artistic tastes which could be so well catered for indoors, but it is important to recognise that the medieval mind could turn to a much larger canvas — the landscape itself. It is curious that archaeologists, in particular, are perfectly willing to accept large-scale landscaping works in prehistory, at least from the Neolithic period onwards, but seem to find it more difficult to recognise similar traits in later times. The ritual or religious nature of so many prehistoric interventions into the landscape (long and round barrows, stone circles and other monuments) not only required substantial investments of time and effort (to say nothing of earth- and stone-moving) but also needed considerable conceptual and intellectual involvement. This was not only on the part of those who 'designed' such landscapes, but also on those who lived with and around them.

We know, of course, that high artistic endeavour was striven for and achieved in medieval literature, poetry, music, painting, sculpture and architecture. In the built environment it is often still possible to appreciate the ways in which several arts could be combined to create an effect which still evokes wonder today. This is especially true of religious buildings, where the combination of the architectural space and features with sculptural and painted iconography created a powerful setting for the liturgy. Why then do we often tend towards literal interpretations of landscape features (often, indeed, seeing them in isolation rather than in combination) rather than looking beyond an apparent function? We must recognise again that a single feature could serve several purposes at once, and that some of these need not be especially 'functional' at all.

This point is particularly well illustrated by the Somersham palace of the medieval bishops of Ely (Taylor 1989). This Cambridgeshire manor had been granted to Ely Abbey towards the end of the tenth century but was transferred to the bishopric on its establishment in 1109. After what may have been a slow start Somersham grew to become an important residence for the bishops, conveniently situated both for Ely itself and also as a staging point on journeys to and from London. The site seems to have been well used for much of the medieval period, but was in decline by the early fifteenth century. It was described as a 'poor howse' by Bishop West in 1520 and was clearly in bad condition when a detailed survey was made in 1588; the See exchanged Somersham manor for Crown lands in 1600, and the ruinous palace buildings were demolished in 1762; a sixteenth-century walled garden is the only structural trace of the palace surviving on the site.

The palace buildings may be long gone, but Somersham is more remarkable for its associated complex of earthworks, cropmarks and the former deer park. The whole ensemble lies to the south of the historic village, which may have been at least partially transplanted to make way for the setting out of the palace and its landscape. One road leads almost due south from the centre of the village where the market place evidently used to be, past the parish church and on to the palace. The road approached the latter on a causeway between two large fish ponds. The smaller of the two has been destroyed by modern housebuilding, but the western one is in very good condition with banks up to 8ft 3in (2.5m) high enclosing an area of about 492ft 2in (150m, east-west) by 328ft (100m). The palace site itself covers approximately 3.5ha and is defined by a substantial but not continuous 'moat': there is a 328ft (100m) gap in the south side which appears to be original and corresponds with the north side of the walled garden (which was thus attached to but lay to the south of the moat). The encircling ditch is in two distinct parts, the western being 42ft 8in (13m) wide and up to 9ft 10in (3m) deep. The eastern section is broader (72ft 2in/22m) but with shallow edges so that there would only have been a 5ft (1.5m) wide stream in its centre. Clearly this 'moat' was not defensive but was intended for effect, and probably picturesque effect at that. Low earthworks and a pond within the ditched area probably belong to the garden of 1.6 ha (4 acres) listed in 1279.

The 'moat', then, was evidently as much an eye-catcher as anything, and it was approached across sheer expanses of water on either side of the causeway from the village centre. Once across the bridge over the 'moat' one would find its interior occupied by not only the palace but also extensive gardens; in the sixteenth century, at least, there would have been a further walled garden to the south. This was by no means the end of the story, however, for there was a much larger area to the south, roughly trapezoidal in shape and now largely reduced by modern agriculture to cropmarks rather than earthworks. The walled garden occupied the north-west sector of this area, while a set of four small ponds occupy the north-east corner. There are further ponds to the south, along with a small 'moat' in the extreme south-east corner, and flat-topped banks appear to have formed the long sides of the 'enclosure'. The latter (and indeed the palace as a whole) sits in the north-east corner of the former deer park which extended to *c*.250ha. A substantial bank and curving hedge-lines define the limits of the park, the ground of which rises quite significantly to the south so that its whole expanse, and the palace itself, could be viewed from the highest ground. Taylor very plausibly sees the 'moat' and all the features in the trapezoidal area to the south of it as part of an entire landscape designed as much to be seen from the park as to look out onto it. To this extent the small 'moat' at the south-east corner of the trapezium might well have acted as a viewing platform or pleasance with a pivotal role between the palace and the park. The subtle use of the natural landform thus becomes a defining element within the design of the palace, its gardens and landscape.

The documentation for the landscaping at Somersham is slender and the site has not been excavated, but Taylor points to parallels both in this country and in continental Europe to support a late thirteenth- or fourteenth-century date which would best suit the evidence available here. Water features, including massive ones, were an important element in its landscaping, and this offers the most immediate point of reference to other places. The remarkable remains at Kenilworth Castle (Warks) undoubtedly provide the most obvious and impressive example of landscape use and exploitation in medieval Britain, using water on a massive scale. This exploits the inflow of numerous streams into the lower land around the castle itself and develops the theme of the large Abbey Pond and a smaller mill pond (both to the east) in the creation of the Great Pool, a shallow mere of enormous area on the opposite side of the castle. The mere and the Lower Pool between it and the Abbey Pool form the backdrop to the earthen forework known as The Brays (indeed the water is taken around this to create a moat). The ensemble dates from the thirteenth century and was further developed by Henry V, who had a great Pleasance built at the opposite end of the mere to the castle in 1414-17. The Pleasance is effectively a moated banqueting house, attached to the Great Pool via a short canal or harbour, and it is virtually the same size as the platform on which the castle itself stands. The whole scheme was refurbished specially for a visit by Elizabeth I in the sixteenth century (Thompson 1964, 1965). The 'gloriet' built at Leeds Castle by Edward I for Queen Eleanor in 1278-90 is another justly famous example of the use of a water feature, in this case in conjunction with what amounts to a palace within the castle reminiscent (in intent at least) of the royal accommodation at the Tower of London and Windsor (**colour plate 19**).

Attention to the overall physical setting can be seen at many other palaces. Bishop's Waltham provides one of the best examples, with the vast ponds on the west side of the palace clearly being more than just 'live larders'. They are also similar to Kenilworth in being disposed on one side only of the site, so that they cannot be seen as a serious element of defence. The Inner Court at Bishop's Waltham is surrounded by a moat, and the outer walls of the twelfth-century south and east ranges within it would have resembled a curtain wall, but it is not clear what if anything would have lined the north and west sides at this date (the surviving buildings here are of the late fourteenth and fifteenth centuries).

We do not know whether this palace was among the castles of Henry de Blois which were slighted in the 1150s, but by the 1180s the site was fit to stage royal councils and from this time onwards it is difficult to see Waltham as anything other than a luxurious residence. The area to the south of the palace and ponds was a park, providing opportunities for hunting, though Bishop Langton (1493-1501) was probably responsible for enclosing a rectangular area of the park immediately to the south of the Inner Court and east of the ponds to form a private walled garden. Much of the precinct wall for this survives, along with two of its octagonal brick-built gazebos (corner turrets). Similar features can be seen at the Lyddington palace of the bishops of Lincoln, the gazebo at the south-west corner of the palace precinct being the first feature to be seen by most visitors. Lyddington also has a fine flight of ponds and associated water channels probably dating from the 1320s to '40s and probably cut through an earlier ridge-and-furrow field system. They are usually described in utilitarian terms as fishponds and they would have functioned well in this way, but their situation on low-lying ground to the east of the palace would have made them an obvious landscape feature as well. An earthwork interpreted as a footpath leads from the direction of the palace to the north-western corner of the ponds.

We need not assume that palace gardens would have to be confined to rural sites: it is quite possible that metropolitan royal and bishop's palaces would have had private gardens, doubtless relatively small in many cases because of the restricted space often involved. The replica medieval garden with its central fountain which has been built in the small space to the south of the great hall at Winchester Castle gives an excellent flavour of what such a garden could have been like. Something more extensive was provided at the Tower of London on a strip of ground outside the defences but still within the city immediately to the north of the castle. Henry III established a pear orchard here in 1262 and in the following year plants were bought for gardens most probably in the same place. The site later became known as the Nine Gardens, and a neatly-presented rectangular area behind the city wall on Tower Hill is clearly labelled as such on the 1597 survey of the Tower. By this time a few houses had been built on the gardens, mainly along the western edge and at the south-west corner next to Edward I's Postern Gate. This encroachment continued, with buildings subsequently put up against the city wall as well, but the overall shape of the Nine Gardens continued to be an important and even determining topographical feature in relation to Tower Hill throughout the post-medieval period; the block can still just about be recognised in the modern townscape of office blocks and Tube station.

Environmental evidence (especially pollen) recovered from medieval soil layers in the Tower moat during 1995-7 demonstrated the presence of exotic planted species such as walnut, lime, spruce, juniper and privet in the vicinity. Seeds and other plant remains probably derived from cessy waste were also found; these included grapes, figs, plums, various berries (eg. strawberry and raspberry) and other fruit such as cherries, apples and pears. By no means all of these need have been grown on the site but the fruit would fit perfectly well with the presence of orchards within the area under the castle's jurisdiction (known as the Tower Liberties) and the pollen are unlikely to be anything other than locally derived. This still does not prove that they come from the orchards to the north: there are candidates within the Tower itself, especially the privy garden in the Outer Ward and Tower Green in the Inner Ward. Given the scale of the relevant areas, though, the Nine Gardens site seems to be the most likely origin for most of these remains.

Gardens continued to be important elements of palace planning in the late medieval and Tudor periods. Relatively few obvious traces of gardens from this era have survived, and the simplicity of their planning and layout relative to later ones (eg. of around 1700) has made them less popular for extensive reconstruction. Nevertheless we know a substantial amount about several Tudor gardens from a combination of historical and archaeological evidence and two of these, at Nonsuch and Hampton Court, deserve extensive description.

At Hampton Court Henry VIII inherited a site which Cardinal Wolsey had already begun to develop, and to that extent the garden and landscape design had to respond to an existing as well as a planned suite of buildings. The physical situation of the Thames-side site was also an important influence, defining the southern edge of a triangular area with the palace on its north side. Here lay 'the most extravagant gardens in England' at the time (Jacques 1995), with a Privy Garden at the east end and the Pond Garden to the west. The latter, though altered by subsequent generations, still survives but the Privy Garden was replaced in the post-medieval period. Traces of it still survive as archaeological features and have allowed a reasonably full reconstruction of its appearance. The eastern side was defined by a boundary wall; parts of the footings of this and two attached pavilions have been excavated, but the precise location of a Banqueting House towards the Thames has not been established. The interior of the main rectangular garden was divided into a series of smaller rectangles on either side of a central path leading away from the façade of the royal apartments to the north, while the smaller triangular Mount Garden between the Privy Garden and the riverside orchard contained a flat-topped conical earthwork with a screw-walk cut into it which gave the area its name. The ensemble was completed by a series of large pavilions and the Water Gallery leading from the centre of the Mount Garden's hypotenuse to a barge house on the river's edge.

Much of the southern part of the gardens and associated structures suffered extensive damage when the surface of the Privy Garden was cut down in 1700/1, and the Water Gallery was removed at this stage (though foundations associated with it were found in the 1990s excavations for the reconstruction of the early eighteenth-century Privy Garden). Excavations in March 2000 also exposed the northern end of the terrace walkway which led along the west side of the Privy Garden. The gardens on the north side of the palace have largely been replaced in subsequent developments, though again traces of them are likely to survive below ground. A partly ornamental orchard lay between the palace buildings and the northern arm of the Tudor moat; timber pavilions can be seen in this orchard on one of Wyngaerde's panoramic views of the site drawn in the 1550s. A great Wilderness lay to the north of the moat in the area which still bears that name. The great expanse of Bushy Park to the north and the palace's Home Park to the east represented the hunting grounds whose potential had attracted Wolsey's and the king's attention to Hampton Court in the first place.

In contrast to Hampton Court, Henry VIII's great palace at Nonsuch was clearly planned from the start in terms of its overall landscape setting. The survey made on the king's behalf before he took control of the site lauded not only the palace site but also its immediate surroundings, and eventually a wide swathe of land (1900 acres/769 hectares or more) was bought along with the ground for the buildings themselves. The grounds formed the basis of the extensive parks which were used for hunting, and a close-set fence was erected around this. Presumably it was complete by 17 November 1538 when £166 13s 4d was paid out so that a thousand deer could be brought to Nonsuch from a number of other royal parks. The palace itself was sited on sloping ground and was terraced into a slight rise within this which would have counteracted the tendency of the area immediately to the north-east to flood in extremely wet weather. The building site was overlooked from the south and west, the former being the vista in Joris Hofnaegel's famous drawing of the palace in 1568, while the land falls away gradually to the north and east. The advantages of this topographical situation were exploited in a number of ways, not least for water supply and drainage (see below), but it was particularly well suited to the laying out of ornamental gardens. These covered around 16 acres (6.48ha): the Privy Garden lay before the south front and the Kitchen Garden was to the east of the palace, while the Wilderness, orchard and Grove of Diana lay to the west. Part of the pattern of borders, knots picked out in box hedges and statuary in the Privy Garden is shown on Speed's engraving of the south front for his 1610 Map of Surrey. The Wilderness and orchard started immediately beyond the walled enclosure around the palace and Privy Garden and would have been anything but wild, though birds and beasts seem to have been a feature. A great variety of trees seem to have been planted, some for their fruit, others as evergreens, and more to create glades and canopies where shade could be had. The Grove of Diana provided a main feature and focus at the west end of the Wilderness, with a fountain, a small 'bandstand', and more statuary relating to the Classical allusion in the title of the place (Dent 1962, 112-23).

The final feature at the west end of the gardens, some 350 yards from the palace, was the Banqueting House (**59**). This was built during 1538-46 and involved the artificial raising of the ground (which already lay at the highest point within the parks) by 3-4ft (0.91-1.22m) through the dumping of clay and gravel. The platform thus created was a very flat octagon in plan, measuring roughly 140-150ft (42.67-45.72m) across and retained by chalk walls faced in brick. Circular 'bastions' covered each of the four corners at the compass points — consciously emulating contemporary miltary architecture — and drains had been included in these to take surface run-off. The drains ended in soak-aways, each of which had a re-used Purbeck marble tombstone fragment at the bottom. The centre of the platform was occupied by the Banqueting House itself, a rectangular building measuring 44ft (13.4m) by 38ft (11.58m). Although this had been demolished to ground level in 1667 the cellars survived in good condition, divided unequally down the middle by a spine wall. As originally built only the larger northern cellar could be reached from the outside, and the southern one must have been accessible directly from the floor above; subsequently a doorway had been punched through the spine wall, perhaps at the same time as the main cellar was divided into two. The western of the two original entrances into the large cellar was also blocked at this time by the insertion of a fireplace and oven, while a drain was also cut through the north wall, running out across the platform and beyond its northern retaining wall. Evidently the cellars were being converted from stores into kitchens: these would originally have been separate, and part of a detached kitchen

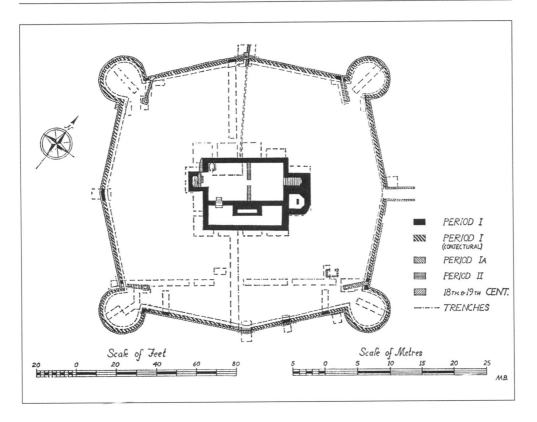

59 Plan of the Banqueting House at Nonsuch Palace excavated in 1959. Drawing courtesy of Prof M. Biddle

block was found some 50 yards to the north of the platform (Biddle 1961, 11-13).

The wider landscape was also important for the contribution in kind that the farmed estates carved out of it made to the overall economy of running the royal or episcopal households. Most palaces would be deliberately and carefully located relative to the estates so that their contribution to the victualling of the court in residence could be maximised. This was one area where the palatial economy differed markedly from that of a monastery, for though both would control extensive areas of land the latter would manage them from a distance, and increasingly farm them out for rent in lieu of produce. The foodstuff from palace farms, by contrast, would be consumed whenever possible, though perishables would doubtless still be sold or traded at market when the household was away from home as must have been the case for much of the time. The estates were also used as a living larder in several ways, notably through the construction of fishponds and in the management of game animals and birds. Indeed, hunting could be an important or even dominant reason for the choice of palace location not only in England but also for Scottish kings (eg. at Falkland). Fish were obviously important for the provision of food but, as we have already seen, game also afforded opportunities for the pleasures of the hunt. The park pale comprising a bank and ditch surrounding hunting land (usually forest) is a characteristic feature of surviving medieval landscapes. The ditch is typically on the inside of the bank so that deer could leap into the enclosure but would find it much more difficult to escape.

At Clarendon Palace much evidence for the hunting which so determined the initial popularity of the site can still be seen on the ground, with parts of the park pale being particularly well defined. This stands today as the typical bank and ditch just described, but medieval documents demonstrate that there would have been a picket fence of closely-set posts around the entire perimeter of the pale as well. The fence probably stood on the crest of the bank, and it must have been intended as much as a statement to anyone tempted towards poaching that the king enjoyed exclusive rights over this particular hunting ground. Timber fencing of any sort requires regular maintenance, as most modern gardeners will readily acknowledge, and this must have been an expensive business over such a long circuit as Clarendon's park pale. Individual posts would have to be replaced as they became rotten (an inevitable fate of earth-set timbers), and there would be occasional need for much more extensive — and expensive — work. In 1359-60, for instance, just over £10 had to be spent on the following:

> new making a paling from the keeper of the forest's kitchen to the gate called Dernegate to enclose the lord king's stables and from the Dernegate to the west gate of the manor and around the perimeter of the keeper of the forest's garden, namely for carpentry, carriage and for various workmen to dig around the whole length of the paling. (PRO E101 460/1, translated by Jeremy Ashbee)

Only a few years later in 1363 a great gale evidently flattened most of the fence (described in the documents as a palisade) on the pale, and caused much other damage to palace buildings as well (PRO E101 460/2). Obtaining sufficient labour to carry out the extensive repairs seems to have been a big problem at this time (James 1988, 39), with the result that work had to continue into the 1370s (eg PRO E101 542/17). The various accounts for repairs describe much of the circuit in topographic terms, providing a useful check on the earthwork evidence.

In the later medieval and Tudor periods royal interest in sports developed in a number of directions. Some of this arose out of the ideas and ideals of chivalry which Edward III cultivated in the aftermath of his victories during the Hundred Years War, eg. at Crécy in 1346, Calais in the following year, and Poitiers in 1356. His initiative to establish an Order of the Round Table in 1344 was soon abandoned but in 1348 he founded the Order of the Garter which still survives — indeed it is the oldest chivalrous movement in the world. Staged tournaments became both testing grounds for battle skills and increasingly popular royal and public entertainments in their own right. It is interesting to note that Bishop Robert Wyville of Salisbury was only able to regain control of Sherborne in 1354 after conceding in principle to settlement of the case by single combat; in the end he had to pay 2500 marks to William, Earl of Montague (who had recently acquired the site from Edward III) and 500 marks to the king. The late medieval kings of Scotland certainly enjoyed such displays; the outer court at Holyrood Palace, for instance, was turned into a tiltyard for tournaments on various occasions, the most notable being the royal wedding of James IV to Margaret Tudor in 1503. Evidently the royal party watched the combat from a gallery, the king's and queen's parties looking out of separate windows (Dunbar 1999, 59).

Henry VIII was a notable enthusiast for the tournament, being a famously capable combatant himself in his younger days. Later in his reign he had to be content with observing the contests, but he did this with typical lavishness at Hampton Court where he built a great Tiltyard for jousting to the north-west of the palace. Parts of the original boundary wall around the Tiltyard survive largely intact, though the area within has long since been turned over to gardens (the hard tennis courts in one corner are an echo of the former sporting use). Furthermore one of the original five viewing towers also survives (**60**). These would have been similar in intent to the Banqueting House at Nonsuch, allowing the king and favoured members of his court to watch the tournament in comfort through massive bay windows. The blocked-up positions of these can still be made out in the north and south walls of the surviving Tiltyard Tower, while the western one (ic. the bay which looked straight out into the yard itself) was opened up again during refurbishment of existing catering facilities in the mid-1990s. Henry VIII was an enthusiast of several other sports as well as the hunt and the tourney, and once again the evidence for these survives above and below ground at Hampton Court. The tennis-play built in 1532-3 still survives (though converted into apartments in 1670), and the king also added one at Windsor where he sited it at the foot of the Round Tower motte (Brindle and Kerr 1997, 46). The Close Bowling Alley at Hampton Court, of about the same date as the tennis-play, was demolished in the eighteenth century. Nevertheless its foundations survive under gardens on the north side of the palace and were examined archaeologically in 1998 (**61**). Tennis courts are also known at several late medieval Scottish palaces (eg. at Dunfermline, where there was also a bowling alley), and indeed one survives largely intact, though renovated several times, at Falkland Palace (Dunbar 1999, fig 6.4).

The bare necessities: service ranges and other functional buildings

Palace life was by no means all about display on the one hand and privacy on the other. At any one there would have been a great deal of 'behind the scenes' activity in progress, at least while the court was in residence. The buildings which housed these activities were integral to life within the palace precinct, and for much of the medieval period there was little attempt to keep them away from the accommodation ranges; there seems to have been little of the compartmentalisation which was evident in the siting of craft or industrial quarters (eg. tanneries) in the contemporary urban context until the fifteenth and sixteenth centuries. Even so we know a great deal about palace service buildings, both archaeologically and historically. In the latter case, for instance, Welsh law books of the twelfth and thirteenth centuries describe a 'typical' layout for a *llys* comprising up to ten buildings. The hall and chamber were there, of course, but the specification also included a privy, a kitchen, a kiln, a granary or barn, a stable, and a kennel (Butler 1987, 49). The kennel, and to some extent the stable, doubtless reflected the general popularity of hunting among the ruling classes of medieval Europe. A probable bakehouse or kitchen (building

60 The Tiltyard Tower at Hampton Court Palace, with the east wall of the tournament ground to the left

D) has been excavated at *Cae Llys*, Rhosyr (Anglesey; Johnstone 1999, 265-7 and fig 14).

Kitchens were probably the single most important service buildings on any medieval site, and a few still survive largely intact. We shall consider the medieval kitchens at Windsor shortly, while there are impressive remains of the medieval kitchens at Farnham in an area of the palace still used in this way (**62**). It is also worth noting the excellent manorial example at Stanton Harcourt, Oxon, and several collegiate ones in Oxford (eg. Christchurch). There are also numerous examples of excavated kitchens such as those of the Benedictine abbey at Eynsham, Oxon. Palace kitchens could expect particularly heavy use as catering would often be on a grandiose scale befitting the wealth and manorial or other resources of the monarch or bishop. On 24 November 1244, for instance, William Ralegh had but recently taken over the Winchester bishopric and he therefore celebrated the Feast of St Edmund in some style. His manors in Berkshire, Buckinghamshire, Hampshire, Surrey and Wiltshire provided hundreds of dishes, bowls, platters and other pottery, along with the livestock to go on them. All available swine had apparently been commandeered by Henry III for the royal Christmas feast, and the sheer variety of fowl consumed at Ralegh's celebrations probably reflects this: peacocks, pheasant, partridge, hens, chickens, woodcock, mallard and plover were among the birds brought in from the manors, while fish, venison hunted specially for the occasion and brawn were also served along with five tuns of wine (Roberts 1989).

Gluttonous displays such as this may have been rare, and in expiation the leftovers would have been distributed among the poor, but they do help to explain the very large scale of many medieval kitchens. The ruinous shell of the kitchen block within the so-

61 The east wall of Henry VIII's Close Bowling Alley at Hampton Court Palace exposed during small-scale trial excavations in 1998, with the existing real tennis court in the background

62 Blocked arcading in the medieval kitchens at Farnham Castle

called 'keep' at Wolvesey, for instance, is about 40ft (12.2m) square internally, divided into three separate rooms. Excavations in the 1960s showed that the interior had been lined with hearths and ranges which had been moved or rebuilt regularly according to need. The great gash in the south wall of the block marks the former position of the main oven range. The kitchen at Bishop's Waltham was remodelled under William of Wykeham in the late fourteenth century and is separated from the bishop's Great Hall to the south by the typical three-room serving area of buttery, pantry and servery. This kitchen is about 50ft (15.25m) long and 28ft (8.53m) wide internally and seems to have comprised a single chamber. Fine remains of ovens can be seen in the west wall, with conspicuous use of brick (**colour plate 20**). Clarendon Palace contains one of the finest excavated sets of kitchen buildings (**63, 64**), some of which are probably of twelfth-century date although the fully developed plan of the complex seems to belong to Henry III's time. At that stage there were two main kitchens on the north and west sides of a small courtyard or cloister immediately to the west of the palace's Great Hall. The north and west kitchens measured 36ft (11m) and 42ft (12.8m) square internally, and four substantial square bases to support piers were found inside the former, suggesting that it may have resembled the well-known abbot's kitchen at Glastonbury Abbey. Little other internal detail was noted in this kitchen, but a central chimney block and a fireplace/oven against the north wall were found in the western one (**64**); this building may be the earlier of the two kitchens and is probably the one referred to as the king's in contemporary documents. Associated buildings or rooms included the salsary (for the

63 Clarendon Palace. View across the kitchen courtyard to the salsary during excavations in the 1930s. Photograph by J. Charlton

preparation of sauces or salting food) and a *'herlebecheria'* (a term of uncertain meaning, but perhaps a scullery or even a slaughterhouse), both of which have been identified on the excavated plan along with areas where kitchen rubbish had been dumped on the steep down-slope immediately to the north of the buildings.

The kitchens at Windsor are probably the most important to have survived at any medieval palace, but the extent to which early fabric remained here only became apparent during the archaeological investigations which followed the great fire of 1992. This had caused extensive damage to surface finishes and structural timberwork, but it also had the secondary effect of leading directly to the exposure of entire wall surfaces which would otherwise have remained hidden. Thus the accepted view that the kitchens had largely been rebuilt in the nineteenth century had to be revised completely when substantial parts of the original buildings were found. Firstly the great fireplaces cut into the twelfth-century curtain wall (which forms the north side of the range) were found to use Bagshot Heath stone which was generally used for external facing: it seems that the original kitchens of *c.*1170 were open-air or at least not fully enclosed. External ovens have also been excavated at King John's Hunting Lodge, Writtle, Essex, associated with a succession of kitchens (Rahtz 1969, 38-51). Henry III seems to have built a great stone kitchen here during the thirteenth century, but nothing of this could be identified largely because of the extensive rebuilding under Edward III from 1357-77. He had the curtain wall both

64 Clarendon Palace. The hearth in the west kitchen photographed during excavations in the 1930s. Photograph by J. Charlton

thickened and raised to take more fireplaces, reconstructed the south wall with new windows, and as we have seen in chapter 2 erected the great lanterned roof. The medieval kitchen range underwent numerous subsequent alterations, and an entirely new one was added in the Kitchen Court to the south during the post-medieval period.

The Tower of London would also have housed several kitchen ranges. The most important of these would have been that attached to the palatial accommodation in the Inmost Ward, and recent research suggests that this would have lain against the inside angle between the Wakefield Tower and the curtain wall which runs northwards from it to the Coldharbour Gate. Like most of the Inmost Ward buildings this kitchen originated in the reign of Henry III (there are several references to work on it during his reign), but the last remains of the palace accommodation here were removed in the late nineteenth century. Therefore we know virtually nothing physically of the castle's great kitchen, but we do know that there would have been several other smaller ones around the castle, all free-standing and attached to other residential ranges in the medieval period.

One such building was unexpectedly revealed during excavations inside the late seventeenth-century New Armouries building during 1999, some 60ft (18.25m) north of the hearth and associated wall discovered in the 1920s. A chalk and Kentish Rag wall was found running parallel to and about 14ft 9in (4.5m) out from the curtain wall; unfortunately neither of the north or south ends could be located in the small-scale work involved, but the structure must have been at least 40ft (12.2m) long. Chalk and other floor layers were found inside the building (the earliest of these went under the wall and therefore must have pre-dated it), and one of these had formed the base for a brick floor: the bricks themselves had been removed but the impressions of them could still be seen in the bedding below. An oven was found immediately to the south of this floor. When the latter was replaced the oven was also taken out of use, in its turn being replaced with a hearth of end-set tiles; this seemed to have been built against a partition inserted into the building across the earlier brick floor. Another tiled hearth was found built hard against and cutting into the face of the inner curtain wall; it seems unlikely, though not impossible, that the two hearths would have been in use together. A building in this general area is documented in the middle of the fourteenth century but neither its exact position not its function is specified, though it is described as a 'pentice' (ie. lean-to). Both of the buildings found in the 1920s and 1990s seem somewhat substantial for such a description, but the term becomes more understandable in the context of such a massive structure as the inner curtain wall: to some extent anything added to this would be a pentice.

Brewhouses and bakehouses were commonly associated with kitchens and halls on medieval sites, as these were, as the names suggest, the buildings where a great deal of food preparation went on, and often on a large scale. These structures have often been excavated on monastic sites, but they are comparatively rare survivals in a palatial context. Probably the best example can be seen in the Inner Court at Bishop's Waltham, where the late fourteenth-century structure erected by Bishop William of Wykeham was remodelled by Henry Beaufort in the middle of the following century. The massive oven range in the north gable is still an impressive sight (**65**).

Storehouses of various shapes and sizes would have been a prerequisite at most palaces, whether for storing fresh and cured foodstuffs or other materials. Such buildings are apt to be replaced or converted to other uses, and because of this medieval examples are not particularly common sights at palaces. At the Tower of London, for instance, the New Armouries building was erected by the Office of Ordnance to the south-east of the White Tower as their main storehouse in the late 1660s. It replaced a range of medieval stores which had been built end-on to Henry III's inner curtain wall on the north side of the castle; the earlier storehouses are clearly shown on the 1597 survey. Soon after the New Armouries had been completed the old ranges were pulled down to make way for one of the Tower's finest post-medieval buildings, the Grand Storehouse, erected during 1688-91 to house spectacular displays of weaponry and other ordnance. This building was burnt out in a major fire in 1841 and was subsequently replaced with the Waterloo Barracks. This sequence of building works might be thought to have destroyed all trace of the medieval buildings, especially when the destructive nature of much Victorian and later service-laying is taken into account. Excavations in 1993, however, showed that chalk walls and floors belonging to the early ranges survived close to the inner curtain. No specific functions could be determined, not least because the nineteenth-century demolition and building work and subsequent insertion of services had done extensive

65 The interior of the great bakehouse/brewhouse at Bishop's Waltham Palace

damage to the stratigraphy within the buildings. Even so their identification with the medieval stores seems clear, not least because chalk only seems to have been used as a major building material in the castle during a restricted period in the thirteenth and fourteenth centuries (Hiller and Keevill 1994).

Much of this storage was associated with the king's wardrobe, initially perhaps a fairly private affair but one which grew into an important and formal office. There are documentary references to the king's wardrobe at the Tower of London from as early as 1211, and Henry III seems to have taken considerable care over the accommodation for this office. Indeed recent research suggests that it may have been provided with the upper chamber in the Wakefield Tower from 1241 onwards. This room had probably been intended for the king's use, perhaps part of his great chamber (*magna camera*) suite, but there seems to have been a change of heart in the 1230s which, among other things, left the Wakefield Tower as a two-storey structure (top-status apartments in towers of the period should have at least three storeys). The Wardrobe certainly seems to have been housed in the upper chamber of the Wakefield from the 1320s, and late in the following decade there is a reference to the repair of 'the round basement below the King's great wardrobe', an excellent description of the arrangements in the Wakefield Tower. The office continued to grow in subsequent centuries, and ultimately an entire range dedicated to and named for the Wardrobe was built during the reign of Henry VIII (who, as we know from his Inventory, had an enormous wealth of personal possessions). This range was long and narrow, running from the Broad Arrow Tower on the inner curtain to the half-round tower adjacent to the south-east corner of the great keep; this half-round structure has been know as the Wardobe Tower ever since, and both it and the long range can be seen clearly on the 1597 survey of the castle. The wardrobe itself (or at least parts of it) still survive below ground, and one of its walls was recorded during a watching brief in 1994.

One type of room was especially important for storage in medieval palaces: the cellar where wine, beer and other provender would be kept. The basement at the White Tower would have been used in this way in its earlier years (later on the basements were used to store a variety of other materials including gunpowder), while many of the surviving medieval undercrofts in both secular and religious contexts would have fulfilled the same function. Some especially fine barrel- and groin-vaulted examples on mercantile and other tenements in cities like Southampton were used for this purpose as well, and there is an especially fine twelfth-century wine cellar (the Castle Vault) at the latter's royal castle. At Clarendon, meanwhile, the crater-like remains of the palace's great wine cellar (known at the time as La Roche, or the rock) are still very impressive even if it is difficult to imagine the full scale of the now-ruinous structure. This was partly excavated in the 1930s and lay to the east of a large courtyard, south of the royal apartments and some distance away from the kitchens and the Great Hall. The cellar consisted of two chambers, the northern one certainly barrel-vaulted; this may have been the full extent of the cellar as built in the twelfth century, with the southern room possibly being an addition in the next century. Entry was from the north via a stairway of 18 steps approached from a square, paved area: the upper stone treads of the stairs had been robbed away in antiquity, but the lower ones were buried deeply-enough to avoid this fate and thus they were revealed during the excavations. The steps were 8ft 4in (2.54m) wide and comprised excellently dressed and carefully set masonry. The surviving ashlar facing of the stair passage's sides was of comparable quality, and evidence for massive double doors were found at the threshold into the cellar. Two round-headed recesses immediately within the doorway, one on either side, were interpreted as lamp holders (**66**).

Many other examples are known from surviving buildings, excavations, or a combination of the two. A late fourteenth- or early fifteenth-century half-cellar, for instance, has been excavated on a manorial site at Bekesbourne (Kent) which was acquired by Canterbury Cathedral Priory in 1443. This half-cellar therefore probably began life in private ownership but was subsequently incorporated into the bishop's palace. A sequence of clay floors was found within the cellar, separated by layers of rubbly soil. Iron nails and discolouration on one of these clay floors suggested that it had in fact supported a planked floor (Tatton-Brown 1980). At Linlithgow Palace, meanwhile, the hall range built by James I of Scotland (1424-37) was extended westward around what became a central courtyard during the later fifteenth and sixteenth centuries (Dunbar 1999, 5-21). The first stage, under James III (1460-88), involved the completion or conversion of the south range and the commencement of the western one, including the construction of a substantial cellar. The latter's floor was excavated in 1987 during improvements to visitor facilities, when in situ paving and a stone 'shelf' were found. The shelf had been built against the west (long) wall of the cellar only, away from the entrances into the chamber from the courtyard (through the east wall) and, via stairs, from rooms to the south and

66 *The stairs down into La Roche, the massive wine cellar at Clarendon Palace, under excavation in the 1930s. Note the niche to hold lamps in the bottom right-hand corner. Photograph by J. Charlton*

above (through the south and north walls respectively). It is very likely that it provided (or supported) wine racks — the chamber is still known as a wine cellar (Caldwell and Lewis 1996, 823-32). The best surviving Tudor cellar in England must be the great wine cellar at Hampton Court where the court's annual consumption of 300 barrels of wine was stored, while some of the 600,000 gallons of ale were kept in the smaller store to the west, now used as the palace's Tudor Kitchen Shop.

Buildings associated with services other than cooking and storage can also be found. At Bishop's Waltham these lay to the north in what became the Outer Court where the necessary agricultural and other service buildings lay. The late Saxon hall here was probably not demolished until the twelfth century, at which point a new boundary wall was laid out. This was not on the same orientation as the earlier structure, but neither was it aligned on the Inner Court buildings or moat; instead it seems to have respected the edge of the great pond. The area seems to have remained free of buildings for quite some time, but the boundary wall was eventually used as one long side of a timber-framed building (probably a barn) with a single aisle in the late thirteenth or early fourteenth century. The aisle was demolished in turn during the late fifteenth century and the timber arcade posts encased in diaper-pattern brickwork. It became known as the Palace Stables and was certainly used for livery in the 1920s; the archaeological evidence for chalk and clay floors and a central drain would be consistent with its use for stabling in the post-medieval period as well, though a map of 1785 shows that it was then in use as a malt house. This building survived until 1967 when it was demolished during roadworks to improve the town's approaches. The gables of a great medieval aisled barn can also be seen at Acton Burnell (Shropshire), where they are the sole reminder of the substantial service complex which would have been built alongside the palace. The barn is on rising ground some distance away from the shell of the residence itself, and although there is no evidence of an intervening moat it is likely that it was part of a court-like arrangement of agricultural and service buildings similar to that documented at Bishop's Waltham.

Water and waste: supply and drainage

A good water supply and adequate drainage were fundamental to the success of most medieval sites, and the skills of the engineers involved in setting out and constructing these is well-known, especially on monastic sites. Palaces did not lag behind in this respect. The simplest method of obtaining water was to sink a well, and this would have the advantage of security from poisoning in sites like Windsor Castle and the Tower of London where defence was important. Both castles do indeed have several wells, eg. in the early twelfth-century Round Tower at Windsor where the fine stone-lined well on the keep's summit was excavated in the early 1990s. Subsequently another well was revealed in the Upper Bailey's Kitchen Court during excavations in the aftermath of the great fire in November 1992. This well is specifically referred to as the 'great well next the great kitchen' in fourteenth-century documents, and it lived up to its description: the internal diameter of the bore was almost 10ft (3m), and it was lined in fine greensand ashlar. This marvellous structure was covered with a brick dome (impressive in its own right) when a new kitchen was built within (and virtually filling) the old Kitchen Court in the late seventeenth century. Access to the well still seems to have been required, however, for a door was provided in the dome along with steps down to it (**67**).

At the Tower of London the well in the basement of the White Tower can still be seen, and a second one is present in the western part of the palace area of the Inmost Ward. Rainwater might also be collected in large cisterns, though more often effort was concentrated on deflecting the rainfall away from walls, especially their heads where damp penetration could cause serious damage. Previously unsuspected guttering was found in the mural passage of the upper floor of the White Tower during 1996 when the existing timber floor over the openings into the passage were being lifted and cleaned. A series of tile-lined intra-mural drains were found which were clearly part of the original Norman construction and were intended to take rainwater off the roof and cast it out on chutes through the upper walls. These gutters lie well below the current wall-tops of the White Tower and, taken with evidence noted in the 1960s and again in 1996 for an earlier roof pitch on the internal faces of the top floor, they appear to prove that the side walls of the keep were originally screens in front of and hiding the entire double-pitched roof.

The White Tower also provides a good demonstration of the care taken over the provision and siting of garderobes (latrines). These are to be found on both the entrance

67 *The seventeenth-century steps down to the Great Well in the Kitchen Court at Windsor castle under excavation in the 1990s. © Crown copyright: English Heritage*

and upper floors of the original building (see above), but evidently not in the basement; all bar one discharged straight out through the north wall onto the ground below. There was a deep and wide ditch here when the White Tower was built, and the intention may have been for the effluent to flow into this. The ditch was filled in during or before the early to mid-thirteenth century (when Henry III massively enlarged the castle to the north), at which point alternative arrangements were presumably planned. In 1996, however, what appeared to be garderobe deposits (ie. cess) were found on the battered plinth of the keep when this was exposed during surface works; these 'layers' were clearly medieval, though no more accurate date than this could be deduced from the stratigraphy and related pottery evidence. The garderobes in the White Tower were disposed thus: two in the larger (western) room on the entrance floor but none in the eastern room, and two in each of the main rooms on the upper floor. One of the two in the upper eastern chamber lay within the thickness of the east wall, not the north, and was accessed through a door in the northern reveal of the first window embrasure at the north end of the chamber; this was therefore the only garderobe not to discharge through the north wall. The presence of a separate passage across the north end of the eastern chamber has recently been proposed on the basis of this garderobe's anomalous position and the orientation of the northern door in the spine wall between the eastern and western chambers (see above).

Garderobes are common enough features of Norman palace sites, not that this should be any surprise; the Latin word *necessarium* which is sometimes used for them in contemporary documents is, after all, a good (even rather prosaic) description. The various chambers in the tower of Bishop Giffard's early twelfth-century West Hall at Wolvesey were supplied with latrines on their west side, for example, flushed by stream water. When Henry de Blois enlarged the palace in the late 1130s he built a large new latrine block at the north end of Giffard's range, at a somewhat inconvenient distance from the great ceremonial space of the new East Hall and its attached chamber block. At Witney Mount House, meanwhile, another early twelfth-century Winchester palace was provided with a substantial garderobe attached to the east side of the great tower which provided the site's dominant feature; the latrine here was not a primary feature, however, but was added in the mid- to late twelfth century. Its long, narrow plan is more reminiscent of Giffard at Wolvesey rather than de Blois, but there seems to have been little need to follow a standard plan in garderobes: Sherborne was provided with a substantial block of them to the north-west of the main courtyard, for instance, whereas most of the examples in Old Sarum's Inner Bailey seem to belong to the smaller, narrower type. To some extent all of these can be seen as communal lavatories similar to the monastic rededorter, and they stand in contrast to the privies more commonly found in the private accommodation of the royal family or episcopate (eg. the single garderobe built on to the south-east corner of Wolvesey's East Hall in the early 1140s and immediately encased in the massive Wymond's Tower).

Elsewhere at the Tower of London, considerable elaboration went into the palace's drainage, especially when the defences were extended during the thirteenth and fourteenth centuries. Henry III, for instance, built great culverted drains under his inner curtain wall immediately to the east of his private water gate on the east side of his apartments in the Wakefield Tower. Part of this drain was exposed to the south of the curtain wall (ie. where it would originally have passed out to the river) during excavations in 1957 and 1992, and it can still be seen. In 1899 the drain was followed northwards as far as the south-west corner of the White Tower, showing that it was the medieval palace's main drain. As we have seen Henry III rarely resided at the Tower, but the extensive records of building work at the castle during his reign make frequent reference to privy garderobes for both the king and queen. The order to build a drain 'like a hollow column' for a privy chamber (possibly the queen's) in November 1238 is notable in this respect (although it is not clear whether the column discharged directly into the river or via the palace's great drain), as is the reference in February 1240 to the construction of a new turret so that a drain should flow into the Thames. This turret must have been on the south-east corner of a rectangular chamber-block built over the inner curtain wall against the east side of the Wakefield Tower; the block projected forwards into the river edge, and its foundations were revealed during excavations in the late 1950s (*see* **40**). Finally, in June 1246 we find the king famously complaining about a malodorous privy in the wardrobe, and entreating that this should be remedied 'even should it cost a hundred pounds . . . before the feast of the translation of St Edward [13 October] when we shall come there' (endnote 4). It should be stressed, however, that this document may not refer to the Tower of London at all: the castle is not mentioned by name, and the complaint occurred at a time when the king made little or no use of the Tower, at least for overnight stays. According to his itinerary the king did not stay at the Tower at all during the 1240s, but as usual he made extensive use of Westminster: indeed, he was there from 8-25 October 1246, and thus spent the relevant feast-day there. Irrespective of where the privy was, the king's impassioned entreaty over its state does show an unsurprising attention to mundane details.

When Edward I added the outer curtain wall in the late 1270s to create the Outer Ward he extended the great drain further to the south so that it carried under his curtain; there is a very clear straight joint between the two different thirteenth-century builds in the culvert (Parnell 1993, plate 14). The latter must have been lengthened yet again when the wharf was built in the fourteenth century. Excavations around St Thomas's Tower in 1958 revealed a second drain of very similar construction about 164ft (50m) to the west. Unfortunately little more is known of this; it has not been seen inside the Tower, but a fine ashlar inspection chamber was found built over it along with a later addition in brick. The almost straight-sided relieving arches for this are very reminiscent of the late fifteenth- and sixteenth-century examples described in chapter 3, and the brickwork was interpreted as a Tudor addition by the excavators.

At the Manor of the More (Herts) the water supply for the house built by the bishops of Winchester and Durham in 1426 was carried from the south in a wooden pipe, the 1ft 3in (0.38m) diameter void of which survived where it had rotted away. Between 1460 and 1470 a brick and tile conduit was built to take the water from its entry point at the gateway over the moat into a cistern which did not survive but must have lain roughly in the centre of the moat platform. This conduit comprised a floor of glazed tiles with brick side walls and, for the most part, a flat tiled or slabbed roof; there was insufficient space to turn a brick vault over the culvert, and spaces had been left in the brickwork of the top wall course so that bars could be laid across it to support the roof. Elsewhere on the platform the water was probably taken round in lead pipes, although these had been robbed out subsequently to leave only the voided trenches behind. Drainage seems to have been back into the moat (Biddle et al 1959, 154-6 and fig 6). A similar scenario pertained at Oatlands House (subsequently Palace), where the private house was provided with a surrounding moat in the late fifteenth century. The inner edge was revetted in brick, and following demolition of the house this was subsequently used as the foundation for a new range when Henry VIII established a palace on the site in 1537. The moat was then culverted and backfilled so that courtyard surfaces could be laid up to the new range. The culvert in the 'old' moat continued to provide drainage, both for rainwater chased into it from downspouts on the walls and from garderobes in semi-octagonal and other projections forward from the range. Substantial brick vaults bridged the moat and its culvert where further buildings ran south-westwards to create a courtyard on this side of the house-turned-palace.

Henry VIII's Nonsuch Palace provides an excellent example of the care taken with water supply and drainage. The water from natural springs rising on the higher ground to the south of the palace was collected at a conduit head and piped down to the palace, where the clean water was fed to a cistern on the second floor of the western tower in the south front. Further pipes led from there to various points in the two main courts and a secondary storage cistern in the kitchens, where a well also provided a back-up water supply. The palace would have had a great need for fresh water, not only for the royal and other private apartments and the kitchens but also for the fountains which were such a feature both of the Inner Court and the Privy Garden (to say nothing of the Grove of Diana and the Banqueting House to the west, but these would have been fed independently). Once used, the waste water was collected in culverted drains which continued to use the natural fall in the land to take the effluent away to the north. Faecal waste, however, was largely confined to the garderobes which ranged along the outer walls of the palace's long sides and along the spine wall in the south range of the Inner Court. A garderobe had also been thoughtfully built into the central spine wall of the Banqueting House, where it was clearly associated with a great chimney. Part of the chimneypiece with fine early Renaissance carving was recovered during excavation of the demolition rubble from within the cellar in 1960. The garderobes were obviously cleared out regularly during the lifetime of the palace, although this vigilance was finally relaxed in the third quarter of the seventeenth century by which time Nonsuch had long since ceased to be a royal palace. Very large assemblages of pottery, clay pipes, glass, metalwork and animal bone were deposited in the shafts and pits of the garderobes then, and this material formed the bulk of the finds other than architectural fragments recovered during the excavations of 1959-60.

At Hampton Court much of the culverted system of water supply and drainage still survives under the palace. There was already a water supply in place at the palace before it passed into the king's hands, but this was inadequate for the needs of the full court and so a new system was established in 1538-45 partly using land taken from the suppressed Merton Priory (which, as we have seen, was a fertile source of materials for Nonsuch as well). Three springs on Coombe Hill some three miles to the east of Hampton Court were provided with new conduit heads, all of which survive, and the three lead pipes from these joined up to head directly for the palace. The pipe had to be reinforced with iron where it went under the Thames, while tampkins (inspection points with stopcock and expansion chamber) were built at intervals to allow leaks to be investigated. Once at the palace the water was taken to storage cisterns in the kitchen area and adjacent to the king's and queen's apartments and thus around the courts in a similar way as at Nonsuch. Here again a fountain was situated in the Inner Court, and this may have acted as a sort of safety valve: the water continued to come whether there was a demand for it or not, so there had to be some sort of overflow system. A fountain was one way of providing this, and in a neat touch at Hampton Court the overrun from the Inner Court fountain fed clean water to the king's fish in the Pond Garden.

Once again at Hampton Court culverts took the waste away, either to the Thames directly or perhaps via the moat (**colour plate 21**). The excavation of a partial section across the latter's north side in 1994 revealed a waterlogged soil at its bottom in what would have been the centre of the moat. This was important in demonstrating that the moat had been wet here at some point in its life, though not necessarily when it was first dug — the dating evidence was not sufficient to prove this. More significantly the soil contained plentiful evidence for the environment in and around the ditch. The wet and oxygen-free conditions had allowed the preservation of organic plant matter and pollen, and these provided a rich harvest for environmental archaeologists. It appeared that there had never been any permanent standing water in this part of the moat, and there was little or no evidence for garderobe waste or other cessy material. This is not entirely surprising as the excavated site is well away from the domestic apartments with their individual garderobes and the House of Ease, a sort of reredort for palace courtiers built over and flushed by (but not into) the moat just before it meets the Thames. Furthermore the excavation was on the opposite side of the palace to the river and thus lay in the least advantageous place possible for finding such waste. The environmental data were very valuable even so. The presence of introduced species such as horse chestnut and others closely related to post-medieval garden and landscape work such as lime suggested that even the primary fills must have been several generations later than the original digging of the moat, showing that it had been kept clean during the Tudor period. It also seems likely that the environment would have highly localised around the circuit of the ditch (Keevill and Bell 1996).

At Bridewell drainage diversions were required during the replanning of the outer courtyard. The two original drains through the eastern range of the principal courtyard excavated in 1978 had been built to take rainwater away from the eaves of the roof: the west ends of the channels through the wall lay at the same height as the courtyard surface, so it could not have serviced that. The water would have passed into the drain through downspouts on the west wall (and presumably the east wall as well as first planned). The channels had clearly been planned from the outset and were carefully built in with the lower masonry of the wall, sloping gradually through it towards the outer courtyard. The clean and unstained state of the drain surfaces was notable and demonstrated that they could barely have been used before they were blocked up when new buildings were erected against the east (outer) side of the range a few years into the construction programme. In contrast the drains which had been chased/cut into the walls to replace them were blackened and stained by years of use.

Garderobes and their chutes were often incorporated into the chimney blocks of late medieval and Tudor buildings. The two had similar requirements which were best served on an external wall face, as we have seen at Nonsuch. These features often contain excellent finds groups, including dumped kitchen waste (again as at Nonsuch), but the regular cleansing of the features means that they are not quite as valuable in archaeological terms for showing what palace life was like as one might hope and expect. In some circumstances the garderobes would be flushed away by running water, as in the Great House of Ease at Hampton Court. Something similar was found if on a considerably smaller scale at the Canterbury palace of Bekesbourne, where a pair of garderobes were offset from but connected directly into a large brick culvert which crossed the site under the main building ranges. An inspection chamber had been provided where the culvert passed out beyond one range into what must have been a courtyard (Tatton-Brown 1980, 45-6 and figs 4 and 6).

Survival: medieval palaces in the post-medieval period

Ultimately the survival of many medieval royal palaces depended on either, but very rarely both, of two factors: the continuing popularity of their location (eg. Hampton Court Palace) or their value as a centre for other arms of government. The Tower of London and Westminster offer especially good examples here, as both lost their palatial roles in the first half of the sixteenth century but manifestly continued in use. The military aspect of the former continued to be important through the Royal Armouries and the Board of Ordnance, while offices such as the Royal Mint also continued to develop both within and, later, in the immediate vicinity of the old castle. Westminster, of course, evolved subtly but completely from being an important expression of royal power into the ultimate one of parliamentary democracy.

Bishops' palaces (and the episcopal estate in general) suffered under the religious troubles of the Reformation. Many bishops gave up properties to Henry VIII in an attempt to curry favour, though not always with any noticeable effect. Thereafter the episcopal residences also either had to evolve (witness the conversion of the Lincoln palace at Lyddington into a bede or almshouse) or wither away. Even some of the most important 'home' palaces within the cathedral cities did not survive intact. The likes of Canterbury and Lincoln have been extensively rebuilt, for instance, and Wolvesey was all but abandoned to the whims of stone robbers for a century before being re-established in the 1680s (the Baroque palace, part of which is still in use by the Bishop of Winchester today). The majority of episcopal palaces away from the diocesan centres either passed into private hands or fell into greater or lesser degrees of ruination.

In some ways it seems odd now that the ruins of old palaces did not attract the same kind of attention as abbeys in the landscape design movement of the eighteenth century and later. We do not find places like Clarendon or Nonsuch — still less Somersham or Bishop's Waltham — becoming features in newly-created parks or the foci of carefully-constructed vistas, even though one might believe them to be tailor-made for such treatment. The development of the Romantic movement led to some revival of interest in the tragic figures of the past, especially in the royal arena where stories of Mary Queen of Scots, Anne Boleyn and others aroused sympathetic passion. A supposedly 1,000 year-old Yew tree at Ankerwycke Priory (Bucks), for instance, gained a reputation as being a trysting-place of Anne and Henry VIII; there was no great evidence for this, but presumably it did no harm to the attempted development of the former nunnery's precinct as a pleasure ground in the early nineteenth century. Little of this sort seems to have befallen palaces, even where (as at Clarendon) they passed into private hands as part of large formerly royal estates. Despite this palaces did become a subject of considerable antiquarian and academic interest during the eighteenth and nineteenth centuries — books could be written on this subject alone — and a considerable body of knowledge was built up accordingly. Here, as in the monastic field, the interest in and romance of ruins gradually metamorphosed into an appreciation of the historical importance of palaces, and thus of their value for studying the people and events of the past. We will explore the uplifting educational value implicit in this attitude in the final chapter.

6   Conclusions

Researching medieval palaces

Hopefully this book will have made it clear that a great deal of archaeological work has been done on medieval palaces, and that the results are both fascinating in their own right and especially valuable when viewed in the light of historical or other evidence. Nevertheless there are gaps in our knowledge at regional, national and international levels that need to be addressed. Research frameworks can be problematical in that they have a tendency to act as straightjackets, but there is little alternative to their adoption if coherent progress is to be made in our understanding of palaces. The greatest immediate priority is to get more national and international surveys of the subject in print in a variety of languages. John Dunbar's recent survey (1999) of late medieval and renaissance Scottish palaces is an excellent example of the potential here, but even this is largely an architectural and historical description. Understandably, the space precludes detailed treatment of archaeological discoveries there in the same way that architectural considerations have been secondary here. The equally recent book on medieval Hungarian royal palaces is another fine example of what is achievable (Zoltán 1999), and we undoubtedly need more of this kind of publication in English. There is little doubt that equivalent publications of British research in other languages would be just as useful.

At a more regional/national level, there are still too many past excavations unpublished in the United Kingdom. One looks back wistfully now at statements made in high optimism in the 1960s with regard to the full publication of such important projects as Nonsuch and Oatlands palaces which then seemed to be imminent (Biddle 1961, 3; Cook 1969, 9). Neither report has yet appeared, though the finds volume for Nonsuch was in press at the time of writing (late spring 2000). The results of several important excavations from the 1950s to the 1970s at the Tower of London have yet to see the light of day, though fortunately more has been realised here through the work of Geoffrey Parnell. A similar picture could be painted at many other palaces (royal and episcopal), and it is not as though more recent generations of excavators have been exempt; the results of excavations at Winchester Palace (Southwark) have yet to appear, for instance. This problem requires urgent attention, and the recent publication of disparate excavations at Whitehall Palace is an example of what can be done in this respect (Thurley 1999).

As for new research, virtually every medieval palace which still survives would repay some further work. This need not always be on a large scale, and limited but targeted excavation can be extremely valuable. The benefits of large-scale projects are inescapable, however, and it is to be hoped that the seeming loss of confidence manifested in the 'let's wait until better techniques are available in the future' attitude does not stop such projects from coming forward. Recent results at places like Windsor Castle and the Tower of London show just how much can be achieved, and who would not cast a longing eye over sites like Clarendon and Bishop's Waltham, to name but two, where so much more could be done? Priorities need to be set carefully, not least because funding will inevitably be the main factor determining whether or not any given site actually does receive archaeological attention in the near future. Site-specific studies will always have their part to play, but there is a strong argument for devising more regional programmes of research. There is great potential for further work in Wales, for instance, building from what has already been achieved in Gwynedd (Johnstone 1999, 275), and every one of the medieval diocese in England, Scotland, Wales and Ireland would repay greater research into their palaces. As ever the best work is likely to be done where archaeologists, historians, architects and others operate closely together in interdisciplinary teams.

It may be legitimate to question the extent to which we can recognise medieval palaces in their own right. Virtually all of the structures, rooms, spaces and features which would have been built at a palace could (and usually would) have been present at contemporary sites of similar status and scale. Monasteries and manors or other seigneurial residences, for instance, would have had their halls, chamber blocks or equivalents, kitchens, service ranges and guest accommodation. Later on, separate apartments for the king and queen in royal palaces would be mirrored in the private rooms of larger secular houses and, indeed, in the abbot's (or equivalent) lodgings in monastic houses. Certainly the trend towards greater personal (and family) privacy during the later medieval period is not confined to the highest-status sites but can also be seen in greater and lesser religious houses, manors, almshouses and other sites. It may not always be easy to say who was the trend-setter (the monarchy, episcopate or magnates) in any given fashion for buildings or living arrangements, but we can say that such fashions were rarely (if ever) solely confined to those exalted levels of society. Palaces, especially the royal ones, did tend to be larger and more grand than the kind of equivalents just listed, but this is not a hard and fast rule and it is equally true that very large and ostentatious buildings were put up by the nobility and others which could be seen as palaces in all but name.

If this is the case, it is surely valid to question the extent to which archaeology alone can define a site as palatial. In the case of Anglo-Saxon period we have already seen that it can be difficult to define a site as a palace rather than of generally high status (chapter 1). Artefacts alone are unlikely to help, as they are all too often poorly represented on any settlement site of this period irrespective of status and top-quality pieces are especially rare: the best were kept for the dead and their burials, it seems. Equally the buildings alone do not appear to satisfy even the excavators that their sites are necessarily in the very top rank. Perhaps there is something here in archaeologists' (and others?) general unease with the concept of high status and royalty, especially in the Anglo-Saxon period when kingship was defined at a local or regional level for much of the time. Doubtless it also has much to do with excavators' understandable reluctance to suggest that their sites are something special or out of the ordinary: a claim of high status is easy to defend, but royalty is more difficult to establish.

It might seem easier to define palaces archaeologically in the post-Conquest period, but here what we have already termed the 'moveable feast' comes into play. Much of the royal or episcopal household's goods travelled with it from place to place, and very probably this would have included the better materials. Top-quality artefacts therefore might well avoid the ignominy of being consigned to the archaeological record altogether, unless they somehow came to be lost down garderobes and in cess-pits, where even the finest jewellery tended to rest unclaimed. At the same time much of the materials carted around by officers of the Wardrobe would have been exactly those which survive least well in normal archaeological conditions: in Britain and much of the rest of Europe we have to rely on waterlogged environments for the preservation of wood, cloth, textiles and so on. Furniture, wooden tableware, bedding, tapestries and similar objects are correspondingly very rarely found during archaeological excavations except as small and often unimpressive fragments. Such pieces do survive, of course, in collections and at palaces, but they do not help us with the question of archaeological recognition.

The finds from excavated medieval palaces, then, need not be particularly remarkable, and there are few if any spectacular collections of artefacts among the published palace excavations. Often, to be sure, there are individual pieces of high quality (the sculpture from Clarendon, for instance) but usually they are not numerous within a single site's collection. Even objects that might seem to define a royal site may not be as significant as they seem at first. The *scintillae* (lead stars which would have been painted gold and attached to a blue or green-painted ceiling or wall) from Clarendon (page 51), for instance, are by no means unique: similar artefacts have also been found on moated sites like Rest Park (Yorks; le Patourel 1973, 90-1) and at Eynsham Abbey (Oxon). The Clarendon pieces only derive additional significance because of the contemporary references to interior decoration at the palace (and others of the same period) which very probably incorporated just such items.

Pottery assemblages from palaces might well include items imported from Europe (in Britain's case), including fine or exotic specimens, and there might well be evidence for rich or unusual foods among the animals bones or seeds from a site, but again these might all be found on contemporary higher-status sites such as monasteries, manors and town houses. Indeed the latter can seem wealthier. It can therefore be difficult to distinguish palaces from contemporary sites purely in terms of their finds. In this context, at least, we might legitimately ask whether the archaeological study of medieval palaces can be seen as in any way distinct from equivalent research into other site-types of this period.

The analysis of palace (or equivalent) groups may well offer the best way of looking at these sites as an archaeological entity. The building campaigns of kings such as Henry III and his son Edward I in the thirteenth and early fourteenth centuries are justly famed for the extent and expense of what was done, and a remarkable amount of this building stock remains for us to study. We can examine the gradual evolution of domestic arrangements in palaces across these reigns (and others), while also looking at the evidence for developing military strategies as expressed in the defensive architecture of the time, as in the defence-in-depth and multi-angled approach into the south-west corner of the Tower of London devised for Edward I in 1275-81. The royal palaces built or acquired over the whole medieval period inevitably represent one of the largest groups of major buildings of any kind in the country (or even in Europe), and they deserve study on that basis if no other. The late medieval/Tudor palaces can be seen as a distinctive group in many ways, but this would hide the potential for interpretation across reigns, decades or centuries from the Conquest to the Dissolution: this would surely be a serious mistake. The geographical spread of palaces at different times from the late eleventh to the mid-sixteenth century is one of the great fascinations of the period, carrying implicit messages about sovereignty through time and the relative importance not only of different parts of the country, but also of the advisability and need (or otherwise) to be seen there.

Similar points can be made regarding the episcopal palaces, though at a different scale in terms of distribution. There were massive variations between bishoprics as to the land, estates and palaces they were granted, bought and built. At one end of the scale were the poorer dioceses such as St Asaph and Bangor in Wales or Carlisle in England (though the latter was rather better off than the first two); at the other were the likes of Canterbury, Lincoln, Salisbury and Winchester — above all Winchester, whose bishops embarked upon building campaigns to rival royalty. The penchant for establishing lodgings in London close to the royal court and government is a further notable aspect, this time across the bishoprics, though the extent and quality of the lodgings was just as subject to variations in wealth of the sees. Once again the greater part of the episcopal building stock survives in some form or another, though less so in London, where the bishops' palaces have not fared so well, and to visit (say) Wolvesey, Bishop's Waltham and Farnham of the Winchester palaces or Old Sarum and Sherborne (**colour plate 22**) of the Salisbury diocese in a single day provides an impressively immediate feeling for the impact that these sites were intended to have. An individual palace may as well be studied against a background of research into the medieval period as a whole: there is usually a more immediate and relevant context within which it should be placed, however, and that is the equivalent sites of the monarch or bishop elsewhere in their lands.

Palaces and landscapes

Palaces could never have existed in total isolation from their surroundings, and of course they were not intended to. On the contrary palatial developments were planned within the context of their urban and rural settings, sometimes to harmonise with it and at others to stand out as a deliberately dominant feature. Important studies of wider palatial contexts are already underway in a number of cases (eg. Clarendon), but there is no doubt that the impact of palace building on landscapes has been under-appreciated in the past. The effects of palaces could have occurred in many ways, for instance through site clearances, quarrying for materials, the creation of emparked landscapes and, increasingly, gardens around the palaces. Such landscaping might well involve substantial physical alteration of the natural environment through earth-moving and working, planting and the creation of water features, but we must also remember that there could be equally significant impacts on existing settlement and communication patterns. Henry VIII's Nonsuch is a good example: not only did construction of the palace necessitate the removal of the church and village of Cuddington, but the establishment of the wider landscape of parks and gardens required that existing roads (some of considerable regional importance) should be closed or diverted around the new royal estate. There are strong echoes here of modern royalty's requirements for security and privacy (eg. closure of footpaths and other security measures around Prince Charles' Highgrove House estate in Gloucestershire).

A future for medieval palaces: access and use

One site, many audiences, one future?

It may seem self-evident that medieval palaces should be preserved for and into the future, but it is not: the archaeological literature already contains enough examples of such sites which have been damaged or even destroyed during modern developments. The Manor of the More at Rickmansworth is one example, but there are many others. It can be difficult to know how to react to such events. There is an inevitable element of shock and anger which arises when an archaeological site (of any type and period) is damaged, but this may be tempered with an understanding of the gains in knowledge which should derive from the physical loss (assuming that archaeologists are allowed to do their work before damage takes place). Indeed much of the information in this book has come from projects which would not have happened without the 'threat' of development, and of course on occasion that threat is lifted and the site lives on. The best way of achieving the preservation of archaeological sites has been discussed intensely in many circles (eg. academic, government, business and public), and there is a general consensus that retaining a monument in situ is always best. Excavation to create a permanent record of a site is accepted as the next-best thing if preservation in situ cannot be achieved for whatever reason (and development is by no means the only one: many sites are vulnerable to natural destructive forces such as erosion). The extent to which excavation can ever provide a truly comprehensive record must be open to doubt, however, because it is rare indeed for any site to be completely dug up in such circumstances. This need not be a problem, but it is a reality which has to be faced.

Many medieval palaces, of course, are offered a strong degree of inherent protection by their owners, notably those which are in state ownership or Guardianship, or through legal designation (eg. as Scheduled Ancient Monuments or Listed Buildings). Virtually by definition these will be among the best sites of their type: they have to be to gain such status. There is no guarantee that such sites will not be subject to damage (deliberate or otherwise) in the future, but it is far less likely to happen.

One of the best ways to offer protection to sites (again of any type and period) is to engender a strong public commitment to them. This must involve a sense of engagement with the monument and a direct interest in it — in short, communal ownership. This is not always easy to achieve, not least because there are still many palaces which are in private hands and where physical access is restricted or simply not possible. Privacy and property laws mean that this can only be respected and accepted, although the threat of loss can lead to remarkable examples of public/popular action, as in the (in)famous case of London's Rose Theatre during the 1980s. No such events have engulfed a palace yet although there have been some good candidates in the past, as in the case of the Manor of the More noted above. At any event it must surely be right to encourage popular interest in archaeological sites, and the success over the years of television programmes such as *Chronicle* and *Time Team* shows that the audience is clearly there. Excavations always attract interest, and the larger the better: 60,000 people visited the work at Nonsuch during July-September 1959, with a further 15,000 in the July-August 1960 season (Biddle 1961, 1). Such figures compare very favourably with the annual visitor returns from all but the top heritage sites today (see below). It is relevant here to ask who the audience is, and we can start to answer this with a diagram.

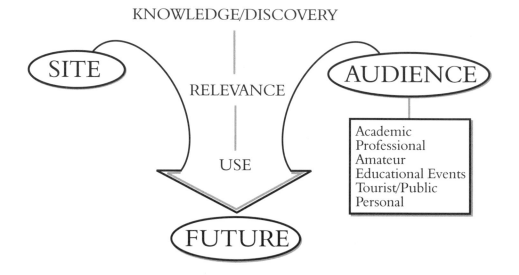

Many of these audiences are quite naturally interrelated. The academic, professional and amateur groups, for example, will all have a strong inherent interest in the past whether as archaeologists, historians, architectural/art historians or other specialists. The educational sector is strongly linked in here, whether in schools through the Key Stages of the National Curriculum in England and its equivalents elsewhere, or through higher education. The event and public audiences are also strongly connected, not least because many in the latter group increasingly gain their experience of archaeological sites through events such as re-enactments (see below). The personal audience is that of anyone who has an individual experience of a palace or other site. That person might well belong in one or more of the other groups, but it is through their own direct involvement that they will gain most from a site. We should accept that this involvement need not include an archaeological, historical or other 'academic' appreciation of a place: for some (perhaps many) people the visual, emotional or other highly personal aspects of a visit may well be far and away the most important, and they are certainly likely to be at least as complex as any learning experience. Last but not least, the business/commercial audience must be catered for: in many cases they are the paymasters, after all, and they may well hold the whole future of a site in their hands. All these groups must interact if the future of archaeological sites is to be assured, and a particular burden of responsibility falls on the first three: they are the ones who must develop that sense of engagement in the others without which ancient monuments will become much more vulnerable.

Access

The accessibility of palaces is highly variable, from those which are open at most times of the year (eg. properties managed by the National Trust, English Heritage and their equivalents) to those which are on private land and cannot be visited without making special arrangements. A relatively small number of palaces fall in between these categories and are open periodically during the year, perhaps once a month. The Winchester bishops' palace at Witney is an example of this. In other cases there are split responsibilities which can be confusing and frustrating. Another Winchester palace, that at Farnham (Surrey), is typical here: the impressive keep is in the hands of English Heritage and is fully open to the public, but the other elements of the medieval palace are either not accessible or are only open once a week. Impressive twelfth- and thirteenth-century fabric and features of the great hall, chapel and kitchens can be examined from outside, along with the magnificent entry tower built in brick by Bishop Waynflete in 1470-5, but the best views are to be had from the south lawn where it is all too easy to feel like a trespasser.

Price may be a deciding factor for many potential visitors to palaces. There are still some sites which can be seen without cost (Acton Burnell in Shropshire and Winchester palace, Southwark, London are two examples among English Heritage's properties), but there is a charge at most of the more impressive sites, whoever owns them. Often entry is inexpensive and even at Kenilworth Castle (Warks) English Heritage will charge a family group of two adults and two children little more than £10. When one moves up to the largest, grandest, most popular and most important sites, however, the laws of supply and demand come into play and charges become more substantial. This is nowhere more true than at the Tower of London (though family and group tickets may soften the burden), while sites such as Dover Castle, Eltham Palace and Hampton Court Palace among state properties and Leeds Castle in the private sector are not far behind. Clearly these are in the major league of tourist attractions, competing not merely in the heritage sector but with the likes of Legoland, Chessington World of Adventures and other theme parks (which are much more expensive). For most visitors the manifest attractions of the Crown Jewels, Yeoman Warders and ravens at the Tower (and equivalents elsewhere) will be enough to justify the admission price, but there will be others for whom that price is simply too high. Unfortunately they will include many in the local and wider communities in Britain, exactly the audience which should have most to gain from direct experience of such sites. The authorities that run these places have responsibilities to those communities as well as to the general paying public, and some worthy initiatives in this respect are described below.

The fabric of historic sites and properties can be susceptible to serious damage through wear and tear from the visitors. Timed and restricted entry arrangements are already in place, especially during peak periods, at some stately homes and even a few palaces such as Kensington Palace, an important post-medieval royal house in London. It is unlikely that such measures will be required in the foreseeable future at the majority of those ruinous or earthwork medieval palaces which are open to the public today, but they cannot be ruled out entirely. The same can even be said of major attractions such as the Tower of London, although here the future cannot be drawn too far ahead.

At the other end of the spectrum, sites can suffer equal or worse damage through neglect. Clarendon, one of the greatest English medieval royal houses, was excavated extensively in the 1930s and periodically on a number of occasions into the 1960s. Most of the excavations were left open with heaps of excavated soil around them, and thereafter the site was largely left to nature. As a result the once-great palace became badly overgrown every summer, while more delicate features such as tiled hearths have suffered the gradual but inexorable decline which besets unconsolidated masonry (compare **64** and **68**). Few people have been able to visit the site, which sits within a private estate, though a few ramblers using footpaths across the area have been aware of the special nature of this particular section of their route. Fortunately a combination of an enlightened attitude from the landowner, academic interest (from King Alfred's College, Winchester) and support (including funding) from English Heritage have led to a change. The palace has been fenced off and the vegetation put under control; a programme of masonry consolidation is under way; the old spoil heaps are being used to fill in excavations which should never have been left open; and best of all, access will now be easier from the public footpaths across the site.

It is conceivable that remote access will offer respite to those sites where visitor pressure is or could become a material threat to the fabric, fixtures and fittings of the palace or similar site. The burgeoning use of the internet has already seen impressive web sites opened by most of the main state agencies and many private equivalents, and it is already possible to access and view important photographic collections remotely (eg. through the National Monuments Records for England, Scotland and Wales). Virtual tours may soon become a reality: the software is already available or being developed, and some impressive VR models have already been produced (eg. for the Tower of London and Rochester Castle), though as yet these have been project-based rather than intended as publicly-usable tools. It is surely only a matter of time, however, before virtual palace and castle tours become available and they will doubtless find a good market, especially in

68 Clarendon Palace today: the condition of the tiled hearth in the west kitchen, May 2000, before consolidation

the international sector where remote access has obvious attractions. Ultimately, of course, most people will not be satisfied with remote access, no matter how virtually real, and will still want to visit sites themselves. Web sites and VR could still help by allowing people to map out their own schedules and routes around sites before they get to them.

Interpretation

Historic and archaeological sites can seem like alien fields to many visitors simply for lack of points of contact, features which are (or might be) familiar to them. This is not because the features are not there, far from it: many of the modern conveniences we take for granted (running water, toilets and drainage, for example) are equally evident at many medieval sites but not necessarily in an immediately recognisable form. The idea and functioning of the medieval garderobe (to take but one example) may be simplicity in itself, but unless one has experience of 'rough' camping or rock festivals it may be extremely difficult to relate this to the modern flush toilet. Even the vast majority of archaeologists are now unfamiliar with the digging of latrine pits: portaloos emptied by lorries have all but replaced the once-ubiquitous elsans and the dubious pleasures of the rota which went with it.

It is not always necessary to understand a site down to its finest details to enjoy it, but an element of education has been inherent in the presentation of historic monuments for many generations. As we pass into the third millennium of the Christian age it is surely right to take stock not only of the monuments of the recently-passed millennium but also of the way we use and interpret them. Proper academic respect for the past must underpin our interpretative efforts, especially where these involve an element of physical reconstruction. This was the case in the early 1990s when Historic Royal Palaces re-presented the medieval palace area in and around the Lanthorn, Wakefield and St Thomas's Towers at the Tower of London. This was highly controversial at the time, not only because some questioned the historical authenticity of specific reconstructed elements such as the candelabrum or throne but also because there were worries over the reversibility of some changes (eg. whether they could be removed without adversely affecting the original fabric). Such arguments can range for many years without resolution — only an eventual act to remove an inserted object will prove the second point one way or the other — but in the meanwhile there seems little doubt that the paying public gains a far better appreciation of the Tower's palatial role through the 1990s interpretation (and the costumed guides which go with it) than previously.

We can look for parallels in a different part of medieval society: the monastery. Fountains Abbey (N Yorks) is one of the greatest historic and archaeological sites in the world, its universal significance recognised in its designation as a World Heritage Site. In some ways the site is easy to appreciate because of the extent of what has survived, but in many specific details the visitor today can feel lost for want of reference points. There is virtually no interpretation on the ground, whether in the form of display boards or even descriptive labels, and even someone familiar with abbeys would find it difficult to recognise the guest houses or infirmaries as such without repeated reference to a guidebook. Clearly we must be sensitive to the needs of the site itself in interpreting it, and there are good practical reasons as well as philosophical ones for not putting up

69 The rebuilt Carthusian monk's cell at Mount Grace Priory, North Yorkshire

extensive signage; nevertheless a feeling persists that in a case like this some visitors, perhaps many, are being sold short. We may contrast this with the evocative and very physical reconstruction of a Carthusian monk's cell and garden at Mount Grace Priory, barely 22 miles (35km) away to the north in the same county (**69**). Fountains attracts over 100,000 visitors a year, Mount Grace perhaps a quarter of that number.

Interpretation also looms very large in the world of education where the value of learning through direct experience is recognised. Here again monastic sites offer a very good model because teachers and other leaders can help their students to make direct comparisons (our points of contact again) between the ancient site they are visiting and the familiar world around them (especially the school; Cooksey 1991). A similar approach can be taken at palaces, whether by looking at the lives of kings and queens or through the everyday existence of the many and varied people who lived alongside and served them. As we have already seen many palace buildings were common to other medieval sites, but equally their functions remain recognisable in students' modern environment: the hall, dining room, kitchens, living and bedrooms, and (always popular and bound to raise a giggle) the toilets. They all become much less a collection of old stones and much more a space that can be recognised, understood and appreciated. Archaeological finds also provide a marvellous way in to the past for children: for one thing there is a palpable sense of excitement in holding things which are hundreds of years old, especially when most children will only have seen such objects before in a museum display case, if at all. Then again even things which might look unfamiliar (mason's marks or initial stamps on clay pipes) can very quickly become relevant and understood if children are encouraged to make the connection with modern trademarks such as the Nike 'tick' or the arching capital M of a certain burger bar. The combination of a site and finds is very close to an educational 'dream ticket'.

Community awareness and involvement can also be encouraged through schools, colleges and other local groups. These approaches have been combined very effectively at the Tower of London in recent years, where an initiative to reach out to the local community in Tower Hamlets, Southwark and other urban boroughs has allowed thousands of children (and many adults) free access to the castle and its collections. School groups have found this especially valuable, not least when preparatory or follow-up visits to the school by the archaeologist have been possible (**70**). Wider community events, especially on the Tower's river Thames foreshore, also provide excellent opportunities for involvement and experience, in this case with an interesting resonance for some Eastenders who remember using the children's beach which was established on the Tower foreshore in the middle decades of the twentieth century. In these educational and community events adults and children have met and talked to archaeologists, handled artefacts, tried simple archaeological or related tasks for themselves, and experienced the wonder of the site itself (**71**). The ability of such a quintessentially British — even more English — site to interest and excite such an audience has been all the more remarkable given the wide ethnic and cultural backgrounds encompassed in these communities and their schools.

Events — history can be fun!

Re-enactments, themed events, costume guides and performances are increasingly being staged against the backdrop of historic sites. In the case of English Heritage's properties in care this is clearly part of a corporate strategy to encourage visitors into its monuments, partially for financial reasons but also because of the organisation's roots in that long-standing British tradition of the educational visit, which need not have anything to do with schools in this context. Such events take place at many properties, and generally the day's entertainment (edutainment?) will have a broadly appropriate theme (eg. medieval music or cookery at a castle or abbey). Some events seem much

70 Messing about on the river: public access was allowed to the Thames foreshore at the Tower of London during a weekend in July 1998. The foreshore is an integral and fascinating part of the monument

more tangentially connected (if at all) with their venue: examples at English Heritage properties in 2000 will include sheepdog demonstrations at Kenilworth Castle, or opportunities to meet a Roman soldier or Civil War surgeon at the medieval bishop's palace in Lincoln (the problem here is specifically with the palace site rather than with Lincoln itself). Equally while some of the military re-enactments can scarcely be accused of inappropriateness to site (eg. 'in situ' re-runs of the Battle of Hastings) others, such as Arthurian battles at Old Sarum, may be on more shaky ground. Some, like the American Civil War battle at Fort Brockhurst (Hants) on 30 April and 1 May 2000, are not so much on shaky ground as the wrong continent.

Does this matter, or are modern audiences sophisticated enough to take their entertainment out of such things at an alternative level to that which they will derive separately from the site itself? Why shouldn't history be fun, even if not necessarily 'right' for a particular place? There is more than a hint of the similar arguments which have raged over period instruments and modern dress/staging in this, but the major difference with events at historic sites must be that these are not just intellectual or critical notions being discussed or played on a blank stage: instead the historic site itself becomes part of the performance, and not merely a backdrop to it. To that extent appropriateness may well be a problem to and for many visitors who do not have, and probably will not be provided with, a yardstick to judge it by. *If* an essentially inappropriate event can be separate in

71 *Tower Hamlets schoolchildren exploring the Salt Tower at the Tower of London with Chris Gidlow of Historic Royal Palaces, November 1999*

people's experience from the site it is played out against, all well and good: if not, its staging must be questioned.

Not all events are equal, however, and some have a quite different focus and justification. One such is the annual fête at Bishop's Waltham, which on at least one occasion has been held within the Inner Court of the bishop's palace (**colour plate 23**). While this inevitably lead to distinctly odd sights — marching bands in penguin suits and a fire engine parked on the guest range — it is also true that it brought in far greater numbers than would otherwise visit the site. It also added a feel of life and business which seemed wholly appropriate to what is normally a quiet location even with visitors in it. The festive market-like air of the day also fitted with the spirit of the place, especially as it was such a community-based event. Finally it was still possible to examine most of the ruins without impediment, as the stalls and displays were virtually all in the open space in between the ruinous ranges (several of the other photographs in this book of the palace were taken on the day of the fête). There simply seemed to be something *right*, not necessarily or easily definable, in allowing such festivities to take place within the medieval ruins.

In the latter pages of this book we have examined audiences, access, interpretation and events at medieval palaces. The combination of these, and especially interpretation, should lead to greater understanding and this in turn should lead to greater respect. That, we must hope, will bring about a climate in which keeping and caring for our historic environment becomes a natural part of individual and corporate life. Only then can the evidence for our past be sustained and enriched for the future.

Endnotes

Chapter 4

1   The intinerary of Henry III was researched by T. Craib who completed his work *c*.1923. It remains in the PRO and has never been published, though a few historians have used it since the 1920s. An edited and annotated version has now been made by Dr Steven Brindle of English Heritage and Stephen Priestley as part of their research into the history of Windsor Castle. I am extremely grateful to Dr Brindle for passing me a copy of their edition and allowing me to use it.

Chapter 5

2   I am extremely grateful to Jeremy Ashbee of Historic Royal Palaces for providing me with information on this interpretation of the garderobe.

3   I am very grateful to Tim Allen of the Oxford Archaeological Unit for this information in advance of its publication.

4   Once again I am indebted to Jeremy Ashbee for these references, and especially the translation which is his.

Gazetteer

Introduction

This gazetteer is intended for readers who wish to see medieval palaces for themselves. It provides short descriptions of a limited number of sites which can be visited and the agencies (where relevant) responsible for their upkeep. Some privately-owned sites are also open to the public either regularly or occasionally, and where appropriate these have been listed as well. Access is difficult or not allowed at many private sites, however, and these have been omitted. The entries for royal palaces are arranged nationally for England, Scotland and Wales; those for episcopal residences are arranged by diocese. The following abbreviations are used: EH for English Heritage, and HS for Historic Scotland; HRP for Historic Royal Palaces; M for municipal (usually local/county council or equivalents); NT for National Trust; P for private. CADW needs no further abbreviation. Counties and their equivalents are included for ease of reference. The following central contact numbers may be useful: CADW, 01222 500200; English Heritage, 020 7973 3000; Historic Scotland, 0131 668 8800; National Trust (England, Wales and Northern Ireland only), 020 8315 1111.

Royal residences

England

Carlisle Castle (Cumbria; EH). The brooding presence of this strategically-vital borders castle owes something to the local stone used and the promontory location. The keep dominates the king's foundation as it always would have done, but royal visits here were usually far more to do with business than pleasure.

Clarendon Palace (Wilts; P). Little now remains standing but the remains are impressive for their sheer extent and the quality of what survives. Main buildings are the Great Hall and associated chambers: the royal chambers to the east, and services (eg. kitchens) to the west. Otherwise the great wine cellar (La Roche) is very impressive. The site is not easy to get to, being approximately two miles off-road in the middle of a large private estate; it is only really accessible by a footpath.

Corfe Castle (Dorset; NT). Magnificent ruins of an important royal castle dominating the Portland area which contained significant sources of stone used in the king's works, especially during the thirteenth century. The Castle itself contains many impressive buildings (notably the early thirteenth-century Gloriette), and is the subject of extensive ongoing archaeological work by the National Trust.

Dover Castle (Kent; EH). One of the most important strategic castles of the medieval realm throughout the period, but containing significant royal accommodation in the late twelfth-century keep, which has one of the best surviving forebuildings in the country, and Henry III's Great Hall, incorporated into a Georgian barrack block which was effectively built around the king's hall.

Eltham Palace (London; EH). Formerly an episcopal residence but taken over by the monarchy in the later medieval period and then extensively developed. The great moat and the late fifteenth-century hall are among the main features, along with luxurious suites of Art Deco rooms from the 1930s.

Guildford Castle (Surrey; M). Intact keep standing on a motte which is somewhat incongruously surrounded by municipal gardens. Other elements of the royal castle survive both above and below ground, and the latter have been the subject of archaeological investigation in recent years. The excellent Castle Arch Museum includes information about this and the castle generally.

Hampton Court Palace (Surrey; HRP). Most complete of Henry VIII's surviving palaces, though the royal accommodation was largely replaced by Sir Christopher Wren for William and Mary at the end of the seventeenth century. The Tudor palace is a mixture of Cardinal Wolsey's and the king's works, with traces of earlier ranges as well. The great western gatehouse dominates the approach to the palace, though the tall Great Hall looms above the roof line as well. The hall, Great Watching Chamber, chapel and kitchens of the Tudor period are all magnificent, while much of the contemporary landscape survives at least in outline; this includes the gardens (though entirely later in planting and layout), the Tiltyard (tournament ground) and further afield the conduit houses and other features of the palace's Tudor water supply.

Kenilworth Castle (Warks; EH). A mixture of magnate and royal residence, Kenilworth is one of England's greatest castles. Its southern aspect is particularly worth seeing from the middle distance. The earthwork remains of the extraordinary 'water landscape' around (but especially to the west of) the castle can also be seen, with Henry V's Pleasance being perhaps the best-known feature.

Leeds Castle (Kent; P). The huge expanses of water and the magnificent Gloriette built by Edward I for his wife Eleanor of Castile are most impressive but the whole castle is well worth visiting.

Ludgershall (Wilts; EH). Fragmentary remains and earthworks of an early twelfth-century hunting lodge.

Norwich (Norfolk; M). One of the most important and best-preserved keeps in the country. Other elements of the castle survive, and extensive excavations were carried out in the 1990s.

Orford Castle (Suffolk; EH). Excellent example of a later thirteenth-century tower/keep built by Henry II and surviving virtually intact. Its surrounding enclosure, formerly defined by walls, now remains as an earthwork.

Portchester Castle (Hants; EH). The twelfth-century keep survives in excellent condition, the later medieval palace ranges rather less so. All are located within the Inner Bailey, set in the north-west corner of the former Roman fortress (part of the late fourth-century Saxon Shore defences).

Scarborough Castle (N Yorks; EH). Extensive defences on a spectacular cliff-edge site. Worth visiting for the twelfth-century keep alone: this was slighted during the Civil War and therefore provides a perfect cross-section through a classic medieval building. The remains of its forebuilding are also important, as is the thirteenth-century barbican defending the castle's entrance.

Tower of London (HRP). One of the great medieval palace-castles, though a careful eye is required to untangle original medieval work from Victorian artifice. The White Tower is still the dominant centre-piece it was always intended to be, and the remains of the medieval palace to its south also contain much of interest. The successive lines of defence established during the twelfth and thirteenth centuries are the other major medieval element still recognisable, while much of the rest is overlain with post-medieval and Victorian trappings of the State offices which succeeded royal use of the site after Henry VIII's time.

Westminster (Palace of; Crown/H M Government, and EH). The Great Hall is the principal remaining feature of the medieval palace. Most of the royal apartments and associated ranges were lost in the great fire during the 1830s which eventually led on to the building of the Houses of Parliament around the Great Hall. The Jewel Tower (EH) was built in the south-west corner of the palace precinct in the 1360s as a private royal treasury, and stands as a lonely reminder of the former extent of London's most important medieval royal residence.

Windsor Castle (Surrey; Crown). Even (or perhaps especially) from the outside Windsor retains the power to inspire awe. Although it occupies only a relatively low promontory it is plenty enough, when taken with the deliberate height of the buildings, to dominate the surroundings. The buildings themselves are a mixture of many phases of royal work (post-medieval as well as earlier). There is a degree of irony in the fact that these phases are far better understood after the extensive campaign of archaeological works carried out following the disastrous fire in 1992, along with equally urgent work on the Round Tower and its motte.

Winchester Castle (Hants; MH). Most of the royal castle and palace has long since been lost to redevelopment, but traces of the city walls and the castle in its south-western corner can still be seen. Henry III's Great Hall (altered in the fourteenth century and later) is the main survival, and it is one of the most important medieval buildings in the country.

Scotland

Scotland has arguably the finest group of palaces in the United Kingdom, though they are predominantly late medieval and early post-medieval in date. Most of them, however, are excellently preserved because the royal court largely moved to London on the succession of James VI to the English throne in 1603.

Doune Castle (Fife and Central; HS). Late fourteenth-century castle built around a central courtyard in the style which became commonly adopted from this period onwards.

Dundonald Castle (Glasgow; HS). Robert II's fine thirteenth-century tower. Built as a summer residence and extensively used as such by the monarch.

Dunfermline Palace (Fife; HS). The eleventh-century Benedictine Abbey became a favoured guest residence for the later medieval Scottish monarchy to the extent that they developed an impressive palace on the west side of the monastic cloister. Parts of this (and the abbey) survive.

Edinburgh Castle (Edinburgh and Lothians; HS). Overtaken by Holyrood in popularity as the city's royal residence towards the end of the medieval period, the castle nevertheless retains important accommodation features along, of course, with much else besides.

Holyrood Palace (Edinburgh and Lothians; HS). Supplanted Edinburgh Castle and became the focus of a building campaign to rival anything in contemporary Europe. As at Dunfermline the palace developed out of guest accommodation on the western side of the parent abbey's cloister, but the palatial remains far outstrip those of the monastery in impressiveness.

Linlithgow Palace (Edinburgh and Lothians; HS). Like Holyrood one of the great late medieval and early post-medieval palaces in Europe, with the courtyard ranges of the royal suites largely intact. The surrounding parkland and its water features are equally important and provide a suitably majestic setting.

Stirling Castle (Central; HS). Another of Scotland's great late medieval royal establishments, in a spectacularly dominant position within the local landscape. The Great Hall is among the largest and finest of the whole period not only in Britain but also in Europe: the other accommodation ranges and defences are scarcely behind it. The earthworks of seventeenth-century formal gardens are also an extremely important survival at the site.

Wales

Most of Wales' royal accommodation survives within castles of Edward I's campaigns and should therefore be seen as English, even intrusive elements.

Beaumaris (Anglesey; CADW). Formidable defences and the partly restored moat of Edward I's castle, built to dominate the island part of the Gwynedd kingdom. The castle also dominated the northern end of the Menai Strait.

Caernarfon (Gwynedd; CADW). Edward I's vast fortress dominating the southern end of the Menai Strait, thus matching Beaumaris in intention. Also strategically important for the control of mainland Gwynedd (especially access between it and Anglesey). Intended as the centre of royal administration in north Wales.

Carreg Cennen Castle (Carmarthenshire; CADW). Began as a Welsh stronghold but refortified by the English in the thirteenth and fourteenth centuries. The hilltop location is as visually impressive and dominant as any.

Caerphilly Castle (Caerphilly; CADW). Begun in 1268 under Henry III, and the largest castle in Wales. It controls the Welsh side of the Severn estuary coastline as well as the strategic route across the south end of the English-Welsh borders.

Conwy Castle (Conwy; CADW). Arguably the greatest of the English castles in Wales, built by Edward I between 1283-7. The military planning and execution of the castle is impressive, while the royal apartments are a palace in miniature.

Criccieth Castle (Gwynedd; CADW). A major stronghold of the great Welsh king, Llewelyn, further strengthened by his Welsh successors but also taken over by Edward I.

Rhuddlan (Denbighshire; CADW). Another of Edward I's great north Welsh castles, but this was also the site of an important royal centre in the Gwynedd kingdom.

Episcopal palaces

Bath and Wells

Acton Burnell (Shropshire; EH). Impressive shell of the late thirteenth-century manor house or palace, with accommodation ranged on several floors. These can be appreciated best from within the building, while the outward appearance of strength was little more than show. Fragments of an associated agricultural court in the adjacent private grounds are not directly accessible but can be seen from the palace.

Wells (Somerset; P). The see palace is still in use, but its impressive curtain walls, moat and entrance can all be viewed from the outside.

Canterbury

Canterbury had one of the most extensive property portfolios of the medieval diocese, but few of its former palaces are easily accessible now. See Thompson 1998, 170-2 for further details.

Canterbury (Kent; P). Fragments of the medieval palace, including windows and fabric of the great hall, can be seen from the outside in its modern successor.

Lambeth Palace (London; P). Medieval remains include thirteenth-century chapel and fifteenth-century gate tower. Occasionally open to parties, but the archiepiscopal use of the palace makes other access difficult.

Durham

Durham (Co Durham; P). See palace still in use but its buildings are impressive even from the outside.

Norham Castle (Northumberland; EH). Massive twelfth-century keep and later defences on a promontory dominating the river Tweed. See Dixon and Marshall for a recent reconsideration of the site. There is also a new site guidebook (published 1998).

Ely

Somersham (Cambs; P). Mostly surviving as earthworks, though with walled garden masonry visible as well. Mostly in private hands, although some of the remains are visible from the road.

Hereford

Hereford (Herefs; P). See palace, with famous hall visible to the south of the cathedral. Blair (1987) describes and interprets the extensive surviving elements of the hall.

Lincoln

Bishop's Palace, Lincoln (Lincs; EH). Extensive remains of the palace which developed over many episcopates to the south of the cathedral. New guidebook being published in 2000.

Lyddington Bede House (Leics; EH). The east-west range of buildings which were converted into almshouses retain important evidence for the medieval palace. The great hall immediately to the north only survives below ground, but has been the subject of some archaeological work. Much of the precinct can be traced, but is largely in private hands.

Newark Castle (Notts; M). Strategically-important castle used throughout the medieval period. Now managed municipally, and has been the focus of extensive community-based work.

Moray, Scotland

Spynie Palace (Grampian; HS). Important episcopal palace with extensive remains of building ranges and curtain walls. Subject of extensive excavations in late 1980s and early 1990s.

Norwich

Norwich (Norfolk; P). Fragments of the medieval see palace survive to the north of the cathedral.

Orkney

Bishop's Palace, Kirkwall (Orkney; HS). Twelfth-century hall-house with later alterations, just to the south of the cathedral. Remains of the post-medieval Earl's palace can also be seen.

Rochester

Rochester Castle (Kent; EH). Massively impressive keep, largely early to mid-twelfth century, on an important strategic site commanding the Medway and the south side of the Thames estuary. The south-east corner tower had to be rebuilt after King John's miners destroyed it during a siege in 1216. The cathedral itself is also an excellent (if perhaps under-appreciated) example of early Norman architecture.

West Malling (Kent; EH). Late eleventh-century tower keep built by Bishop Gundulf, who also had important connections not only with the see but also with the Tower of London.

St David's

Lamphey (Pembs; CADW). Gateway gives access to well-preserved remains of extensive palace within high perimeter wall. Inner gate tower, hall remains and arcading reminiscent of the see palace are among the main features of the site, while there are traces of associated agricultural buildings (barns etc) as well.

St David's (Pembs; CADW). Mainly fourteenth-century remains of the see palace survive to the west of the cathedral and within its precinct defences. The highly decorated open arcades below the crenellation are a particularly fine architectural feature of the site.

Salisbury

Old Sarum (Wilts; EH). Dramatic siting within an Iron Age hillfort, and complex remains of both the original cathedral, its successive see palaces in the Inner and Outer Baileys, with 'new' Salisbury and its cathedral visible to the south. The palace complex built around a courtyard on the Inner Bailey is the main visible feature of the episcopal residence and is worth comparison with Sherborne (below).

Sherborne (Dorset; EH). Imposing defences and palace ruins to the east of and overlooking the town which was the diocesan centre until its removal to Old Sarum after the Conquest. Like the see palace, the residential remains are disposed around a central courtyard.

Winchester

Bishop's Waltham (Hants; EH). Multi-period remains of a residence which was often preferred even to the see palace itself. The bishops' accommodation in the West Tower is reasonably well preserved, the rest of their chambers less so. The hall and attached services are excellent despite extensive ruination, while the bakehouse/brewhouse is one of the finest of its kind in any medieval context. The remaining part of the guest range is also a remarkably complete survival, at least in its upper storey. It is interesting to compare this with Lyddington Bede House.

Farnham (Surrey; EH and P). Massively-defended shell keep with extensive later medieval and Tudor work. This part of the site is managed by EH and can be visited from late spring to early winter. The adjacent palace accommodation is now part of a conference centre but some of the main rooms (eg the great hall) can be visited on Wednesdays.

Winchester Palace (Southwark, London; EH). Fragments of the hall block survive both in plan and elevation (long south wall and west gable with excellent rose window) visible from the roadside. The palace was incorporated in commercial developments in the post-medieval period, and was the subject of excavations in the 1980s. Such an important site seems incongruously sited now in an urban backstreet, but it is one of the few episcopal residences in the capital which has visible remains left.

Witney (Oxon; P). Massively thick foundations with deeply-splayed windows and central supporting column, left exposed after excavations in 1984 and displayed under a very modern-looking tent structure. Within grounds of private house, but open occasional weekends during year by arrangement with local historical and archaeological group.

Wolvesey Palace (Hants; EH). See palace adjacent to the cathedral, and with the existing palace incorporating the chapel of its medieval predecessor. The ruins of the twelfth-century and later building campaigns provide one of the most rewarding visits to an episcopal residence. The West and East Halls would be reason enough individually for a visit, but seen together and with the wealth of other structures and detail they make this a most rewarding site.

York

York (P). The see palace lay to the north-west of the cathedral. Part of a twelfth-century arcade and a two-storey chapel of the early to mid-thirteenth century are all that remain today.

Glossary

Palace, *n.*, official residence of sovereign, president, archbishop, or bishop; splendid mansion, spacious building. F f. L [origin French from Latin] *palatium. Oxford Dictionary of Current English* 1985. The second part relates to the post-medieval and modern usage of the term palace. The word 'president' (as we understand it politically) would have little or no meaning in the medieval word, but otherwise the first part of the definition is simple and appropriate.

The following glossary may be useful to readers unfamiliar with some of the more technical terms and words used in the book, but it is not intended to be comprehensive.

Arcade	series of arches, open or filled in, which can be inter-linked.
Ashlar	square dressed blocks of stone laid in regular courses, usually with fine vertical joints.
Bailey	fortified enclosure forming part or all of a castle.
Barbican	additional layer of defences, usually outside an entrance tower. Often capable of functioning virtually independently of the main curtain walls, towers etc of the castle or palace.
Bastion	general term for a defensive structure projecting from the main line of defence.
Batter	wall face inclining back from the vertical plane.
Baulk	strip of earth left unexcavated within an archaeological excavation or between trenches.
Berm	strip or ledge of land between the outside of a defensive wall and adjoining moat.
Blind arcade	an arcade incorporated into a wall face but without opening through it, i.e. the arches are not windows but are part of the masonry face.

Chamfer	surface formed by cutting off a square edge, usually at a 45 angle.
Course	a layer of stones laid in the horizontal plane within a wall.
Curtain wall	fortified wall enclosing a castle, a castle bailey, or one of its parts.

Dendrochronology
the technique of dating wood by matching its annual growth rings to a known sequence; timbers of oak and beech are especially good for this technique, but some species such as elm are completely unsuitable.

Forebuilding	structure in front of and usually attached to the keep, containing the stairs up to the main (often only) entrance. The forebuilding could usually be isolated from the keep to protect the latter.
Garderobe	toilet, usually extremely simple in form and discharging either through a shaft within a wall or directly out from it. The effluent would be flushed away by a stream or artificial water channel, or taken into a deep, often stone-lined pit which would be cleaned out periodically.
Keep	tower of exceptional size and strength, usually residential as well as defensible.
Pilaster	a square column or buttress built with an external wall face, both to give greater strength and also for decorative effect. A classic feature of Norman architecture.
Pipe Roll	annual accounts rendered by the sheriff of each county to the king or, in some cases (eg Winchester), the bishop; there are many equivalent document types (eg Liberate Rolls) which performed similar functions under different arms of the royal administration.
Plinth	one or more courses projecting forward at the bottom of a wall, often including a chamfer and/or decorative mouldings.
Postern	a secondary door.
Quoin	dressed stone blocks used at the external corners of building to provide structural strength.
Revetment	wall or construction shoring up and defining a slope, such as the edge of a moat.
Shore	a supporting member, often timber, in a building.

Sole plate   horizontal timber forming the base of a structure with framing built off it, as in a house or bridge.

Sondage   small excavation, usually to dig deeper within a limited area of a larger trench.

Stratigraphy   the method by which archaeologists understand the way in which soil layers, structures etc were built up on any given site in the past. Lower layers are usually earlier than those above them, while features such as pits and ditches may also cut into and therefore be later than soil layers. The individual soils, features and structures are given unique identifications known as *context numbers*, and the interaction between any two of these is known as a *stratigraphic relationship*. Dating evidence such as pottery, coins and dendrochronology is used to establish the chronology (i.e. time-frame) of the stratigraphy.

String course   horizontal band of masonry intended to provide a stable building platform as the stonework is built up. Most valuable structurally in rubble work, but often used to decorative effect as well especially when projecting from the wall face and embellished with ornament.

Undercroft   basement under domestic or other chambers, usually vaulted. Need not be wholly or at all below ground, as principal chambers were often raised at first-floor level over a ground-floor undercroft.

Bibliography

Barker P.A., 1986, *Understanding Archaeological Excavations* Batsford, London

Beresford G., 1987, *Goltho: the Development of an Early Medieval Manor c.850-1150* London

Biddle M., 1961, 'Nonsuch Palace 1959-60: an interim report', *Surrey Archaeol Collections* 58, 1-20

Biddle M., 1986, *Wolvesey, the Old Bishop's Palace, Winchester, Hampshire* London

Biddle M., Barfield L. and Millard A., 1959, 'The excavation of the Manor of the More, Rickmansworth, Hertfordshire', *Archaeol J* 116, 136-99

Binski P., 1986, *The Painted Chamber at Westminster* London

Bird J., Hassall M. and Sheldon H. (eds.), *Interpreting Roman London*, Oxbow Monograph 58

Blagg T., 1996, 'Monumental architecture in Roman London', in Bird et al (eds.), 43-8

Blair J., 1987, 'The twelfth-century bishop's palace at Hereford', *Med Arch* 31, 59-71

Bonney D. and Dunn C., 1989, 'Earthwork castles and settlement at Hamstead Marshall, Berkshire', in Bowden et al (eds.), 173-82

Bowden M., MacKay D. and Topping P. (eds.), 1989, *From Cornwall to Caithness*, BAR Brit Ser 1989

Brigham T., 1998, 'The port of Roman London', in Watson (ed.), 23-34

Brindle S. and Kerr B., 1997, *Windsor Revealed: New Light on the History of the Castle* London

Butler L., 1987, 'Domestic buildings in Wales and the evidence of the Welsh laws', *Med Arch* 31, 47-58

Caldwell D. and Lewis J., 1996, 'Linlithgow Palace: an excavation in the west range and a note on finds from the palace', *Proc Soc Antiqs Scotland* 126, 823-70

Clark, A.J., *Seeing Beneath the Soil* Batsford, London

Colvin H. (ed.), 1963, *The History of the King's Works: the Middle Ages* London

Colvin H. (ed.), 1975 (Pt 1) and 1982 (Pt 2), *The History of the King's Works: 1485-1660* London

Cook A., 1969, 'Oatlands Palace excavations 1968, interim report', *Surrey Archaeol Collections* 16, 1-9

Cooksey, 1991, *English Heritage Teacher's Guide to Using Abbeys* London

Cox E., Owen O. and Pringle D., 1998, 'The discovery of medieval deposits beneath the earl's Palace, Kirkwall, Orkney', *Proc Soc Antiq Scot* 128, 567-80

Cunliffe B., 1973, 'Chalton, evolution of a landscape', *Antiq J* 53, 173-90

Davison B., 1977, 'Excavations at Sulgrave, Northamptonshire', *Archaeol J* 134, 105-14

Dent J., 1962, *The Quest for Nonsuch* London

Dixon P. and Marshall P., 1993, 'The great tower in the twelfth century: the case of the Norham Castle', *Archaeol J* 150, 410-32

Dunbar J., 1999, *Scottish Royal Palaces: the Architecture of the Royal Residences during the Late Medieval and Early Renaissance Periods* East Lothian

Edwards N., 1997 (ed.), *Landscape and Settlment in Medieval Wales*, Oxbow Monograph 81

English Heritage 1991, *Exploring Our Past* London

English Heritage 1998, *Dendrochronology* London

Gadd D. and Dyson T., 1981, 'Bridewell Palace: excavations at 9-11 Bridewell Place and 1-3 Tudor Street, City of London, 1978', *Post-Med Archaeol* 15, 1-79

Hare J., 1988, 'Bishop's Waltham Palace, Hampshire: William of Wykeham, Henry Beaufort and the transformation of a medieval episcopal palace', *Arch J* 145, 222-54

Hare J., 1993, *Bishop's Waltham Palace* London

Harvey J., 1981, *Medieval Gardens* London

Hassall T., 1986, 'The Oxford region from the conversion to the Conquest', in G. Briggs, J. Cook and T. Rowley (eds.), *The Archaeology of the Oxford Region*, 109-14

Hiller J. and Keevill G., 1994, 'Recent archaeological work at the Tower of London', *Trans London and Middlesex Archaeol Soc* 45, 147-81

Hinchcliffe J., 1986, 'An early medieval settlement at Cowage Farm, Foxley, near Malmesbury', *Archaeol J* 143, 240-59

Hope-Taylor B., 1977, *Yeavering: an Anglo-Saxon Centre of Early Northumbria* London

Impey E., 1998, 'The western entrance to the Tower of London, 1240-1241', *Trans London and Middlesex Archaeol Soc* 48, 59-76

Impey E., 1999, 'The seigneurial residence in Normandy, 1125-1225: an Anglo-Norman Tradition?', *Med Arch* 43, 45-73

Impey E. and Parnell G., 2000, *The Tower of London: the Official Illustrated History* London

Jacques D., 1995, The history of the Privy Garden, in S. Thurley, 1995?, 23-42.

James S., Marshall A. and Millett M., 1984, 'An early medieval building tradition', *Archaeol J* 141, 216-42

James T. Beaumont, 1990, *The Palaces of Medieval England* London

James T. Beaumont and Robinson A.M., 1988, *Clarendon Palace: the History and Archaeology of a Medieval Palace and Hunting Lodge near Salisbury, Wiltshire*, Soc Antiqs Res rep 45

Johnstone N., 1997, 'An investigation into the location of the Royal Courts of thirteenth-century Gwynedd', in Edwards, 1997, 55-69

Johnstone N., 1999, 'Cae Llys, Rhosyr: a court of the princes of Gwynedd', *Studia Celtica* 33, 251-95

Jones B., 1984, *Past Imperfect: the Story of Rescue Archaeology* London

Keevill G., 1997, 'The Tower of London', *Current Archaeology* 154, 384-7

Keevill G. and Bell C., 1996, 'Archaeological investigation of the moat at Hampton Court Palace', *Trans London and Middlesex Archaeol Soc* 47, 145-56

Keevill G. and Linford N., 1998, 'Landscape with gardens: aerial, topographical and geophysical survey at Hamstead Marshall, Berkshire', in Pattison (ed.), 13-22

Lapper I. and Parnell G., 2000, *Landmarks in History: the Tower of London, a 2000-year History* Oxford

Le Patourel H., 1973, *The Moated Sites of Yorkshire*, Soc Med Arch Monograph 5

Lewis E., 1985, 'Excavations in Bishop's Waltham, 1967-78', *Proc Hants Field Club* 41, 81-126

Longley D., 1997, 'The Royal Courts of the Welsh Princes of Gwynedd, AD 400-1283', in Edwards, 1997, 41-54

Millett M., and James S., 1983, 'Excavations at Cowdery's Down, Basingstoke, Hampshire, 1978-79', *Archaeol J* 140, 151-279

Musty J., 1990, 'Brick kilns and brick and tile suppliers to Hampton Court Palace', *Archaeol J* 147, 411-19

Nenk B., Margeson S. and Hurley M., 1992, 'Medieval Britain and Ireland in 1991', *Med Archaeol* 36

Oxley J. (ed.), 1986, *Excavations at Southampton Castle* Southampton

Parnell G., 1983, 'Excavations at the Salt Tower, Tower of London, 1976', *Trans London and Middlesex Archaeol Soc* 34, 95-106

Parnell G., 1993, *The Tower of London* London

Parnell G., 1999, *The Royal Menagerie at the Tower of London* London

Pattison P. (ed.), 1998, *There by Design: Field Archaeology in Parks and Gardens* London

Rahtz P., 1969, *Excavations at King John's Hunting Lodge, Writtle, Essex, 1955-7*, Society for Medieval Archaeology Monograph 3

Rahtz P., 1979, *The Saxon and Medieval Palaces at Cheddar* BAR, Oxford

Riall N., 1994, *Henry of Blois, Bishop of Winchester: a Patron of the 12th-century Renaissance*, Hampshire Papers 5, Hampshire County Council

Roberts E., 1989, 'Bishop Ralegh's banquet, 1244', *Hants Filed Club Newsletter* 12

Roberts E., 1993, 'William of Wykeham's house at East Meon, Hants', *Archaeol J* 150, 456-81

Rosevear A., 1995, *The King's Highway - Recorded Journeys Through the Thames Valley*, RUTV 9

Society for Medieval Archaeology, 1987, 'Archaeology and the Middle Ages: recommendations by the Society for Medieval Archaeology to the Historic Buildings and Monuments Commission for England', *Med Arch* 31, 1-12

Steane J., 1993 (1st edition), *The Archaeology of the Medieval English Monarchy* London

Stephenson D., 1984, *The Governance of Gwynedd* Cardiff

Stocker D., 1991, *St Mary's Guildhall, Lincoln: the Survey and Excavation of a Medieval Building Complex*, The Archaeology of Lincoln 12-1

Tatton-Brown T., 1980, 'History of the 'Bishop's Palace' at Bekesbourne', *Arch Cant* 96, 30-57

Tatton-Brown T., 1982, 'The Great Hall of the archbishop's palace', in British Archaeological Association, *Medieval Art and Architecture at Canterbury before 1220*

Taylor A.J., 1996, *The Jewel Tower, Westminster* London

Taylor C.C., 1989, 'Somersham Palace, Cambridgeshire: a medieval landscape for pleasure?', in Bowden et al (eds.), 211-24

Taylor C.C., 1997, 'The place of analytical fieldwork in garden archaeology', *Journal of Garden History* 17.1, 18-25

Taylor C.C., 1998, 'From recording to recognition', in Pattison (ed.), 1-6

Thompson M., 1964, 'Reclamation of waste ground for the Pleasance at Kenilworth Castle', *Med Arch* 8, 222-3

Thompson M., 1965, 'Two levels of the Mere at Kenilworth Castle', *Med Arch* 9, 156-61

Thompson M., 1987, *Farnham Castle Keep, Surrey* London

Thompson M., 1998, *Medieval Bishops' Houses in England and Wales* Aldershot

Thurley S., 1993, *The Royal Palaces of Tudor England* London

Thurley S. (ed.), 1995, *The King's Privy Garden at Hampton Court Palace 1689-1995* London

Thurley S., 1999, *Whitehall Palace: an Architectural History of the Royal Apartments, 1240-1690* London

Watson B. (ed.), 1998, *Roman London: Recent Archaeological Work*, Journal of Roman Archaeology Supplementary Series 24

White P., 1986, *Sherborne Old Castle* London

Wilson D., 1982, *Air Photo Interpretation for Archaeologists* Batsford, London

Woodfield C. and P., 1981-2, 'The palace of the Bishops of Lincoln at Lyddington', *Leics Arch and Hist Soc Transactions* 57, 1-16

Woodfield C. and P., 1988, *Lyddington Bede House* London

Youngs S., Clark J. and Barry T., 1987, 'Medieval Britain and Ireland in 1986', *Med Archaeol* 31

Zoltán E. (translator), 1999, *Medium Regni: medieval Hungarian Royal Seats* Budapest

Index

This index covers principal place names only (eg not including sub-divisions of places such as individual towers) although places like London and Winchester which are mentioned on most pages have been excluded for clarity. Counties and regions are generally not included as separate entries except where there are important and specific textual references (such as Gwynedd). Only historic personal names have been included. No Gazetteer entries have been included in the index. Text illustrations are indexed in bold at the end of each entry; colour plates are prefixed CP.